GULLIVER'S AFTERLIVES

GULLIVER'S AFTERLIVES

300 Years of Transmedia Adaptation

Daniel Cook

BLOOMSBURY ACADEMIC
LONDON · NEW YORK · OXFORD · NEW DELHI · SYDNEY

BLOOMSBURY ACADEMIC
Bloomsbury Publishing Plc, 50 Bedford Square, London, WC1B 3DP, UK
Bloomsbury Publishing Inc, 1359 Broadway, New York, NY 10018, USA
Bloomsbury Publishing Ireland, 29 Earlsfort Terrace, Dublin 2, D02 AY28, Ireland

BLOOMSBURY, BLOOMSBURY ACADEMIC and the Diana logo are trademarks
of Bloomsbury Publishing Plc

First published in Great Britain 2026

A catalogue record for this book is available from the Library of Congress.

A catalog record for this book is available from the Library of Congress.

ISBN: HB: 978-1-3504-6437-7
PB: 978-1-3504-6438-4
ePDF: 978-1-3504-6439-1
eBook: 978-1-3504-6440-7

Typeset by Deanta Global Publishing Services, Chennai, India
Printed and bound in Great Britain

For product safety related questions contact productsafety@bloomsbury.com.

To find out more about our authors and books visit www.bloomsbury.com and
sign up for our newsletters.

CONTENTS

FIGURES

ACKNOWLEDGEMENTS

This book benefited from the skills and kindness of many archivists and library staff members at multiple institutions throughout the world, most notably the universities of Dundee, Oxford and Cambridge, Trinity College Dublin, the University of Toronto, the University of Pennsylvania, Ohio State University, Yale University, Harvard University, the New York Public Library, the Library of Congress, the V&A, the British Library, the National Library of Scotland and the National Library of Ireland. I also relied on the labour of the curators, content creators and support staff involved with the online repositories and resources listed in the Bibliography. For the allocation of a Maddock Research Fellowship at Marsh's Library in Dublin, I'm thankful to Dr Phillip and Mrs Niamh Maddock and to Amy Boylan, the assistant librarian. Board members of both The British Society for Eighteenth-Century Studies (BSECS) and the Bodleian Library kindly awarded me a BSECS-Bodleian Visiting Fellowship at Oxford, where I explored the Herbert Davis archive among other unique holdings. I also spent considerable time at the Lewis Walpole Library in Connecticut, where I received expert guidance from Sue Walker and the residential team. Early and related versions of some chapters of this book were delivered as panel presentations at three annual BSECS conferences. I also tried out some material at the Eighteenth-Century Literature & Culture Research Seminar at Oxford, and I'm grateful to Ros Ballaster, Christine Gerrard and David Francis Taylor, as well as the attendees, for their conviviality and feedback. At Yale, I delivered two papers focused on their Gulliverian holdings. Andrew Hiscock and Lisa Hopkins kindly invited me to discuss my research during its final stages at the Sheffield Hallam/Bangor Early Modern Seminar, and I'm thankful to them and the audience for their help.

Parts of the first and second chapters of *Gulliver's Afterlives* build on material previously presented in my journal article 'Mrs Gulliver's Travels: Minor-Character Elaboration in Theory and Practice', which appeared in the 2024 issue of *Critical Quarterly*, and a chapter titled 'Further Voyages' for *The Cambridge Companion to Gulliver's Travels* (Cambridge: Cambridge University Press, 2023), a book that I co-edited with Nick Seager. I want to thank the editors of each piece for their care and attention. For ongoing support of my work more generally, I'm mightily thankful to Nick. In recent years, Jakub Lipski has generously furnished numerous avenues for my research on literary adaptation, particularly as it pertains to eighteenth-century literature. My colleague Chris Murray provided vital guidance on comics and film scholarship. Before writing this book, I had the pleasure of helping Moto Shibata with small queries related to his serialized translation of *Travels* into Japanese. In turn, he kindly sent me a copy of *Travelogue G*, a collection of Asa Hiramatsu's illustrations for that edition. Hermann J. Real has long been an enthusiastic benefactor of many generations of Swift scholars throughout the world, and I'm especially thankful to him and the team at the Ehrenpreis Centre for Swift Studies in Münster. Lucy Brown and Aanchal Vij at Bloomsbury provided invaluable support throughout the publishing process. The anonymous reviewers delivered detailed and wholly constructive reports, and for that I am very honoured. Final thanks are reserved, always and forever, for Laura, Julia, Dougie and Maisie.

INTRODUCTION

Ahead of a performance of Shakespeare's *Measure for Measure* (1604) at Lincoln's Inn Fields on 25 May 1727, the *Daily Journal* reported that a well-dressed guest would be in attendance: Captain Lemuel Gulliver.[1] Two stage boxes would be kept for the ship captain and his company, and the Master of the House promised that no one would disturb them. Barely six months after the appearance of his debut book, *Travels into Several Remote Nations of the World* (1726), the author-explorer had already become a celebrity – despite being a fictional character conjured up by the satirist Jonathan Swift. Centuries later and still famous, Gulliver cameoed in two of the biggest science fiction franchises on the planet, *Doctor Who* (in 1968) and *Star Trek* (in 1990). Celebrated contemporary poets Alexander Pope and John Gay wrote in his name, and, in the twentieth century, Wole Soyinka adopted Gulliver as an alter ego for political prisoner verse. Members of Swift's circle and their enemies produced pseudonymous prose extensions of *Travels* shortly after its initial publication. Fanfiction arrived early. Horace Walpole enclosed Gulliverian stories in private correspondence before the century was out, and online fora such as Archive of Our Own continue to engage with *Travels* and related works. Cartoonists from William Hogarth, in the early eighteenth century, to Martin Rowson, in the twenty-first, have seized on the character's mobility across the political spectrum. Harlequin Gullivers and other types of theatrical clones amused scores of Victorian audiences across the country, and Lilliputian pantomimes still appear most Christmases. A major puppet theatre in Romania, Teatrul de Păpuși Gulliver, has borne his name since 1995, and Gulliverian puppetry has long been popular across the wider world.

In the last 120-odd years, ever since the advent of moving pictures, Gulliver has headlined at least forty-eight films and television series produced in many languages, including but not limited to English,

French, German, Hindi, Italian, Japanese, Portuguese, Russian, Spanish and Ukrainian. Max Fleischer rotoscoped him during America's Golden Age of animation, and modern namesakes have loomed out of the big screen in 3D movies, more recently. The leading purveyor of syndicated cartoons in the second half of the twentieth century, Hanna-Barbera, produced for him and a concocted offspring two separate series a decade apart. The highest-profile graphic novelist working today, Alan Moore, gave Gulliver his own fellowship of public domain characters in *The League of Extraordinary Gentlemen* (1999–2021). (Moore also gave him terminal cancer.) Gilberton's *Classics Illustrated* and Marvel Comics, among other leading industry stables from multiple countries, adapted Gulliver's story in comic book form many times during the previous century and continue to do so. Novelists throughout the world have taken him – or his family – on further adventures, to new countries and unknown solar systems, deep into the future. Gulliver's afterlife extends well beyond narrative media. Travel agencies, moving companies, bookshops, toy shops, cafes and other vendors keep punning on the explorer's name and the title of the book more popularly known as *Gulliver's Travels*. Theme parks and fairgrounds bearing his brand have popped up across Europe in recent decades, while wood or iron effigies can still be found in differing states of disrepair across the globe. Examining disparate engagements with Swift's literary properties, *Gulliver's Afterlives* serves two main aims. First, to reposition *Travels* within a longer history of cultural adaptation. Second, to model a creative reception of early transmedia characters using the protagonist of one of the most enduring works of fiction.

Born in Nottinghamshire in or around the year 1661, Lemuel Gulliver studied at the universities of Cambridge and Leyden before practising medicine in London.[2] Despite starting a family with Mary Burton, in 1688, he took to the seas in 1699. Sixteen years later, after encountering miniature people at war, benevolent giants, a flying island, shades of the illustrious dead, decrepit immortals, sorcerers, savages, pirates and talking horses, he failed to resettle among his own kind. Publishing his memoirs in 1726 proved to be the beginning of an unending story, despite the author-explorer's protest, in a substantially revised and now-standard edition that appeared in 1735, against a relentless stream of unofficial extensions. He was right. Over the previous nine years, Gulliverian texts had proliferated across the marketplace, in books, pamphlets, broadsheets and periodicals. *Travels* was widely serialized within weeks of initial publication. As a result, the book 'bore so considerable a Share in almost every Conversation', observed *The Penny London Post* on 25 November 1726. Three days later, *Parker's Penny Post* similarly claimed that 'for their Variety of Wit and pleasant Diversion, [the *Travels* had] become the general Entertainment of Town and Country'.[3] And Gay famously proclaimed that Swift's work, in some form or other, had been 'universally read, from the Cabinet-council to the Nursery'.[4] A master of a ship, somewhat unexpectedly, claimed to know Gulliver personally, according to Lord Scarborough, a friend of Swift's friend John Arbuthnot – the author-explorer lived in Wapping, apparently, not nearby Rotherhithe (Redriff). (Gulliver's Wharf can now be found in the first of those London districts and Gulliver Street in the second.) The physical comedy of the book delighted Augusta of Saxe-Gotha-Altenburg, the Princess of Wales. Another more earnest contemporary reader went immediately to a map in search of Lilliput.[5] Cultural saturation seemed inevitable. Instead, the opposite has happened.

Gulliver's Travels and transmedia archaeology

A solely book-born character, Gulliver came before the emergence of the technologies that underpin modern transmedia storytelling, though he falls more securely under the broader category of transfictionality, which Richard Saint-Gelais identifies as an occurrence in which two or more texts 'share elements such as characters, imaginary locations, or fictional worlds'.[6] (As we shall see, Gulliver crossed media, not just the same textual medium, almost immediately after the publication of *Travels*.) Transmedia storytelling, as defined by Lars Elleström, describes 'narrative in different media types working together to form a larger whole'.[7] While 'working together' – like Saint-Gelais's notion of transfictional sharing – does not fully rule out contrarian storytelling, such as parody or fraudulent continuations, the focus on concertedness aligns with Henry Jenkins's field-defining model of convergence culture, in which transmedia storytelling becomes 'a process where integral elements of a fiction get dispersed systematically across multiple delivery channels for the purpose of creating a unified and coordinated entertainment experience'.[8] Belatedly dispersed across multiple books, stage plays, games and films, among other channels, Gulliver therefore helps us test both the scope and boundaries of the field. Put another way, Swift's *Travels* and related works form an unlikely but key case study for transmedia storytelling precisely because of the main character's uncoordinated familiarity. First, a large and diverse body of materials have accrued over many years, though much of it has been ignored by literary scholars and cultural historians alike. Second, a deep dive into this material *in toto* allows us to introduce older models of characterization into current debates within transmedia studies. Third, pursuing Gulliver's unsystematic portability across creative environments better reveals actual practice by secondary authors and artists over a long period of time. More accurately, there have been phases of concerted storytelling involving Gulliver and his world. A notable example of this arose during the Silver Age of media convergence, that is, mid-twentieth-century reworkings of *Travels* on film by Fleischer Studios along with tie-in comics, games, merchandise and promotional materials. Crucially for my argument, though, the concerted storytelling came as early as 1727, when supplementary poems produced by members of the author's circle in the voices of various characters were included in a new, authoritative edition of *Travels*. Before that, Gulliver had already appeared in satirical prints and newspaper gossip columns. Far from re-describing *Travels*, all engagements have, from the beginning, added something new to the central character and his world, either by resetting the material or revising it.

If Gulliver does not quite fit the requirement of systematic dispersal, he should still play a prominent role in the historicizing of transmediality, or transmedia archaeology, for which Paolo Bertetti has identified three different but interwoven approaches. The first, 'a textual, narratologic (and sometimes semiotic) approach', examines the ways in which narratives are organized as transmedia expansions.[9] The second explicitly connects the different forms of transmedia storytelling to formative industrial and cultural contexts. The third focuses on audiences, including participatory cultures such as fanfiction.[10] This study will prioritize the first approach because the long-lived developments of character and other narratological elements require the most sustained attention, and, as discussed, Gulliver and his world preceded both the mass industrialization and digitization of cultural production. Where relevant I will nevertheless outline the commercial contexts in which adaptive works have been produced and consumed. For consistency, this subsidiary approach will entail considering competing expectations associated with the diverse formal settings displayed only as far as it concerns characterization. Indirectly, this also means we can reassess the complexities of genre long associated with literary analyses of *Travels* – beyond the satirical, political and philosophical origins, the nominal protagonist has been shunted into children's adventure stories and science fiction, among other frameworks. Outside the present treatment, tracing Gulliver's value within different participatory cultures would enhance an understanding of the transfictional function of established literary properties. This further research might include more extensive examinations of board and video games, fanfiction fora and entertainment ephemera. In sum, *Gulliver's Afterlives* uses the contrarian pluralism of Lemuel Gulliver, the nominal if sometimes absent author and varying types of character, and usually a mixture, to explore different models of adaptation and appropriation as practised by artists and authors (and other types of creators) over the past three hundred years. Primarily focused on prose and poetry produced in the eighteenth and nineteenth centuries but taking in contemporary examples of the same kind too, Chapter 1 attends to continuations and spinoffs produced in the name of Gulliver, that is, a posthumous author (a ghostwriter, or a ghost-as-writer). Mainly using works from the twentieth and twenty-first centuries, Chapter 2 maps out Gulliver's voyages beyond *Travels*, along with refocalizations on different characters and namesakes. Chapter 3 looks at visual Gulliveriana, beginning with the scant description of the character and official portraits in *Travels* and taking in illustrated books, comics and graphic novels. In Chapter 4 we will consider the most famous and some of the most overlooked iterations of Gulliver in performative media, ranging from Victorian pantomimes to silent-era shorts through to recent feature-length films and games. A short Conclusion takes stock of this study's findings.

Travels (and the culture-text that it has spawned) suits Matthew Freeman's tripartite model of transmedia storytelling: character-building, world-building, and authorship.[11] Just as The Wizard of Oz has the Land of Oz and Batman the noirish city of Gotham, so Gulliver remains chiefly associated with Lilliput. And yet, as a fantastical voyager, Gulliver perpetually transcends worlds, not least of all the various and vastly different nations and planets to which Swift and other authors, scripters and artists have taken him – and will keep taking him. As the nominal writer of *Travels*, Gulliver commingles the commonly contrary functions of *author* and *character*, and this poses a procedural problem for creators or creative teams. Reworkings in pictorial or performative media sometimes prefer Gulliver the character over Gulliver the author, particularly when reframing the material as an adventure story. Some show Gulliver in the act of composition, as though forever writing himself into existence, or even an already published version of the book ahead of the actual voyaging. In Rowson's graphic novel, *Gulliver's Travels: Adapted & Updated* (2012), we glimpse in passing the front covers of two versions of *Travels*, an eighteenth-century edition and a twentieth-century comic. Not only has Gulliver been taken on further adventures, other texts have also been attributed to him, from mock-medical treatises centred on his surgical expertise to satirical ballads. Gulliver is not an isolated case – Robinson Crusoe, a contemporaneous author-explorer, immediately comes to mind. But the peculiar range of his further travels and ghostwritten works demands fuller attention. Considering Swift's properties in the twinned purviews of transfictional and transmedial storytelling also shows how we can move canonical works away from intertextual models of adaptation in which singular relationships between texts become privileged and undue emphasis gets placed on teleological engagement by an ideal consumer. Rather than 'operating as a simple process of selling serialised chapters', Freeman suggests that 'transmedia storytelling is perhaps better theorised as either a strategic or an emergent/contingent form of *expansive intertextuality*'.[12] The afterlife of a character is rarely as coordinated as even this theoretical recalibration would suggest, however, particularly when dealing with one that long postdates the first author or authors. We engage with established stories dispersed across multiple platforms asynchronously and within personalized environments. Swift, as Gulliver, could complain in real time about the proliferation of unofficial extensions of his memoirs, and conversations about *Travels* may well have occupied cabinet councils and the nurseries. These early extensions were largely contrarian, and the conversations were disjointed or unrecorded. Butting up against Jenkins's notion of modern media convergence, the story centred on or written in the name of Gulliver has always been fragmented and dispersed – like found objects for cultural archaeologists.

If 'Gulliveriana', a collective term for creative and critical responses to Swift's *Travels*, forms an imagined museum on a Brobdingnagian scale, then the following account would be a more targeted Lilliputian exhibition within that museum. In it we will see many curiosities and familiar items that, when looked at together, reveal congruences and contradictions in theories and practices of appropriation from the eighteenth century to the present. Many of these museum pieces have become famous in their own right, not least of all the films and comics produced by notable studios. Some pieces have had to be dug out. As early as 1738, buried in a footnote to an entry on Samuel Butler's *Hudibras* (1663) in a new edition of Pierre Bayle's *General Dictionary*, we find an attack on the relentlessness of Gulliverian imitations: 'The moment after the famous Captain Lemuel Gulliver came abroad, many claimed kindred to him [. . .] and fatigued the public with their stupid adventures'.[13] Ironically, one of Bayle's English editors, John Lockman, had played a part in the perpetuation of Gulliver's legacy as the translator of Pierre-François Guyot Desfontaines's widely read follow-up, *Le Nouveau Gulliver, ou Voyage de Jean Gulliver, fils du capitaine Gulliver* (1730). Fearful of being obscured by such extensions rather than being buoyed by them, Swift's Gulliver, in the final stages of his infamous account of Houyhnhnm-Land, had warned readers about the travellers who will soon add 'many new Discoveries of their own, jostle me out of Vogue, and stand in my Place; making the World forget that ever I was an Author'.[14] Expressed as a warning, such words also encouraged engagement. Secondary authors have taken Gulliver on multiple 'fifth' voyages. Others have 'completed' Gulliver's account with implied if not actual death. Most of them have prolonged the travels and the nominal hero's despair indefinitely. Presented as a Lucianic, Rabelaisian or Scriblerian satire in scope and tone, within the confines of the original book at least, the expanded life of Gulliver quickly became and remains an adaptable if reductive paradigm of the fantastical adventure story, a favourite among audiences of all ages around the world still.[15]

As an authored work of fiction, Swift's *Travels* invites but resists closure. By his own claim, Gulliver could not rely on the surety of the written word ascribed to his pen. Whenever we refer to Brobdingnag and cognate terms, we are condoning errors introduced during the printing process, some of them deliberately and with faux authority (it's *Brobdingrag*, the pseudonymous author tardily reveals in a prefatory letter added to the 1735 edition, and thereby endorsing the reality of an entirely fabricated place [*GT*, 13]). Gulliver's fictional print agent (his cousin Richard Sympson), the printers (Benjamin Motte Jr's team working independently across four sites in London or George Faulkner's in Dublin), Motte's appointed bowdlerizer (the Reverend Andrew Tooke), and Swift's literary friends (Pope, Gay and Arbuthnot) had hands in the production of the received text. Some of these hands were under the control of Swift and his circle – counting Sympson, another speaking character. In the self-referential attack on the print trade added to the front of the revised edition, Gulliver criticized his cousin for allowing his book to be 'loaded up' with extensions of all kinds ('Libels, and Keys, and Reflections, and Memoirs, and Second Parts' [*GT*, 11]). Intriguingly, he ignored a ubiquitous type of textual reworking, abridgements, which appeared as early as 1727. Arguably the most commonly adopted such variation of Swift's original, *The Adventures of Captain Gulliver* (republished by Francis Newbery and his associates throughout the 1770s and into the next century) popularized the ongoing tradition of detaching Lilliput and Brobdingnag from the rest of the story and reframing the genre. And it is this version, or something like it, that consumers have long had in mind when thinking of *Travels*. What we refer to as Swift's *Travels*, including here in the present study, is a palimpsest of endless iterations. Can we identify it as 'a book'? It has been refitted for every conceivable textual or audiovisual format, after all, and many people will have first engaged with Gulliver outside of his published memoirs.

Lemuel Gulliver: A character study

Reconsidered within the purviews of transfictional and transmedial storytelling, Gulliver readily fits Jan-Noël Thon's transmedia character template, which singularly contains the 'physical, mental, and social characteristics' that 'any work-specific character sharing the same name may or may not exhibit, but would initially be expected to exhibit via a character-specific version of the principle of minimal departure'.[16] Relatedly, he also fits Thon's notion of a more generic transmedia character type, as a fantastical voyager or, more mundanely, a feckless sea captain. Whereas his attributed corpus of writing shifts in shape and size after the initial publication of *Travels*, Gulliver's own body and related accoutrements (such as the iconic tricorne hat) anchor the character across space and time. With the transmedia templates in place, however implicit, some continuations can refer to Gulliver without confirming his current status, let alone featuring him. Sometimes we glimpse implied parts of his body and clothing, such as his giant buckled shoes and white stockings in advertising campaigns. In such circumstances we might refer to the spectre of Gulliver's character or perhaps its papery corpse. In Deidre Lynch's terms, Gulliver is a textual entity whom readers or viewers experience as simultaneously 'dead *and* alive', an object and a subject.[17] We might also refer to Gulliver's clones, bodied characters that share little beyond a name or ones flung far into the future. Sometimes secondary authors invoke the spirit of Gulliver, such as when he ghostwrites hidden voyages, the manuscript accounts of which were purportedly recovered from his actual writing desk. Often, in animations or advertisements especially, the character's form becomes part of the medium. In one of the most famous such examples Gulliver sleeps for roughly a third of the 1939 cartoon adaptation produced by Fleischer Studios. The rotoscoped body merges with the verdant landscape, much to the alarm of an unsuspecting and highly kinetic Lilliputian who takes over the role of protagonist. Fully formed but versatile, Lemuel Gulliver was born for transmedia storytelling.

In Brian Richardson's schema, Gulliver would be a 'transtextual' character as fictional men bearing his name have appeared in texts that are not perceived as a continuous series but rather a suite of works produced by different authors, scripters and artists.[18] Richardson considers such characters to be entirely separate entities, though he would accommodate 'authentic' variations.[19] Or, as Marie-Laure Ryan might instead have it, Gulliver is multiple, uncoalescing versions of a 'transfictional' character able to cross mutually exclusive fictional worlds.[20] Such conflicting views about both the ontology and portability of characters points to a larger uncertainty in transmedia studies about the importance of continuity against multiplicity, that is, the extent to which narratological elements rely on plausible resemblances to be understood as forming a storied unity. More specifically, we might wonder if Gulliver upholds or contradicts Bertetti's claim that transmedia characters are always accretive in that new iterations add elements to a solidified figure.[21] Freeman similarly insists that 'transmedia storytelling must ultimately produce a series of media texts that function not as *versions* of the same fiction, as in adaptation, but rather as continuing *extensions* of the same story'.[22] For Tobias Kunz and Lukas R. A. Wilde transmedia characters are 'shaped by regularity'.[23] Richardson prioritizes 'plausible continuation'.[24] Belatedly dispersed across multiple text and media systems, Gulliver complicates the scope of a transmedia study. At the very least, we must embrace a paradox: long-lived characters can be consistent in different ways. Whereas the author-explorer's words usually appear verbatim or at least superficially paraphrased, depending on the immediate verbal or visual context, his physical form has retained a regular if not quite plausible shape for much of his cultural afterlife.

Lemuel Gulliver usually looks like a fortysomething light-skinned man. Increasingly, though, he has been aged down (and sometimes way up) or given brown skin (as in Hindi comics and films). In a recent stage performance by Unicorn Theatre he became a woman of colour for the first time, albeit under a new name: Grace Gulliver. His relationships and friendships have changed a lot. In the 1996 television series starring Ted Danson in the lead role, they keep Gulliver's former employer, Dr Bates, alive well beyond the first few pages of the source material and repurpose him as a belligerent love rival. A family man in *Travels*, Gulliver is depicted in adaptations or new works as either extremely loving, and therefore tragic, or as aloof and perhaps villainous. To account for the contradictory roles Gulliver has played in extensions and reworkings we might attend to narrative motifs, in which at least two competing actions operate at once (usually discovery and interaction). The most famous type of instance sees an alarmed or charmed Gulliver tethered by small ropes and flanked by hostile Lilliputians. Then there's the bewildered Brobdingnagians peering over the little human performing a ludicrously grandiose gesture. Large or small, young or old, kind or cruel, Gulliver, the character that we have inherited, speaks through actions as much as in words. Despite the textual pluralism built into *Travels* and its initial publishing contexts, we are dealing with a recognizable, if not conventionally consistent, lead character.[25] Frederik N. Smith goes so far as to argue that Gulliver's own storytelling comprises multiple voices under a singular I, including that of the 'epic boaster', the satirist, and the political theorist.[26] Less convincingly, Loyd Douglas identified six distinct Gullivers spread over the course of *Travels*.[27] Even the two portraits of Gulliver provided in the official editions are clearly of different men (as discussed in Chapter 3 of the present study). For the entirety of the author-explorer's travels, he has a wife and children back home; we learn only in passing that a daughter, Betty, now has a family of her own (and a life outside her father's memoirs). We can guess Gulliver's date of birth based on his schooling, but his official death date remains unknown.

Beyond biographical particulars, *what* is Gulliver? Is he a type, or perhaps types (a middle-class Englishman, a traveller, a surgeon, a linguist, a fool, a trickster, a madman, a misanthrope)? An allegorical personage or a satiric ingénu?[28] Is he an actor (an enactor of established text) or a writer (a creator of stories), or a Crusoean hybrid of the two?

Many adaptations and reworkings foreground the actions over the words. Some extensions pointedly favour his writer status instead and go so far as to link the scribbling to dishonesty or madness as part of an elaboration of the core storyline. Comic book and film adaptations of *Travels* often present Gulliver as an already famous character before (re) tracing his story.[29] With the development of film and comics as popular art forms, Gulliver increasingly became heroic – and usually gained a more rugged appearance suited to arduous sea voyages. Long before this, with the commercial success of the 'Lilliputian' series curated by Newbery's son, John Newbery, the term became a synonym for children from the 1750s onwards. According to Lionel Basney, this lexical shift suggests Gulliver took on the role of mentor to younger adventurers as the fantastical worlds created by Swift gained greater interest among more diverse audiences.[30] If so, for all its breadth and depth, Gulliver's mainstream cultural afterlife has obscured the different, contradictory character functions that Swift and others have conferred on him. To the original Lilliputians, he is a selfish monster and also a one-man war machine. For the Blefuscudians, he embodies a malevolent force of nature that rips through their fleet of ships. The miniature man is a mechanical plaything to the King of Brobdingnag, a rival entertainer to the court's dwarf, and a living doll to the farmer's daughter, Glumdalclitch. Like many personlike entities, Gulliver has a name, a body, a family, and a timeline.[31] None of these elements are consistent in Swift's *Travels*, let alone across the three centuries' worth of extensions and retellings that followed it. Swift's Gulliver is both Dr Gulliver and Captain Gulliver; more recently, he has become Lem or plain Mr Gulliver. To some he is also Grildrig or a Nardac, or, like Frankenstein's Creature, defined by his physical description, namely, Quinbus Flestrin (Man-Mountain) and a *lusus naturae* (a freak of nature). In the first two canonical voyages his body shifts in scale relative to those around him. By implication, it also shrinks after an abstemious diet among the Houyhnhnms. And he sires many more children beyond the pages of *Travels*.

Arguably Gulliver becomes *more* of a character after the fact, if we endorse novelistic definitions implicitly upheld by the few scholars who have addressed the personhood of the original version of the protagonist.[32] Claude Rawson insists Swift's Gulliver is not a character because he lacks intellectual or moral consistency.[33] Robert C. Elliott similarly notes that Gulliver's character does not 'develop'; 'it simply changes'.[34] This changeableness, for David Fishelov, renders this 'chameleon-like figure' an 'ad-hoc character' at best.[35] Denis Donoghue posits an unsolvable paradox: Gulliver is one of the most memorable characters in all fiction precisely because he has virtually no character, that is, no inner life.[36] Taking Gulliver's characterlessness as read, Lionel Basney reduces him to the in-text function of a 'friendly camera'.[37] Such denials of Gulliver's ontological presence rest on the assumption that literary characters 'have to be deep, well-rounded, psychologically complex, or unified to count as characters', in the words of Rita Felski.[38] Far from being a consistent entity, Gulliver respawns in different character formats across and beyond *Travels*: he's a ravenous monster, a child's plaything, a freak of nature, a gentle Yahoo, and more. As these precedents had been established in the source text, the competing versions adopted in adaptations or extensions must be equally valid in design, if not necessarily in execution. With that premise in mind, Amie L. Thomasson's notion of the abstract artefact provides us with a pertinent alternative to the personhood model of fictional character more appropriate for realist literature.[39] Characters are abstract because they do not exist in our world, but they are artefacts because they depend on our works for existence. The word *character* still implies impersonation, the mimicry of a person, or personation, agency in action rather than an agent of plot: one puts on a character, or one has character.[40]

Figure may be a more appropriate term for a non-realist character, despite the inartistic connotations. A literary figure, like a mass-produced action figure or doll, is an object to which a plot happens; its familiar appearance endows it with wider cultural value. Despite the insinuation of passivity, it can still offer emotional or intellectual worth to the imaginative user, particularly where the narrative motifs can be performed in reminiscence of prior reading or viewing experiences. Even if Gulliver changes in some fundamental ways, his actions invariably do not. He is perpetually tied to the Lilliputian beach. Giant wasps and rats keep attacking him. And he keeps discovering the same or similarly bizarre nations. This narratorial tension between personlike character and toylike figure remains implicit in Swift's original text but becomes more apparent and perambulates in remediation and new transmedial storytelling. In comics and graphic novels, as we shall see in the penultimate chapter, Gulliver more readily conforms to this definition of figure as narrative object, especially when in Brobdingnag. In films, as discussed in the final chapter, Gulliver looks and acts like a fleshed-out character, but not always convincingly so. The equal plausibility of this seeming contradiction indicates why medium specificity matters in character studies, as Peter Lamarque reminds us.[41] Far from being a sign of mimetic failure, incompleteness distinguishes characters as abstract artefacts from real persons. After all, so Thomas Docherty theorizes, if a character is immune to change they are effectively 'dead'.[42] Or, in Lynch's critique of the personhood model, a character's ontological deficit – its not dying – mirrors its 'never living'.[43] If character creation must always be teleological, as Baruch Hochman argues, literary figures in my schema participate in the personlike act of dying, often multiply so, but repeatedly defraud death.[44]

Like Frankenstein's Creature, Dracula, Sherlock Holmes, Tarzan, Batman and Superman, among the other (more usual) suspects, the book-born Lemuel Gulliver ought to be treated as a serial figure who crosses an unfixable approximation of real-world time and space. Serial figures, according to Shane Denson and Ruth Mayer, do not develop according to a linear biography but rather undergo a virtual beginning with each repetition, revision or reboot of their stories.[45] This anti-linearity finally justifies the paradoxical motif of the already published book that appears in some visual reimaginings of *Travels*. A serial figure needs no explanation, introduction or elaborate framing, as Denson and Mayer argue, though it needs a starting point: it is '*familiar*, even if one has never dealt explicitly with the figure before'.[46] Such figures coexist with rather than displace their variants, regardless of any lingering murderous intentions among later versions, like clones tied to yet independent from the source material. Here I depart from David A. Brewer's migratory model of a social canon, in which readers engage with characters as though they were 'old friends' capable of living beyond the boundaries of text.[47] Implicit in Brewer's historicized account of eighteenth-century engagements with literature is a personhood notion of character, which suggests singularity and ultimately proprietary authorship. Serial figuration instead thrives on infinite movement. This, I wish to demonstrate, is not a new phenomenon in literature.

Gulliver's further travels

Transformation trumps mere transplantation in transfictional and transmedial storytelling. Constant modification is the norm.[48] Even now characters can be subject to limited copyright protection, but they remain prone to parody, pastiche and other types of disfigurement too.[49] Of Gulliver's multiple creators, co-creators and re-creators, surprisingly few have attempted to align with Swift's prototype too rigidly, after all – though a transmedia theorist such as Freeman would insist that this further indicates that 'variation' must be just as important as 'sameness'.[50] Here, *variation* is complicated by competing aesthetic and commercial contexts beyond the original publication of *Travels*; or, put another way, *sameness* can refer to different house styles adopted by creative teams focused on their own series or catalogues. Among the secondary creators we might list unacknowledged collaborators such as Arbuthnot and Pope, who, in the early days, brought different eighteenth-century forms and genres to bear on Swift's properties, through to illustrators, abridgers and continuers, some of whom carry their own cultural cachet into the Gulliverian multiverse. Others are jobbing artists operating in different media entirely and in line with the guidelines of the companies for whom they have worked (Gilberton, Fleischer Studios, Hanna-Barbera, Toei Animation, the BBC and more). We nevertheless often find Gérard Genette's author-centric 'contract of transposition' deployed in the paratextual elements of overt Gulliverian adaptations: 'from' or 'inspired by' the 'classic tale by Jonathan Swift' and the like.[51] Notice of this contract appears conspicuously on title pages or in the framing narrative of a film, where the act of writing itself is often prominent. Or, if that performative motif has been left out, often along with the first-person voiceover, Gulliver defaults to being the enactor instead.

The adaptative process seemingly prioritizes either Gulliver as an active author or Gulliver as the narrativized subject, though in most substantial reworkings such figurations invariably overlap at specific junctures. The format of the material matters in different ways too. As discussed in Chapter 1, some book-length Gulliveriana imitates the original, most notoriously Samuel Richardson's *Travels into Several Remote Nations of the World. Vol. III* (1727; hereafter *Volume III*), which appeared only a few months after Swift's *Travels*, and was bound with it in unsuspecting foreign-language editions for decades to come. More recent 'found' extensions examined in Chapter 2 include Volter Kilpi's *Gulliver's Voyage to Phantomimia* (1939, 2020), an unfinished time-travel adventure, Kurt Friedlaender's *A Voyage to Springistan* (1972), from a manuscript in Swift's hand 'recovered' from an Irish castle, and John Paul Brady's *A Voyage to Inishneefa* (1987), which had been 'discovered' in Swift's writing desk in Dublin. Matthew Hodgart's *A New Voyage to the Country of the Houyhnhnms* (1970), another modern 'Fifth Part', mimics the typography of the original and brings back old characters. But, like its contemporaneous expansions, it made little attempt to conform to the original's social setting. Gulliver's pliability has been a significant aspect of his longevity among authors and artists. For early satirists in the periodical press, the character provided generic shorthand. For many filmmakers, the author-explorer has been a convenient adventure hero perpetually nabbed from the public domain. But, as I will suggest, the sometimes exploitative, sometimes incidental use of Gulliver in these and other creative engagements better reveals the true value of his cultural standing than largely reverential straight adaptations have, as explored in Chapter 4.

Many of the commercial outputs bury their supplementary authorship or, at least, rely on the dispersed labour of a production team and therefore do not consciously participate in the combative demands of literary adaptation. As we shall see in Chapter 3, some advertising agencies jettison Gulliver entirely, replacing him with a tethered egg or motor vehicles in an intriguing instance of an adapted narrative motif. (In such cases the aura of Gulliver induces a different type of generic shorthand, that of the ensnared hero or folkish monster.) In other cases, where the secondary author or artist happens to be a notable practitioner in their own field, the production requires us to understand specific stylistic and formal contexts, whether it's John Arbuthnot's Scriblerian comedy or Alan Moore's metafictional gamesmanship. Some, such as Martin Rowson's scatological, satirical aesthetic, align with the brand, if not the style, of Swift's *Travels* after ingenious refitting. Others seem to contradict it until we consider the implied audience. Discussing the now-iconic rotoscoped film produced by the Fleischer brothers at the outset of the Golden Age of animation, Charles Solomon criticized their choice of source material ('*Gulliver* was a sophisticated, episodic satire that most Americans had read in English classes, if they had read it at all').[52] However, this viewpoint ignores the abridged versions and children's books long consumed by impressionable readers, a young Max Fleischer among them. Rather than limited adaptations that endorse or transform a singular source, transfictional and transmedial works are treated throughout the present study as collective but uncoalescing guest texts tied symbiotically to the expanding host material (to adopt David Cowart's terms).[53] The grinning, thoughtless Gulliver of the 1939 animation had a precedent in Newbery's widely circulated abridgement, *The Adventures of Captain Gulliver*, whether he knew it or not.

Instead of privileging like-for-like links between works, the creative reception modelled here considers authorial and artistic aesthetics within the overlapping horizons of literary, cultural and economic expectations. Within the comfort of our homes, we can find Gulliver in a veritable treasure trove of books, games, comics and live-action or animated films (including digital representations of all these things). If we could traverse time and space, we would find him in real civic spaces – libraries, bookshops, cinemas, theme parks and fast-food restaurants. He haunts public artworks, murals, advertisements, postcards, puzzles, magazines, memes and all sorts of entertainment ephemera. In the *Doctor Who* serial *The Mind Robber* (1968), the second Doctor stumbles across an embodied figment of the author-explorer on a strange planet where fictional beings come to life; in the *Star Trek* novel *Gulliver's Fugitives* (1990), by contrast, a schoolgirl cherishes a fragment of a copy of *Travels*, desperate to keep its words alive in a future where imagination has been outlawed. Ensconced within popular franchises, the latter examples encapsulate the two major forms in which Swift's literary properties linger in our collective imagination, as an eighteenth-century everyman named Lemuel Gulliver and a cherished book (*Gulliver's Travels*), both of which can be opened up creatively for vastly different purposes. If adopting Christian Moraru's distinction between counterwriting and underwriting, though, like Cowart's theory of literary symbiosis, it was coined for a typology of Postmodern narrative, we will notice a skewing towards the latter in the accumulation of Gulliveriana over the past three hundred years.[54] Counterwriting equates with rupture, even dissent: one finds this most compellingly expressed in recent feminist refocalizations that critique Gulliver's neglect of his barely mentioned family. Underwriting more deferentially endorses the host text, expanding its heterocosm (literally, other world) within implied parameters or else carefully demarcated alternative universes. Grown-up but still missing her Grildrig, the titular heroine of Leo Sonderegger's 2000 sequel *Glumdalclitch* creates a museum in his honour; in effect, she monumentalizes the singularly Brobdingnagian Gulliver.

Any Gulliverian museum would be messy and incomplete, according to Jacques Derrida's archontic principle of endless expansion, particularly if and when we bring in participatory cultures such as fanfiction.[55] Curating a metaphorical museum that challenges the negative connotations associated with propriety models of authorship, that is, *appropriation* (which implies theft or exploitation) or the *derivative* (which implies mere imitation), I have favoured archontic selectiveness over canonical restrictiveness, or abstract artefacts over rounded, personlike characters. My process relies on an extensive engagement with non-academic resources found online and throughout the world, from *Ads of the World* to YouTube, as well as established library holdings. Many perishable items have been lost or have eluded catalogues outright. What remains can still reveal much about Gulliver's ongoing appeal to authors and artists working in different forms and genres, both popular and literary alike. Swivelling my attention between Gulliver as a figure and as a fictive author, I prioritize continuations and reworkings that include him (whether as a character or narrator, or both) or are attributed to him (as an author who may or may not also appear within the book or text). A sizeable portion of Gulliveriana produced over the past three centuries refocuses the narrative, typically through established characters (Glumdalclitch or Mary Gulliver) or familial or appointed descendants (John Gulliver or Michael Pine). Other works revisit Lilliput or Laputa, often many years after Lemuel Gulliver's first discovery of those places. Much of that hefty body of materials lies just beyond our immediate scope, though I will allude to it in passing where common ground can be found. This book will feature little to no discussion of adaptations or extensions that exclude Gulliver, even cherished classics such as T. H. White's *Mistress Masham's Repose* (1946), or its own spawning, or Hayao Miyazaki's influential anime *Laputa: Castle in the Sky* (1986). We can barely find room for one of the most inventive Gulliverian texts of recent times, Adam Roberts's metafictional novel *Swiftly: A Novel* (2008), in which Jonathan Swift displaces Lemuel Gulliver as a literary figure. The world of Gulliveriana is impossibly large, and, as with any archive of found objects, it keeps growing.

1 THE GHOST WRITER

In August 1796, almost seventy years after the initial publication of *Gulliver's Travels*, the spirit of the eponymous explorer-turned-author remained restless. Having communed with him, Felix Phantom (Francisco Solano Constancio) reported in *The Ghost* that this 'worthy Phantom complains much of the injustice done him by the mutilated state in which his ingenious and authentic Travels have been given to the world'. Gulliver's notional creator, Jonathan Swift, has finally been outed as yet another plagiarist: 'like another Defoe, he pretended that my friend's real adventures were the inventions of his own brain'.[1] This is a common enough trick among secondary authors even today: challenge the primary author's claims to ownership while endorsing the artistic legitimacy of their own, unauthorized contribution, and perhaps angling for further commissions subject to demand. Whatever the motivations might be, such enforced collaboration also helps establish the public persona – and perhaps social personhood – of a character. Constancio and Swift both present Gulliver as a fussy writer worried about the previous and future treatment of his materials.[2] Viewed through the modern lens of transmedial storytelling, this late-eighteenth-century example exemplifies what an unsystematic dispersal of characters and other narratological elements could look like before the age of media convergence. Broadening this focus on unsystematic dispersal across the eighteenth and nineteenth centuries, while also taking in modern examples of the same kind, this chapter comprises readings of continuations and spinoffs produced in the name of Gulliver by friends, enemies and those with no immediate connection to Swift. The first section, 'Gulliveriana', establishes key terms and challenges. The next section, 'Original omissions', analyses the diverse range of works written in the name of Gulliver. This includes a fraudulent third volume of *Travels* in 1727, by the printer and novelist Samuel Richardson, and expansions such as *Memoirs of the Court of Lilliput* (1727), *A Cursory View of the History of Lilliput for these last forty three Years* (1727) and *An*

Account of the State of Learning in the Empire of Lilliput (1728). Bizarre authorial attributions to Gulliver, like the mock-medical treatise *The Anatomist Dissected, or the Man-Midwife finely brought to Bed* (1727) and Henry Fielding's *The Masquerade, A Poem* (1728), feature in the final section, 'Gulliver's voices', alongside official Lilliputian poems written by members of Swift's circle. We end with an expedited literary history of later 'found' Gulliveriana, ranging from a chapter in Mortimer Collins's comical novel *Squire Silchester's Whim* (1873) to Louis Hermann's *In the Sealed Cave* (1935) to twenty-first-century ventriloquizations.

At turns accretive and contrarian, these prose and poetic engagements with the host material will be considered in competing formal and generic settings. Constancio's Phantom takes an ingenious extra step in referencing a notable authority who, in the *Review* earlier in the century, had publicly complained about those scribblers who stole intellectual property.[3] Fearing the theft of his most famous creation, Robinson Crusoe, Daniel Defoe killed off his lead character in a book-length continuation a year after giving him life in print. Robinsonades kept appearing, however, and they continue to do so.[4] Miguel de Cervantes had resorted to charactercide a little over a century earlier, in the 1615 sequel to *Don Quixote* (1605), and has been just as unsuccessful in foreshortening the afterlife of his titular protagonist. Chastened by these cautionary examples, Gulliver undertakes a counterintuitive solution by publishing *more*, beyond the grave, through Felix Phantom. More here means missing rather than new pieces: 'I now present my readers with a passage which has been left out in chap. 5. of the Voyage to Laputa'.[5] Ironically, this posthumous mode of publishing attempts to prevent Gulliver from falling into the type of authorship mocked at the conclusion of another of Swift's major prose satires, *A Tale of a Tub* (1704): 'I am now trying an Experiment very frequent among Modern Authors; which is, to *write upon Nothing*; When the Subject is utterly exhausted, to let the Pen still move on; by some called, the Ghost of Wit, delighting to walk after the Death of its Body'.[6] Trapped into a timeless existence of underwriting, that is, recovering putatively missing material, Gulliver the author no longer belonged to the late Dean Swift. The venerability of the connection would nevertheless continue to serve him well, no less than now, in comics, graphic novels and movies alike (as we shall see in upcoming chapters). Constancio's coup failed.

A rival cleric-poet, Jonathan Smedley, tried a different approach. He spent an entire book, which he opportunistically titled *Gulliveriana*

(1728), splicing together Gulliver and Swift to expose the pointlessness of pseudonymous satire in an age of celebrity authorship (signing letters as 'Jonathan Gulliver', providing biographical information about 'The Reverend Captain *Gulliver*', and so on). Amid a deluge of parodic poems, essays, letters and journals, Smedley also mockingly hinted at forthcoming, damning publications, such as a paper called '*Gulliver's Reasons*, *viz.* for *Ingratitude*, for *Irreligion*, for *Turning*, for *Returning*, and to serve any *Turn*, to be bound up with the *Tale of a Tub*'.[7] On the whole, though, secondary authors have bought into the ruse of Gulliver's singular authorial presence. An unknown scribe put a journalist's pen into Gulliver's hand as early as 1728. *Applebee's Original Weekly Journal* featured on its front pages from 13 April through 5 October a series of letters signed 'L. Gulliver'. Seventeen of these letters are extant – there may have been many more.[8] Certainly, the final known letter does not definitively close the narrative of the continuation. We might note that the periodical series picks up from the unofficial *Travels into Several Remote Nations of the World. Vol. III* (1727; hereafter *Volume III*), which had been quietly ushered into print by Samuel Richardson (without a printer's or bookseller's name). There we had left Gulliver in France making a misjudged investment in the Mississippi Company, John Law's real-life counterpart to the similarly disastrous South Sea Company that once fascinated Swift. The Applebee Gulliver manages to recover a large part of his investment, gaining further narrative traction upfront, as well as low-key legitimating the fraudulent attachment of *Volume III* to Swift's original two volumes of *Travels*.

Cynically, we might presume the avatar of Gulliver provided a convenient writing prompt, regardless of the immediate source. More curiously still, the financial crisis at the outset of the decade had lost its topicality by 1728, even if this linked the Gulliver sequence to a persistent theme of the periodical's earlier output. This anomaly suggests the secondary author had broader satirical interests in mind, namely, an attack on institutional corruption. If so, the serial format suited his varied interests better than a novel would: 'that I should Weekly transcribe so much of my remaining Travels and Adventures, with such miscellaneous Pieces and Remarks thereon, as I could with Conveniency and Justice of the Original' (V.221). The final clause in that sentence signals a canonical respect for Swift's authorial property, but, equally, the fuller statement pushes the passage closer to *Serious Reflections of Robinson Crusoe* (1720), Defoe's non-narrative extension of *Robinson Crusoe* (1719), than to a sequel comprising further voyages. After all, the three volumes (Swift's and Richardson's) only cover 'some Part' of the character's life, though more will come. The Applebee Gulliver 'fills in' gaps left in Swift's original by adding a more detailed account of financial corruption, albeit more directly and without the satirical ruse of the necessity of simplified cultural translation. However, the expansion of worlds teased in the initial letter largely falls away, either by design or because the series fell out of favour with the editorship or its readers:

> Those who are inclin'd to a Life of Gallantry and Diversion, will in the Relation of my Travel thro' the Land of *Noibla*, meet with many amusing and pleasant Accounts of the Freedoms and Amours of the Natives of that Kingdom, the superiour Order of its Inhabitants, generally speaking, indulging themselves in all manner of Pleasures, amongst which, Love is not the least; the Ladies of that Country being as susceptible of that Passion, as they are in any Parts of *Europe*. (V.222)

The gleeful hinting at scandalous content largely responds to other unofficial Gulliverian texts, it must be said, such as the salacious *Memoirs of the Court of Lilliput*, which itself expanded on small, coy hints in Swift's original, including implausible sexual relationships insinuated by enemies at court. To query the fidelity of the Applebee Gulliver, along with the Gullivers of *Volume III* and *Memoirs*, would miss the salient point in the critical purview of transfictional or transmedial storytelling: Lemuel Gulliver has never been a consistent character, and secondary authors have made little investment in adhering to the original template. We find Gulliver alive and well in the periodical press as late as 1844, in *Blackwood's Edinburgh Magazine*, where he introduces a free transcription of the proceedings of a meeting of Houyhnhnms on a timely topic unknowable to Swift or his character: The Corn Laws.[9] Another strategy entailed returning to Lilliput, ostensibly to verify Gulliver's initial findings but really to find new resonances between the fictional nation and the foibles of modern British politics. Adopting the mask of Gulliver's re-voyaging grandson and thereby discovering 'many States and Empires beside those of *Lilliput* and *Blefuscu*', a youngish Samuel Johnson circumvented a parliamentary privilege that forbade the verbatim reporting of debates with his allegorical column for *The Gentleman's Magazine* between 1738 and 1746. Familiar yet inexhaustible, Gulliver provided convenient coding to other satirists. It did not matter that the original author-explorer had probably felt 'the unexpected Stroke of sudden Death' or was at least too lazy to complete his account of Lilliput.[10] If anything, Gulliver's implied personhood got in the way of contemporary concerns – so Johnson cut him out while retaining his spirit.

Gulliveriana

Expanding the intellectual, emotional or political scope of *Travels*, the early Gulliveriana imposed more recognizably character-like qualities upon the nominal protagonist, and more explicitly than Swift had allowed. To solve this paradox we need to trace Gulliver's largely unarticulated function as a ghostwriter of his own further works. In the next chapter we will consider how this character-centric dynamic plays out in nominal further voyages, and after that we will unpick the ontological tension between *character* and *figure* in word-and-image adaptations and retellings. Here we will explore post-*Travels* writings attributed to the pen of Lemuel Gulliver. Intriguingly, Richardson aside, few secondary authors have tried to ventriloquize Swift's voice too closely (and in that case *Volume III* cannibalized the works of other authors to achieve this effect). Many of them have turned to different and largely inappropriate forms, such as ballads and other types of poetry, scandal memoirs and periodical prose – despite Gulliver's expressed disdain for poetry and scandal memoirs (and the arts and popular entertainment more generally) in *Travels*.[11] Many explored ideas not previously expressed by Swift's character, while yet others flatly contradict his stated principles, biases or assumptions. Returning to the original text, we must note that Gulliver's authorial voice jostled against other ghostwriters involved in the production of his memoirs, not all of whom were created by Swift.

In the 1735 version of *Travels* (and most subsequent editions) an Advertisement responds to the paratext that immediately follows it, Gulliver's open letter to his print agent Richard Sympson (another character created by Swift and his circle), in which he complains that unauthorized interpolations had been added to the memoirs.[12] The 'publisher' blames '*a Person since deceased*' for the mangled state of the first edition (*GT*, 5). Although not named here, that man was a real person: the Reverend Andrew Tooke, whom Benjamin Motte Jr had enlisted to bowdlerize the manuscript prior to the printing of the London edition in 1726.[13] While noting the authoritative corrections, the publisher stops short of claiming the new edition could be definitive: the corrections come from a transcription of '*a most intimate Friend of the Authors*', the unnamed Charles Ford, a trusted acquaintance of Swift.[14] In 'A Letter from Capt. Gulliver, to his Cousin Sympson', which immediately follows this statement, the author-explorer demands that the print agent acknowledges the mistakes, inscribing such errors into perpetuity rather than burying them beneath final correction. Gulliver the author, in other words, already signals a lack of control over his materials. Evidently, the author-explorer has a life beyond the laying down of his pen ahead of the 1726 publication of his memoirs. But his 'authorial quest', in Alan D. Chalmers's words, 'leaves him almost as insubstantial as he was before he began it'.[15] Beyond this metanarrative of writing and rewriting, and even unwriting, the true ghostwriter – Swift – would have been conscious of his own lack of control in real terms. After all, the erroneous versions remained in circulation.

Considered within the remit of novelistic characterization, the 1735 letter presented to the reader a 'bitter, ranting Gulliver strikingly at odds with the opening pages of the main text', as Stephen Karian has observed.[16] The Gulliver of the prefatory letter has evidently been changed by his experiences in Houyhnhnm-Land insofar as he now detests the 'human Species' and cannot fathom the benefits of lying ('*the thing that was not*' [*GT*, 8–9]). Crucially, however, Gulliver understands that such change can be reversed against his will: 'since my last Return, some Corruptions of my *Yahoo* Nature have revived in me by conversing with a few of your Species' (*GT*, 14). As a book-born character, Gulliver is trapped in an endless loop of dawning misanthropy that Gulliver the author cannot stop. The loop is interrupted by another paratext, Sympson's letter ('The Publisher to the Reader'), in which different versions of Gulliver have been presented to the public since its first appearance in 1726. Indeed, Sympson's letter contradicts Gulliver's own in terms of form and function. Reluctant to publish *Travels*, Gulliver nevertheless hopes it will reform the species, an 'absurd' project, so he comes to realize: 'I have now done with all such visionary Schemes for ever'. Sympson similarly believes the book has a social function but considers it 'a better Entertainment to our young Noblemen, than the common Scribbles of Politicks and Party' (*GT*, 16). To that end, he candidly 'resolved to fit' – or refit – the manuscript for the general reader, removing the lengthy material that would have made it a more literal kind of travel memoir, such as descriptions of the weather and management of the ships. And, whereas Gulliver considered the manuscript 'all destroyed', Sympson has the 'whole Work' to hand, ready for inspection by any unusually attentive hypothetical reader that might request to see it.

Authorship does not necessarily equate to ownership. In fact, Sympson appoints himself as the custodian of *Travels*: 'This Volume would have been at least twice as large, if I had not made bold to strike out innumerable Passages'. The editor's pen unwrites any version of *Travels* that falls short of a market-focused, novelistic ideal. If Sympson can destroy unwritten material that only existed in a fictional universe, such material could be restored or rewritten (that is, written), either by the author himself or self-appointed appropriators. The Applebee Gulliver had made a similar claim about his manuscript, which 'would swell beyond my present Design'.[17] The vagueness of Sympson's phrase 'innumerable Passages' goads adapters into counterfeiting the seemingly missing pieces in any shape or size they plausibly could. The fictive print agent also alludes to the prevailing culture of abridgement and chapbooking, which directly affected *Travels* as early as 1727. The first abridger of Swift's *Travels* claimed the project would help readers by lessening the expense of the purchase without causing 'Injury to the celebrated Author' (he was right about the financials, at least: the abridgement cost three shillings, the original eight shillings and sixpence).[18] More than that, he takes for granted that 'a faithful Abridgement' was not only possible but made the book more readable on both moral and aesthetic grounds: 'some Passages in the Original, which the Generality of Mankind have thought immodest and indecent, are entirely omitted, and many trivial Circumstances contracted into a very narrow Compass' (ii). If not quite displacing Swift's original, abridgements only gained in commercial value. Omitting the third and fourth voyages and duly setting a major precedent, Francis Newbery's *The Adventures of Captain Gulliver, in a Voyage to the Islands of Lilliput and Brobdignag* [sic] (1772) remained in print for the next thirty years before losing out to other low-cost abridgements.[19]

While textual cuts in abridgements were usually pragmatic, by definition, some alterations were clearly ideological. As Julian Fung has shown, many condensers softened Part IV, which featured the voyage to Houyhnhnm-Land.[20] And different versions of *Travels* attracted different readerships. Some were foreign-language retellings attuned to local interests.[21] Many abridgements and textbook editions were aimed at English-speaking children or readers of English as a second language.[22] Modern specialists in book publishing for schoolchildren, such as

Ladybird and Usborne, routinely include boldly illustrated *Travels* in their catalogues.[23] The bestselling novelist Jonathan Coe recently reworked the material for a young, modern audience as part of a 'Save the Story' campaign ('Unforgettable stories retold by today's greatest writers').[24] *The Story of Gulliver* (2013) remixes all four voyages into chapter book form, in the third person, and positions Gulliver as a folkloric figure: 'Almost 300 years ago, there lived a man with a strange name' (7). Swift wrote 'to make people think', Coe reasons in an afterword ('Where is this story from?' [89–90]), and this universalism keeps the subject matter relevant. Expansions rather than abridgements worried Gulliver, who complained in his open letter to Sympson about the 'Libels, and Keys, and Reflections, and Memoirs, and Second Parts' loaded up on *Travels*, including a fraudulent *Volume III*, that appeared in the meantime (*GT*, 11). Secondary authors expanded the world of Gulliver through multiple fifth voyages, spinoffs, mock treatises, in-character verse exchanges, and much more for many more years to come. Using Jeanne K. Welcher and George E. Bush Jr's eight-volume collection of pre-1800 Gulliveriana as a guide, close to two hundred imitative or supplementary works were produced and reproduced between late 1726 and 1730 and well over a hundred in each of the following two decades, the 1730s and 1740s. In 1726 alone we have twenty-six Gulliver-related publications, a remarkable feat when we recall that Swift's book first appeared as late as October of that year. In 1727 the figure leaps up to sixty-eight items. Between three and four hundred original visual Gulliverian pieces alone were produced in the century after the appearance of *Travels*. Six hundred or more performances (music, dance and drama) reached audiences of thousands across the world throughout the eighteenth century.[25] In the subsequent centuries, up to the present day, such performances have spread well beyond our ability to count them.

Representing a multimedia, word-and-image (and sometimes wordless) body of materials, 'Gulliveriana' must remain a broad term, even if we can discount the loosest reworkings, nominal homages, or incidental references. Some Gulliveriana is Gulliveriana in name only – Gulliver became a convenient pseudonym for up-and-coming satirists, as in a medical spoof of Nathaniel St André's calamitous account of the case of Mary Toft, who had convinced several doctors that she gave birth to rabbits, *A Short Narrative of an Extraordinary Delivery of Rabbets* (1727). Enlisting Gulliver's authority as a famous surgeon, *The Anatomist Dissected, or the Man-Midwife finely brought to Bed* (also 1727) conflates real-world quackery with Swift's mock-academy at Lagado. In 1730 and 1731, six writings under the pseudonym Martin Gulliver and one under Martinus Gulliverianus appeared in Dublin. There's also an alleged brother, Ephraim Gulliver. There have been many Lemuel Gullivers Jr too, as we shall see in the next chapter. Most Gulliverian works signal a formal connection with *Travels*, whether they revisit old settings, fill in perceived gaps in the narrative, or provide additional, non-narrative material. To take a familiar example, *Modern Gulliver's Travels* (1796) opens with a discussion of the infamous traveller's romance with a Blefuscudian lady, which, we learn, had been omitted in the prior book on the grounds of moral decency. Filling in this omission, the secondary author picks up a small hint in Swift's book, thereby legitimising his new endeavours. *An Account of the State of Learning in the Empire of Lilliput* (1728) claims on its title page to be '*Faithfully Transcribed out of* Captain LEMUEL GULLIVER'S *General Description of the Empire of* Lilliput, *mention'd in the 69th Page of the First Volume of his Travels*', which marks out its affiliation with the original publication with teasing precision.[26]

With John Arbuthnot (the most likely author of *Account*) and Alexander Pope (author of official Lilliputian poems) and other members of Swift's circle in mind, Welcher distinguishes complicit Gulliverian writers from opportunists: 'His friends caught his spirit of self-imitation, echoed it for his delight, passed it on. The genuine alter egos of Swift entered into mock complicity with Gulliver. The fake ones functioned as Gulliver clones'.[27] A distinction between 'genuine' alter egos and 'fake' clones is inherently problematic, but it does capture a conundrum within the study of Gulliveriana and, by extension, allographic sequels (that is, supplementary texts not written by the original author). To what extent is the field shaped by the authors, whether primary or secondary, whether outsiders or allies, or by the consumers? Or, in terms of Brian Richardson's notion of 'transtextual' characterization, to what extent can 'authentic' variations plausibly differ from a common template?[28] To what extent is mock-complicity akin to authoritative status? How much creative leeway would a complicit secondary author have, and would it be more or less than for an outsider? Can authorship be outsourced without the reader's awareness? Welcher and Bush acknowledge over sixty significant responses to *Travels* that endeavour 'to reproduce something of its style, intent, and design'.[29] This definition is also problematic because it fails to accommodate partisanship in anti-Swiftian, contra-Swiftian and de-Swiftian responses, and it would rely on a narrow consensus on what the original intentions and targets are. It also presupposes that those original intentions and targets remain fixed and therefore unadaptable. Without some adjustment, this definition also poses a problem for modern studies of transmedia storytelling that assume the dispersal of characters and their worlds needs to be systematic. Nicholas Seager provides a compelling solution. Gulliverian sequels are, he writes, 'prose fictions that accept the fictional world detailed in Swift's original, and which supplement it in some way – accretive, rather than analogous works'.[30] The accretive need not be consistent, but there must be at least some implicit working together, however contrarian.

Keeping Seager's imperative in mind, we can map the dominant formal elements of *Travels* onto Matthew Freeman's historicized model of transmedia storytelling, which comprises character-building, world-building and authorship.[31] In addition to being immediately strewn across competing authorial contexts, Gulliver inherently complicates both character-building and world-building since he is both the main character and nominal author, that is, the world-builder. And it is precisely this complication that has always attracted an array of highly inventive creative responses. Would the new Gullivers have to fall in line with their prototype? If so, do we only mean the book-born original or also the always uncoalescing versions that fit Marie-Laure Ryan's 'transfictional' model of character?[32] If the latter, would the same open-ended logic apply to other, less prominent characters, such as Mary Gulliver? Or does the specificity of their functions within Gulliver's world-building demand yet more regularity? How do we, or unsuspecting readers, distinguish between imitation and imposter Gullivers when the initial print version of *Travels* was editorially compromised (by the claim of Swift's Gulliver)? Do we need to? Gulliveriana, I suggest, is not always tethered to Gulliver's voyages, but it is collectively haunted by them. We might go so far as to call Gulliver-less imitations 'Gulliveriads' and set them alongside Robinsonades, in which new characters similarly displace Robinson Crusoe. Some unannounced Gulliveriads thrive on a more substantial engagement with Swift's materials than some explicitly marked, opportunistic Gulliveriana, where the action might be slight or the satire less severe, even if the original period, characters and setting are retained for the purposes of audience recognition. Does *Travels* have a replicable plot? Or does it have four separate plots if we take the voyages on their own terms? Is a fifth voyage implied or entirely closed off by the misanthropic memoirist?

Reflecting on the wide appeal of *Travels* for secondary authors, David A. Brewer considers the plotlessness of the original to be the key: 'There is no actual story behind the bulk of Gulliver's plot. Or rather, there are as many stories as there are readers'. All they need to do, he continues, 'is not to contradict the *Travels* themselves too egregiously'.[33] We do not need words to convey the plot. A salient example came early, in Germany: Georg Philipp Telemann's *Gulliver Suite* for two violins (serialized in his biweekly periodical for amateur musicians, *Der Getreue Music-Meister*, in 1728). The movements focus on the fantastical elements of the remote nations, using massive divergences in the music to at turns convey the littleness of the Lilliputians (through a flurry of quasihemidemisemiquavers), the gigantism of the Brobdingnagians (through plodding semibreves), the intrusive tapping of the flappers (through agitated notes amid soporific reverie), and the order of the Houyhnhnms against the chaos of the Yahoos. Relying on an audience's general understanding of *Travels*, the violinists can still replay iconic scenes involving the central character and plot, such as when they take 256 notes to depict Gulliver's mingled bemusement and alarm when tied to the Lilliputian beach.[34] *Travelogue G* (2022) gathers all seventy-seven of Asa Hiramatsu's illustrations that featured alongside Motoyuki Shibata's serialized translation of *Travels* into Japanese for the Friday evening edition of *The Asahi Shimbun* and adds twenty new ones.[35] Read as a practically wordless treatment of *Travels*, Hiramatsu's collection remixes and revises imagery from a dense and complex Gulliverian museum to convey the story's competing emotional tones and character dynamics, examine famous and some lesser-touched narrative motifs, and foreground some concrete ways in which Swift speaks to eighteenth-century and modern political concerns. Bits of Gulliver prove sufficient for retelling certain set pieces in *Travelogue G*, but some imagery precludes him and even the *Travels* entirely. Near the start of the third voyage, for example, Hiramatsu patches an approximation of a facsimile of an entry in the *Drapier's Letters* (1724–25) over images of the Lindalino rebellion, thereby visually linking the fictional text with Swift's political writing about Ireland. Whether rendered in sound or images, Gulliveriana does not need a full-bodied Gulliver; he lurks in the shadows regardless. Having established some common terms and issues, we will now explore the ways in which authors have filled in and filled out Gulliver's world in his name. In the subsequent chapter we will explore proleptic continuations attributed to Gulliver's offspring, time-forwarded Gullivers, and other, non-Gulliverian explorers turned authors.

Original omissions

On 26 August 1727, *The British Journal* advertised the imminent publication of a book by a certain Captain Alexander Smith, an authorial figure known for a bestselling history of the lives of modern criminals.[36] The new book, they claimed, would overturn the recent *Travels* written by an imposter 'who falsely usurps the Name, Stile and Title, of Capt. Gulliver'.[37] No such book has been found, though Smedley includes a large section in *Gulliveriana* where he mockingly speculates about the contents of the multiple folio volumes forthcoming from the 'unworthy Author', Smith, supplementing the extra Libels, Keys, Reflections, Memoirs and Second Parts later identified by Gulliver with 'many original Papers and Records, secret Histories and Memoirs, Sermons and Ballads'.[38] Ensconced within a rival's extended, if niche, gibe against Swift's literary pretensions, the dubious association with Smith speaks to the complex manner in which a market-focused model of adaptation proves useful for understanding the generic assumptions of different forms of textual afterlives. In particular, Linda Hutcheon's notion that an adapted text provides a 'reservoir of instructions' for secondary authors rubs against the more historically entrenched treatment of adapters as 'raiders'.[39] In other words, moving away from a singular text-to-text understanding allows us to appreciate the messiness of literary reworking in the eighteenth century, when published materials were considered convenient fodder and perhaps culturally important but not necessarily eternally canonical. Seen in this environment, we can better appreciate the uncoordinated but vitalizing practices of those creators who helped disperse Swift's properties across different print and media settings.

One such raider is Samuel Richardson, who, in the same month he printed the abridged version of *Travels* for J. Stone and R. Long, produced an unauthorized *Volume III* for the original book. Despite appearances, the text Richardson raided most egregiously is actually Denis Vairasse's *The History of the Sevarites or Sevarambi: A Nation inhabiting part of the third Continent, Commonly called, Terrae Australes Incognitae* (1675), which had not been reprinted in English since 1700.[40] *Volume III*, as Nicholas Seager notes, adopts the structural pattern of Swift's book, which we might identify as the reservoir of instructions. Part I starts with a blatant imitation of Swift, a second voyage to Brobdingnag, which comprises about two chapters. The extensive plagiarism from Vairasse comes as early as page 51 and occupies the rest of Part I. Part II is almost entirely derivative, though none of it is a straightforward raiding. Rather, it abridges Vairasse. With regards to the Gulliverian material, which includes a return to worlds and characters created by Swift, Richardson's prose narrative was actually the first book to extend the story chronologically beyond where the first two volumes end. After embarking from Brobdingnag, Gulliver finds (to him and most, if not all, his readers) new lands, Sporunda and Sevarambia. Adhering to an author-as-owner paradigm, Walter Scott was not alone in dismissing *Volume III* as an 'impudent' imposition.[41] But, in terms of unsystematic transmedia storytelling, such impositions lingered among readers. French, Dutch and German versions appeared in 1728. There were more than a dozen printings of all three volumes together as one work across Europe before 1740. As late as the 1790s, the first Spanish version of *Travels* still contained *Volume III*. No mere book-historical anomaly, *Volume III* should also be read as a 're-envisioning' of *Travels*.[42] It is at once a forgery and a 'genuine' continuation, in Welcher's terms.[43]

Wittily, the introduction to *Volume III* outlines an authorial motivation that became commonplace in Gulliver's 'further' travels, the fear of being forgotten: 'I am terribly afraid some more fortunate Mortal will tread the Paths I have gone before'. Swift's Gulliver had expressed such a concern at the culmination of the account of the fourth voyage, though the new amplification insinuates a more mercenary angle. More than mere supplementation, when viewed in an expanded authorial context, Richardson's Gulliver worries about being overwritten when the hypothetical next traveller renames 'the Countries I have discover'd'.[44] Richardson cannily prolongs Gulliver's quarrel with his print agent, Sympson (here Simpson, a friend rather than a cousin). Claiming the 'Editor of my former Volumes' now avoids him, he references the alleged bulkiness of the original, which 'would be considerably increas'd, if he had printed my Course of Sailing, and many Sea-Terms' (*Volume III*, 6). That is, Richardson countersigns Swift's belated paratextual joke about superfluous, unwritten materials. We might identify this as the paradox of enforced collaboration. Read as a sequel, however illegitimate in proprietorial terms, Richardson's book both endorses and extends the ending of *Travels*. We had left Gulliver in the company of his horses. By

Volume III his respect for his 'Companions in the Stables' has 'augmented daily' (7). After a lengthy account of various attempts to educate his horses (now named Lmnfrimpnmo and Trtpmpfnic), Richardson's Gulliver realizes he must take them to Houyhnhnm-Land – not because, as Swift had it, the character recognizes that he was regaining his Yahoo habits among his own kind but for the opposite reason. Indifferent to his wife's newly discovered affair with the groom, as to feel otherwise entails 'thinking like a *Yahooh*', he seeks a return to 'that delightful Country' (14–15). The new adventure, via 'A Second Voyage to Brobdingnag', is bolted onto published reports of the old one ('I find mention'd in my last Page but Two of my second Volume . . .'). But, unlike Swift, Richardson practically kills off Gulliver at the conclusion of the book, where, now widowed, the eponymous hero expressly awaits the ultimate end: 'as Death is a Tax laid upon us, I think the sooner it is paid, the better' (159). A fourth volume now seemed unlikely. Familiarity segues into compulsory amplification and then newly acquired closure.

Published at around the same time, *Memoirs of the Court of Lilliput* builds on Swift's property in a different way: the title page calls it 'omitted' material. The Preface also hints that there are yet more scandalous supplements waiting to be published from Gulliver's time in other lands: '*I publish at present but that part which relates to* Lilliput, *and shall proceed gradually with the Memoirs of the several Kingdoms he resided at in their due order*'.[45] Market forces would decide if further material of this amatory kind was needed: not now, came the answer; or perhaps this addition proved sufficient (unlike most early Gulliveriana, it quickly reached a third edition). Read in an adaptative authorial context as a legitimate if unauthoritative expansion of *Travels*, *Memoirs* consolidates the unsettling threat of further, perhaps unmasked satiric swiping. It also introduces more characters and settings and re-engages with enduring Swiftian targets (projectors, legal inequalities and the like). Like *Volume III*, *Memoirs* implies a familiar relationship with the original character-as-author, and therefore a real person, as well as with Gulliver's print agent. In fact, *Memoirs* adds a further paratextual character, its alleged publisher Lucas Bennet, who claims he received from Sympson – another character who has been gifted personhood – '*the original Papers under Mr.* Lemuel Gulliver*'s own Hand*' (vii). In spite of the found-manuscript motif that remains popular among secondary authors today, however, *Memoirs* eschews any sustained semblance of being an autographic sequel. An anti-Swiftian parody by proxy, in its mockery of prominent members of the Dean's circle, *Memoirs* was publicly associated with Eliza Haywood in Pope's *Dunciad*.[46] Like Haywood's attributed novellas, *Memoirs* certainly smuggles in metafictional jokes under the guise of amatory fiction: 'Booksellers build fine Houses out of needy Authors Brains, just as they do here' (65). Judged as an illegitimate extension, moreover, it cleverly inverts the values of *Travels* while filling in its apparent redactions. Gulliver becomes gossipy, and the spotlight shifts to private intrigues, not public office failures. While Swift's account includes some bashful if boastful remarks about Gulliver's exposed penis in Lilliput and the like, the new author (still in the voice of Gulliver) lingers over the romantic intrigues of the Lilliputians: 'her Passion rising to the most extravagant height, and his desire of publishing her Frailty, not interior' (26). In terms of embodiment within the narrative, Gulliver's gargantuan size rendered him a useful war machine in Swift's original. Here, the Man Mountain uses his body to thwart a nocturnal sexual assault about to be committed by an established court enemy, Skyresh (here Skyris) Bolgolam.

Written instead in the voice of an unknown author who presents the pamphlet as a recovered document (from '*the Papers of a deceased Friend of mine*'), *A Cursory View of the History of Lilliput for these last forty three Years* (1727) challenges Gulliver's account outright. In the words of the editor: '*I must observe to the Reader, that in those Places where my Friend and* Mr. Gulliver *differ, I am of opinion the latter was mistaken*'.[47] Some 'corrections' offered here are whimsically benign and, from a world-building perspective, welcome. Whereas the original Gulliver identifies only two kingdoms which Lilliputians called the two great empires of the world, the new author '*has often assured me, there were divers other Monarchies and Republicks composed of the same sort of Men*' (V.110). Other changes speak to Whiggish principles. Swift's fictional equivalent of the future George II plays to both Whigs and Tories, as signified by his hobbling gait (one high heel, one low), but *A Cursory View* dismisses this as an error of interpretation. The only 'Orthodox' Lilliputians are Slamecksan, or Low Church Whigs, and the Tramecksan Lilliputians are disguised Catholics controlled by Jacobites ('they palpably labour'd against the true Interest of the People and the Royal Family' [V.116, 123]). Corrections notwithstanding, the new pamphlet assumes no prior knowledge ('The *Lilliputians* [. . .] are Men about six Inches high'), suggesting it can feasibly stand apart from the original. *A Cursory View* relies on and yet moves beyond the original property; it is, in the pleasingly paradoxical phrasing of Welcher and Bush, 'mildly independent'.[48] Put another way, this prose extension exemplifies the at turns accretive and contrarian reframing of *Travels* when considered through the lens of transfictional storytelling.

Often attributed to a prominent member of Swift's literary circle, John Arbuthnot, *An Account of the State of Learning in the Empire of Lilliput* (1728) modifies Gulliver's material more explicitly.[49] The title page claims the pamphlet has been '*Faithfully Transcribed*' out of Gulliver's '*General Description of the Empire of* Lilliput': it appears to be an elliptic continuation, to adopt Gérard Genette's term for describing works that expand parts of the original rather than extend it.[50] Like *Memoirs*, *Account* revisits familiar targets, though it mocks them more blatantly. The pedantic librarian Bullum, who is clearly modelled on the Royal Librarian, Richard Bentley, frustrates Gulliver's research: 'Bullum, as I heard afterwards, was in great Wrath, and loaded me with many opprobrious Names, for refusing to hear his Speech out, and daring to treat a Man of his Learning with so little respect'.[51] Amusingly, as Seager notices, the 'greater Work' filled in by *Account* amounts to merely thirty-seven pages: 'The joke here is *against* the desire for more'.[52] And a substantial part of the miniature account, as prominently highlighted on the title page, is given to an improbable biography of Bullum. Promised five hundred books – an erroneous 'Interpolation' in the emperor's order (an erratic Bentleyan emendation), the librarian now claims – Gulliver receives only five. Amid generic titles (e.g. 'A Collection of Poetry'), we have titillating callbacks to Swift's most celebrated scenes ('A Dissertation upon *Tramescans* and *Slamescans*, or High-heel'd and Low heel'd Shoes' and 'A Bundle of Controversies concerning the primitive way of breaking Eggs').[53] Because the Lilliputian context seems extraneous, we might dismiss *Memoirs* from our Gulliverian museum as it merely hijacks the popularity of *Travels*. (In the context of creative reception, such hijacking nevertheless extends the reach of Swift's properties in its own way.) *Account*, meanwhile, deposits supplementary material into the Gulliverian archive while appropriating the smallness conceit to make Swiftian jokes against vainglorious scholars. Intertextually, it expands the Lilliputian language to include such words as Glomflastru and Mulro, having just reminded the reader of Swift's own comical coinages on the previous page (Nardacs, Glumglums and Hurgos).[54] Mercenary motives, and perhaps literary merit, aside, one consistent way to judge Gulliveriana would be to consider the contrasting contributions it makes to Swift's heterocosm. *Account* at once fills in and fills out the first part of

Travels. Memoirs repurposes it. *Volume III* embellishes and then closes it. *A Cursory View* reboots it.

Gulliver's voices

Other early Gulliveriana borrowed Gulliver's voice but largely neglected his voyages. *The Anatomist Dissected* appeared just weeks after *Travels*. In his new role as Surgeon and Anatomist to the Kings of Lilliput and Blefuscu, and Fellow of the Academy of Sciences in Balnibarbi, Gulliver weighs in on a real-life British hoax involving Mary Toft, who purportedly gave birth to a litter of rabbits. Ingeniously, the author of *The Anatomist Dissected* inverts the power dynamic between the texts: rather than relying on the success of *Travels*, they insist *Travels* 'has been so neglected of late' precisely because of the maniacal fascination with the hoax in the press, and hence Gulliver's opportunistic turn from travel memoirs to medical treatises.[55] Gulliver, the absent family man, becomes the ironic author of a seemingly popular though now rare pamphlet, *The Pleasures and Felicity of Marriage* (the first known extant edition, nominally the second, was published in 1745; earlier versions, if they existed, must have been 'read to pieces').[56] In 1749 he had a small but important cameo as a translator in Denis Diderot's *Les Bijoux Indiscrets, or, The Indiscreet Toys*. No mere transfictional character press-ganged into non-narrative environments, Gulliver had become a communal avatar of jobbing authorship and a ghostwriter (an unbounded fictional author but also a phantom scribe working beyond the grave).

Poets ventriloquized Gulliver, his wife, and other characters. As with the prose works explored above, often these poems expanded the scope of *Travels* by returning to old scenes. Others were entirely ornamental. An unlikely balladist, the ship's surgeon turned memoirist is the alleged author of *An Excellent New Ballad on the Wedding of Pritty Miss S—lly to Jolly Old J—o* (1730), a conventional-looking piece of street verse that addresses a common theme in literature focused on social mores in the period, namely, problems associated with large age gaps in romantic relationships. Conscripted to Edmund Curll's army of hacks, 'Captain Gulliver' is belatedly given *The Totness Address Transversed* (1727), Joseph Mitchell's loose appropriation of an anonymous and entirely Gulliver-less satirical poem printed for H. Whitridge. Credited as Poet Laureate to the King of Lilliput, though now living in 'my garret in Grub-street',

Lemuel Gulliver leads Henry Fielding's early squib, *The Masquerade, A Poem* (1728). Unlike the Curllian piece, the latter poem makes explicit reference to *Travels*, though it does not reboot, rework, or revisit it in any extended way. Gulliver's vocabulary has been permanently shaped by his experiences in the several strange nations: 'A lady in a velvet hood [. . .] flapp'd me on the shoulder', which recalls the flappers of Laputa. But the London theatre scene has now taken his full interest: 'The criticks wou'd be apt to bark, / Was I to leave them in the dark / As to my dress'.[57] Not merely eking out a textual existence beyond *Travels*, Gulliver, like any other transmedia character, has respawned and then developed within a specific environment.

As in *The Pleasures and Felicity of Marriage*, Gulliver the author has (in Fielding's hands) left Lilliput and the other countries far behind. Really, *The Masquerade* satirizes its dedicatee (C—t H—D—G—R), the Swiss impresario 'Count' John James (Johann Jacob) Heidegger, who had gained notoriety in England for his garish but evidently well-attended masquerade balls.[58] A more invasive form of appropriation was modelled by 'Signor Corolini' (likely Curll or his team) in a series of four printed 'keys', which were quickly gathered into a single volume and even bound into copies of *Travels*. Throughout, Corolini summarizes *Travels* piece by piece and either quotes or loosely paraphrases Gulliver's words. He puts additional poetry into the lead character's mouth, on the title page of the third pamphlet: 'Laputians *here behold with wond'ring Eyes, / And see the* STOCKS *in* Balnibarbi *rise*'. And he brings him into the real world, as imputed in an aside to the real-world author and addressee, Swift: 'Now, Mr. Dean, if you and I should ever live to see our Friend *Lemuel* at *Redriff*, we will shew him five Volumes in Folio *Framed* by an *Englishman*, and *Spun* only out of his own Brain'.[59] Caring little for intellectual property, Curll teasingly references Defoe's spirited defence of proprietorial authorship, the brats of a singular author's brain.[60] Acknowledging a character's text-bound existence even while modifying the words attributed to him, this sort of engagement threatens Gulliver's portability across diverse formal and generic settings. In other words, Gulliver the character becomes trapped in the book that birthed him. Largely a critical digest with elaborating elements, however, Corolini's keys also enhance attempts to endow Gulliver the author with personhood as found in periodical appropriations of this facet of Swift's creation, such as the Applebee series. Such an ontological contradiction speaks to the complexities built into the author-explorer when viewed within the expansive purview of transmedia storytelling (expressly Freeman's model comprising character-building, world-building and authorship).

Pieces 'commissioned' from Gulliver the author dwindled, but 'found' Gulliverian texts kept appearing. The editor of the blandly titled *Sequel to Gulliver's Travels* (1830) claims it is simply based on an unpublished epilogue (or a eulogy, in their words) from the end of *Travels*. Having 'hinted' at the close of the ninth chapter of the fourth voyage (in Swift's text) that 'I should in a short time publish a whole volume by itself upon the manners and virtues of this excellent people', the Houyhnhnms, Gulliver now resolves to 'redeem' his promise.[61] Rather than extending the narrative, *Sequel* fills out the description of the Houyhnhnms – despite the title, we would identify it as an elliptic continuation. More recent ventriloquizations of Gulliver include Conrad Peregrinus's (Kurt Friedlaender) *A Voyage to Springistan* (1972), from a German translation of a manuscript in Swift's hand 'recovered' from an Irish castle, and John Paul Brady's *A Voyage to Inishneefa* (1987), which had been 'discovered' in Swift's writing desk in Saint Patrick's Hospital in Dublin. Offering a suggestive parallel with Swift's Struldbruggs, Justus Franz Wittkop's *Gullivers letzte Reise: die Insel der Vergänglichen* (*Gulliver's Last Voyage: The Island of the Mortals* [1941]) takes the protagonist to the Island of the Mortals, whose inhabitants live for only thirty days. Volter Kilpi's *Gulliver's Voyage to Phantomimia* (left unfinished in 1939) hurled its narrator two centuries into the future via a vortex near the North Pole.

Adhering to the ruse that he found the phoney manuscript collected by Kilpi and then translated into Finnish, Douglas Robinson 'transcreated' the work back into Swiftian English. This elaborate authorial framing neatly explains its formal divergences without losing its spirit. Matthew Hodgart's *A New Voyage to the Country of the Houyhnhnms* (1970), another 'Fifth Part', mimics the typography of the original book, including capitalization and italicization, and brings back old characters (Yahoos and Houyhnhnms). Wittily, the blurb claims the manuscript upon which Hodgart's work is based had been written in 1744, 'the last year of Swift's life': it does not explicitly purport to be an authentic Gulliverian text, though like Smedley's *Gulliveriana* it references the true – and very famous – author of the source material. That is, Hodgart bypasses the fictional conceit of Gulliver as a real author sustained in the early Gulliveriana. The references to the American college sit-ins of the 1960s (the 'Great Shit-In') reveal its modern provenance. Ironically, the textual introduction, written in the voice of (and signed by) the real-life literary scholar Hodgart, refers to '*Incontrovertible evidence concerning the handwriting and other matters*' that will appear in a (non-existent) separate volume.[62] Fake authorship hides in plain sight in this playful homage to a satirical master. Even the manuscript of *Travels* did not have on it the overly cautious hand of Swift. This is a teasing overcorrection aimed at fellow bibliophiles.

A more character-centric ventriloquization, Alison Fell's *The Mistress of Lilliput or The Pursuit* (1999) comes back to the site of the first voyage but instead refocuses the point of view to that of Mary Gulliver and a sentient doll, Lady Mary.[63] Lauren Chater takes this minor-character elaboration further still in her lengthy novel *Gulliver's Wife* (2020), where Mary's life independent of and with her conniving husband has been extensively filled out.[64] Chater also switches the true romantic interest to Richard Sympson, whom Swift had confined to the paratextual matter that, chronologically speaking, came after Gulliver's adventures. Erga Netz has just begun a multibook series devoted to reworking *Travels* from Mary Burton-Gulliver's perspective. The first published book, *Oh, Gulliver! Mrs Gulliver and the Secret of Size* (2023), explores the discrepancy between the author-explorer's highly sexualized adventures in Lilliput and the travails of the woman he has left behind (not least of all the miscarriages she suffers alone, a counterfactual detail entirely omitted in the official record). As early as 1727, the abandoned Mrs Gulliver had aired her grievances as a neglected wife in Pope's 'Mary Gulliver to Capt. Lemuel Gulliver', one of five poems added to the second edition of *Travels*.[65] Desperate to reunite with her husband, she publicly declares herself willing to indulge his hippophilia and other habits: 'I'd call thee *Houyhnhnm*, that high sounding Name, / Thy Children's Noses all should twang the same' (*GT*, 586). The generic precedent set, the approaches taken by the authors could nevertheless not be more different when it comes to the question of what to do with a character who is hardly visible in the source text.

In the modern novels by Fell and Chater, Mary tracks down her husband, at once exploring ground new to her yet long familiar to the reader. Netz's *Oh, Gulliver!* largely keeps the Gullivers apart while recounting their separate if tandem life stories. Formally and in tone, Pope's epistle, Fell's *The Mistress* and Netz's *Oh, Gulliver!* recalibrate the barely sketched relationship between the Gullivers in starkly different ways. Nominally an editor who revises the otherwise sanitized version of her husband's account, Netz's Mary is a co-author who inserts elaborate fantasies about Gulliver's erotic experiences with multiple Lilliputians, among other things. Fell's Mary now gains agency overseas in her lived storytelling. Pope's version of the character merely demands to be heard at home. Although written in the third person, *The Mistress* contains free indirect discourse and extensive dialogue, allowing for emotional insights or dramatic exchanges between the Gullivers to arise as needed. Begging affection from her husband ('What, touch me not? what, shun a Wife's Embrace?' [*GT*, 582]), in a one-way verse conversation, Pope's Mary more conspicuously becomes a figure of fun. As Brewer observes, the poem 'recasts Gulliver's misanthropic repulsion toward his wife as bawdy farce'.[66] Considered within the burgeoning field of anti-Gulliver Gulliveriana, alternatively, Mary exposes her husband's dereliction of duty: 'to see / The *Groom* and *Sorrel Mare* preferr'd to me!' (*GT*, 584). Despite their formal differences, Fell's and Pope's texts together draw attention to the sexlessness of the original Gullivers. Netz explores their sexualities outside their vexed marriage (a potential new husband has entered this Mary's world, a hosier named John Lowsley). Under the auspices of an expanded authorial purview, by outlining different narratorial perspectives, such examples also advance the character-building and world-building of *Travels* as a transmedia culture-text *avant la lettre*.

While overtly engaging with Swift's material, the Lilliputian ode enjoyed a lengthy afterlife of its own, aesthetically (as part of a wider poetics of transgression that prioritized an oxymoronic compound of high and low art) and materially (in being made available in print beyond the bound pages of *Travels*).[67] Not long after adding them to his re-set *Travels*, Motte issued the poems in a separate collection, *Several Copies of Verses on Occasion of Mr. Gulliver's Travels* (1727), in a large print run. Pirated reprints quickly circulated in Dublin. *Two Lilliputian Odes* (also 1727) soon followed. The first ode, the bawdy 'On the Engine with which Captain *Gulliver* extinguish'd the Flames in the Royal Palace', replays an infamous scene in Swift's Lilliput, while the second, 'Inviting a Bookseller to a Coffee-House, where the Author was', explicitly adopts the authorial persona of one of Pope's paratextual poems – 'Sure as I am Titty Tit', Lilliput's Poet Laureate. Members of Swift's circle revelled in the prosodic absurdity of the form, beyond the prose-shaped *Travels*, according to an insider, John Arbuthnot.[68] John Gay's 'The Man-Mountain's Answer to the Lilliputian Verses' responded to the first of the official-looking Lilliputian poems attached to *Travels* and so helped to extend the mystique of Gulliver among the early reading public. To attentive readers of *Travels*, the poem compounds the metafictional jocularity of the first verses. Titty Tit's 'To Quinbus Flestrin the Man-Mountain. An Ode' foolishly equates the scale of the subject with his literary ambitions: 'So shall I, / Lofty Poet, touch the Sky' (*GT*, 575). The lines are literally too short to reach epic heights. An unlikely, philistine poet in *Travels*, Gulliver (in Gay's hands) humbles Titty Tit and poetasters more generally:

> To be free
> From jeopardy,
> Careless found,
> You might bound,
> Little poet! to the ground.[69]

Outsiders used the micro-genre against Jonathan Swift as a public figure more specifically. Smedley smuggled into *Gulliveriana*, a patchwork pastiche of the works of his celebrated rival cleric-poet, 'A Lilliputian Ode; In Imitation of, and humbly Inscrib'd to, Captain Gulliver', in which he mockingly conflates Swift's littleness conceit (taken from *Travels*) with his scatological style (as exhibited in the published poems):

> *Eccho* too!
> Nasty Verse!
> Things so *true*
> To rehearse.[70]

Most extant early Lilliputian and Brobdingnagian verses display an incidental connection to *Travels* rather than participate in concerted character-building or world-building. Pertinent exceptions include the five poems by Pope, which enhance the perspectives of Gulliverian characters, such as the Lilliputians' mind-bending awe in 'To Quinbus Flestrin the Man-Mountain': 'Can our Eyes / Reach thy Size?' (*GT*, 574). 'The Words of the King of Brobdingnag', conversely, considers the opposite point of view: 'In Miniature see *Nature*'s Power appear' (*GT*, 587). 'The Lamentation of Glumdalclitch for the Loss of Grildrig', a mock-pastoral, captures the young giantess's extreme distress: 'She wept, she blubber'd, and she tore her Hair' (*GT*, 576).[71] In *Dreams in Lilliput* (1790), a collection of instructive verses for children, and *Lilliput Lyrics* (1899) alike, references to *Travels* have become barely noticeable. The same can be said of plenty of prose works for young audiences that appeared towards the end of the eighteenth century and into the nineteenth, such as *The Lilliputian History* (1800). *The Lilliputian Library, or Gulliver's Museum* (1782) poses a more complex case. In a medley of lectures, poems, fables and jokes, Lilliputius Gulliver reworks his kinsman's materials while adding copious items to the Gulliverian archive, usually by appropriating Aesop and other enduring authors. Within a section on voyages, he rewrites the first two parts of *Travels* in a simplified, third-person format: it is a reboot from within. (According to the fanfiction theorist Sheenagh Pugh, third-person narration has long been a hallmark of the mode.)[72]

While modern authors tend to favour the form of prose when retelling Gulliver's life story, a powerful character-focused approach can be found among Wole Soyinka's prison verses published in 1972.[73] Adopting the voice of Gulliver in 'Gulliver', Soyinka revisits that initial entrapment in Lilliput with which *Travels* practically begins. He turns the self-deluded monster who revels in frightening the tiny assailants into 'an alien hulk' conscious of its own dehumanization as a political prisoner. To Swift's carefree Gulliver, the volley of needle-like arrows barely proved inconvenient. To the new speaker, they carry a 'full-fanged, venom-bodied' threat. And, in the political poem, the dwarfish captors are not merely risible; they are 'Peacock vain, mannikin cruel, sycophant'. Soyinka's Gulliver speaks back to power from a lived experience the original character could not fathom. The Polish poet Ernest Bryll found in Gulliver's fantastical experiences suitable imagery for his emotional state, particularly the most famous narrative motif associated with Lilliput, in 'Guliver' (1958): 'Every thought of mine is torn like hair, / Tightened like a string'.[74] Sylvia Plath was another particularly attentive mid-century reader of *Travels*, as frequent references to Lilliput and Brobdingnag in her verse attest.[75] This includes a 1962 poem nakedly titled 'Gulliver' (and formerly known as 'Gulliver in Lilliput'), which scholars have interpreted as a response to petty, thoughtless critics ('Unlike you, / With no strings attached').[76] Towards the end of the Soviet era, a number of poets turned to Gulliver, such as Yakov Andreev, for whom, in 1988, Gulliver stood for the people 'who lost their lives in the Soviet Gulags'.[77] Nikolai Lisovoi, a year later, used Gulliver to represent a group governed by a minority that abuses its power.[78] As this brief history of Gulliverian poetry reveals, the source material lent itself to all kinds of responses, from the silly to the satirical to the serious. Poetry might be a more economical medium, especially in the diminutive Lilliputian mode, but the more fanciful satirists – as opposed to the political commentators – have usually relied on prose when embedding their Gulliverian squibs in larger works. World-building could occur in the most unlikely of places.

In the second volume of Mortimer Collins's comical novel *Squire Silchester's Whim* (1873), the eponymous Squire casually declares to an assembled group of friends that 'I have some odd old manuscripts in my library', noting that one of them will particularly appeal to Miss Louisa.[79] The next chapter, chapter five, comprises the 'Fifth Voyage' of Captain Lemuel Gulliver, to whom the Squire thinks he must be 'in some way or other' related, hence explaining why he has a manuscript in the original 'hand and style of an ancient mariner' (I.49). The manuscript, abridged for the immediate audience, tells of Gulliver's undocumented journey to Amazonia in May 1715, which plausibly falls within Swift's established timeline. The Squire presents Amazonia as a utopia benignly ruled by young women who have descended from expatriate English feminists. In the new country girls can fight just as well as the boys (though they deem it uncivilized) and, by means of their superior intellect, the women keep the men in complete subjection. A witness to this society, Gulliver extrapolates that, with women in charge, there would be no war, litigation, robbery, violence, drunkenness or indecency. He fails to hear the casual sexism of his own words, however. The Amazonians choose their queens based on intellect and beauty. And the general populace is full of learned and gifted poets. Gulliver nevertheless refers to the military as 'pretty' and calls one teenage girl 'a very pretty little thing' (I.51, 53). We might ascribe this lapse in awareness to a lack of character development. Or, in narratological terms, we might argue that the narrator moves to a more enlightened position only after he interacts with the inhabitants, in accordance with personhood models of characterization. Unlike Swift's Gulliver, after all, Collins's author-explorer longs to return to his wife. Collins's mock-Gulliverian travelogue, in sum, serves a flighty function within *Squire Silchester's Whim* while also evidencing some residual Swiftian concerns. As a satirical aside within a novel, the late Victorian text enlists the eighteenth-century character to comment on the long-entrenched mistreatment of British women.

At the turn of the new century, Lewis Jesse Bridgman produced a markedly different type of book in Gulliver's name, *Gulliver's Bird Book* (*c.*1901). Lieutenant John Gulliver of the British Marines, so the introduction claims, had recently amused his shipmates with 'some drawings'.[80] Such drawings were purportedly produced by the original Lemuel Gulliver, along with hidden text newly revealed by the heat of the lamplight (not simply – glibly – offering a found work, Bridgman ingeniously brings in the trope of revealed text to establish a bookish lineage). *Gulliver's Bird Book* is essentially a bonus voyage in an offbeat register. Familiar and yet reformatted, the additional tale lacks any explicit connections with the previous voyages: Gulliver begins, abruptly, 'I had been many months in the country of the Grand Vizier, and still found new and surprising things every day' (1). Along with increased levels of reported speech, there are liberal sprinklings of songs and visual gags somewhat alien to *Travels*. Familial, in its nominal connection between Lemuel and John, and yet unrelated to the satirical scope of the original, the word-and-image appendage retains and even prolongs its animal-themed absurdism in a sort of confused supplementary reboot of a famous character and his unacknowledged kin. A later, more earnest example of found Gulliveriana, Louis Hermann's *In the Sealed Cave* (1935), describes a chance discovery of further documents written by Lemuel Gulliver and handed through his descendants (from his son John Gulliver down to Ithiel Samways, a reclusive sailor). Largely narrated in the third person and in the present tense, the novel includes lengthy snippets in Gulliver's own voice. In a further if already well-established manoeuvre of bringing Gulliver into existence within our reality, the narrator also describes an 'authentic correspondence' between the voyager and Jonathan Swift, the handwriting of whom he had compared with documents in the British Museum.[81] We are, in effect, reading the words not merely of a fictional explorer-author but of a dead man. Or, like the narrator, we are witnessing a literary spirit subsumed into the additional account two centuries later: 'We left Gulliver sitting in shirt and breeches with the six identical half-men curiously squatting near him at the altar fire' (50). Hermann's Gulliver is at once a scholarly authority and a flesh-and-blood character with unusual levels of personhood; a reflective anthropologist rather than a mere adventurer is driven hither and thither by plot.

In a short creative deconstruction of Gulliver's first voyage enticingly titled 'Gulliver: The Story of a Tall Man' (another 1935 work, as it happens), the American novelist Thomas Wolfe (who himself stood tall at six feet six inches) instead reduces the subjectivity of Swift's lead character while replaying the usual narrative motifs:

He awakes at morning in a foreign land, his ship is wrecked, his comrades drowned, and he forsaken: a regiment of tiny creatures are swarming up across his body, they shoot their tiny arrows at his face and bind him down with countless weavings of a thread-like cord, and the terrific legend of his life among the pygmies becomes the instrument by which another giant whipped the folly, baseness, and corruption in the lives of men with the scorpion lash of the most savage allegory ever written.[82]

Neither Gulliver the author nor Gulliver the explorer can be said to exist here, the story's namechecking title notwithstanding. And yet, the trace presence of each facet of Swift's creation haunts the rebooted narrative. Depersonalized, the passage still captures the Gulliverian character's oscillating fears and bemusement. Other secondary authors have felt compelled to address, or at least hint at, Lemuel Gulliver's death. A brief family tree at the beginning of Hermann's *In the Sealed Cave* lists Gulliver's death date, 1731, as an incidental detail. Alan Moore killed off Gulliver again in 2007: in *Black Dossier*, a spinoff from *The League of Extraordinary Gentlemen* graphic novel series, we learn by the by that Gulliver had died of cancer as late as 1799. As my analyses of diverse eighteenth- and nineteenth-century engagements demonstrate, Gulliver was a remarkably transportable character even before the rise of media convergence culture. Long untethered from his own memoirs and bodily remains, beyond a hand that ceaselessly writes, the ghostwriter (the ghost-as-writer) remains restless.

2 NEW VOYAGES

Over the past 300 years many writers have prolonged the adventures of Lemuel Gulliver and his family. Many have taken them to uncharted places, some back to former haunts. Others have relied on a future-flung Gulliver or a clonish namesake. As with the allographic works explicitly attributed to Swift's main protagonist, as discussed in the previous chapter, accounts of these additional voyages occurred across an array of formats and genres, chiefly but not only novels and short stories, and with a scattered preference for political commentary, feminist refocalization, whimsical satire and metafictional science fiction. The first section, 'After Travels', attends to works that essentially press-ganged Gulliver into anachronistic political contexts. This comprises early periodical pieces as well as book-length 'fifth' voyages, such as Matthew Hodgart's *A New Voyage to the Country of the Houyhnhnms* (1970), Kurt Friedlaender's *A Voyage to Springistan* (1972), and John Paul Brady's *A Voyage to Inishneefa* (1987). The next sections, 'Mrs Gulliver' and 'Home and abroad', focus on late-twentieth-century refocalizations, namely, John Kessel's 'Gulliver at Home' (1997), Karen Joy Fowler's 'The Travails' (1999) and Alison Fell's *The Mistress of Lilliput or The Pursuit* (1999). Davy King's 'The Woman Gulliver Left Behind' (1978) came before this set, and the most recent examples analysed here are Lauren Chater's *Gulliver's Wife* (2020) and Erga Netz's *Oh, Gulliver! Mrs Gulliver and the Secret of Size* (2023). 'Gulliver's clones', the penultimate section, picks out numerous namesakes and copycats that have become associated with Gulliver and his world since the eighteenth century. This includes self-declared sons, grandsons, great-grandsons and other types of notional descendants. Non-Gullivers with little explicit connection to Swift's world-building nevertheless trace similar elements, ranging from a prose satire centred on the fantastical voyager Murtagh McDermot in *A Trip to the Moon* (1728) to the twee conferral of the title 'Gulliver' on young Omar by displaced Lilliputians in Michael Morpurgo's *Boy Giant* (2019). The final section, 'Spaced out', addresses the complex ways in which two notable transmedia franchises,

Doctor Who and *Star Trek*, have both rigidly adhered to the eighteenth-century character template and yet reduced Swift's Gulliver to a textual ghost and a hallucinated vision, respectively, and thereby recalibrated his value as an agent of plot for modern audiences.

In sum, this chapter explores the variety of sequels, minor-character elaborations and other types of continuations that have appeared in different reading contexts for the past three centuries, and which claimed to differing degrees of plausibility an affinity with *Travels*, often for contradictory purposes. While these creative engagements have largely relied on Swift's template, or the world-building that has accreted around it over the years, not all have treated Lemuel Gulliver as a personlike character. Some, particularly the Mary Gulliver fictions, have strategically rounded out the flaws of Gulliver, as a feckless husband and father based on small hints of marital strife in the source text, in order to tell an unlikely type of story (a romance). Many science fiction authors all but reduced him to an incidental if still coherent figure so that new plots could unfold. Beyond our reach in this chapter, there is a long tradition of writing Gulliver out of Gulliveriana. Among Horace Walpole's extant Gulliverian materials printed or privately circulated in correspondence during the second half of the eighteenth century, we find a science fiction fairy tale set in the year 2000096 and an epistolary account of a newly discovered land of giants that, according to the author, should not be read as 'some political allegory' or a 'new-vamped edition of Swift's Brobdignags [*sic*]'.[1] The latter story refers to the Patagonian giants, whose mythical presence had become topical news again in 1766 when John Byron and his crew returned from their circumnavigation of South America two months before Walpole took up his Gulliverian pen. An impressionable nine-year-old when *Travels* was first published, Walpole, in middle age, clearly still considered Swift's work to be the benchmark against which fantastical or hoaxing voyages should be judged. In Chapter 1, we traced across different environments the consolidated and contradictory uses of Gulliver as a handy avatar of jobbing authorship but also a ghost-as-writer producing additional, or reproducing lost, works beyond the grave. The continuations in which he figures as an author-explorer (or separately as an author or explorer) are similarly accretive and contrarian, particularly when they expressly return to the source text or to the more famous of its companion works. Rarely do they cohere in the systematic way demanded by modern transmedia storytelling. Yet, Lemuel Gulliver's immediate and sustained fame cannot be denied. Even

Gulliver-less or Gulliver-lessened Gulliveriana relies on Swift's original character-building or world-building. As a familiar culture-text, *Travels* has always retained high entertainment value.

After *Travels*

An early indication of his burgeoning fame, Gulliver cameoed throughout the British periodical press shortly after debuting in print. Hampshire Yahoo, for one, casually refers to 'my new Friend Mr. *Gulliver*' in a letter to the editor of *The London Journal* (Saturday 26 November 1726).[2] For half a decade, between 1727 and 1733, Gulliver and his *Travels* were frequently mentioned, or otherwise more substantially engaged with, in *The Craftsman*, the anti-Whig vehicle of the out-of-favour Tory politician Henry St John, 1st Viscount Bolingbroke. Of the two dozen periodical pieces that carry specific Gulliverian marks, as defined by Jeanne K. Welcher and George E. Bush Jr, a letter from Rica to Usbeck – the made-up noblemen borrowed from Montesquieu's *Persian Letters* (1721) – holds special interest.[3] In letter no. 150, Rica describes Gulliver's journey to an unknown nation. The inhabitants of Grimbagria, we learn, have fallen into corruption and greed. The '*great Emperor*' wants the best for his subjects, but, under the current ministry, 'his Desires are daily contravened by *Art*, by *Fraud*, by *Corruption*. This they call *Policy*—' (V.96). A corrupt and long-employed leader, Shamgrigg is a thinly veiled caricature of the British Prime Minister, Sir Robert Walpole, who resembles another Walpolean politician residing in Swift's Lilliput, Flimnap.[4] Within this new formal setting, periodical satire, the modification of Swift's fictional properties remains plausible enough. Crucially, though, they are appropriated for political rather than strictly literary means. At best, the contribution to transfictional character-building or world-building here seems incidental – but it is a contribution nevertheless.

Even when he was absent, Gulliver's name alone could feasibly occasion further – and arguably more forceful because it is condensed – satirical commentary on eighteenth-century politics. A Dublin magazine, *The Flapper*, took its title from the attendants (flappers) tasked with keeping the absentminded Laputans alert. In the first issue, the author identifies Captain Lemuel Gulliver as the only 'genuine' authority on Laputa before dismissing him as prejudiced and therefore 'erroneous'.[5] Considered in the context of historicized transmedia storytelling, this example indicates that an enduring character can fulfil a purpose beyond the secondary work that does not service the central narrative. Other periodical extensions treated the author-explorer as a passive figure ready to be flung on further journeys subject to readerly interest. 'Gulliver's Last Voyage', which belatedly appeared in *The Monthly Review* for July 1903, picks up straight after Swift's *Travels*. Weary of London life after sojourning with the Houyhnhnms, Gulliver undertook a fresh voyage on 31 March 1716. We have a familiar enough premise: by the end of the new first chapter, Gulliver has been set adrift more than five thousand miles from the coast of Africa by uncaring shipmates. On the Internecine Islands he discovers communities divided. Soon enough, the historical framework gets abandoned, however. Anachronisms silently propel us to the present day (a motor car, among them) and ultimately to an extended critique of the Secretary of State for the Colonies, Joseph Chamberlain ('the Great Chamberlain'), who, in real life, had recently instigated the Second Boer War for imperialist gains. Chamberlain's opposition to free trade in 1903 became literalized in the Internecine Islands, where 'a sufficiently high wall—called in those parts a *tariff*' prevents the constituent islands from prospering.[6] That same year, a satirical novel, *Gulliver Joe* by the absurdly named 'Jonathan Quick, Dean of St Rattrick's', conflated Gulliver with Chamberlain in the role of author-explorer: 'I was so completely and entirely bound by these same *Promises* that I was at first unable to move'.[7] In such examples, the additional world-building aligns with live political debates instead of extending Swift's properties as such. The central character, though, must still be shaped by regularity to ensure readerly recognition.

Another, more extended type of continuation centred on Gulliver and his world modifies in bespoke ways the character templates established in *Travels*, including the specifics of Gulliver's personality and appearance as well as the broader narratological function of a fantastical voyager. Typically, for creative variety if nothing else, this also entails adjusting to varying degrees of severity the format of the story, the world-building or established plot points. Multiple 'last' voyages have occurred in single-volume book form, as in *Gulliver's Last Voyage, describing Ballymugland, or the Floating Island* (1825). Divided into chapters, each with header summaries, this book loosely mimics the format of Swift's *Travels*. We begin with a blunt announcement of the death of the author-explorer's wife, however, leaping us beyond the original timeline while consolidating

Gulliver's personhood. Bored on his own, Gulliver takes up the government's call for experienced mariners to visit a mysterious island in the Pacific that can apparently move. This Gulliver is an irrepressible adventurer who favours 'an enterprise that might involve danger', even if he spends most of the novella passively observing the people he encounters.[8] To the standard list of humans and parahumans encountered by Swift's Gulliver we can now add Humguffs and Tonguewaggers. Another two-party system tied to the Fugfugs and the Antifugs can be placed alongside the Slamecksans and the Tramecksans of the original. In sum, this voyage bluntly expands *Travels* without troubling its internal boundaries. If anything, the existential angst that clouds the original author-explorer has lost its tragic edge, inadvertently highlighting Swift's subtle character treatment. While these types of continuations are not necessarily less political or localized to specific concerns, their attention to plausible world-building indicates a more concerted, if belated, effort to disperse Gulliver across multiple cultural environments.

The last voyage premise in extended book form reemerged in the mid-twentieth century with a trio of works that did more insistently trouble the spatial and temporal boundaries – and the outline characterization – set by Swift. Considered within the purview of transtextual storytelling, such modifications ultimately enhance rather than erode an established character and his world. Even when they facetiously threaten to complete his story for good, the authors of these works implicitly acknowledge that Gulliver's endless seriality is both a product and prolonger of his accreted fame. At once an appropriation and an extension, Matthew Hodgart's *A New Voyage to the Country of the Houyhnhnms* (1970) was 'edited' from a made-up 1744 manuscript. In it, Gulliver has 'returned' to the final strange nation – though 'things are different now', as the Sorel Nag nonchalantly concedes.[9] The New Yahoos, now likened to present-day students amid the American college riots of the 1960s, are nevertheless no less scatological. By the end of *New Voyage*, Gulliver's misanthropy has definitively descended into madness: 'I have crept into a Bin, that formerly held Oats, and have pulled the Cover over my Head; and now I sit in the Dark, scribbling, scribbling . . .' (91). The final ellipses ingeniously capture the unwritten, or yet-to-be-written, Gulliveriana that lay ahead. This Gulliver, though, has been silenced; the narratorial loop in which the original had been caught has now been cut. John Paul Brady's *A Voyage to Inishneefa* (1987) finishes on a softer note that implies a character-centric sense of an ending, even peace: 'A man could live a secure and contented life in England as nowhere else on the globe'.[10] We find precedent for a happier hero (or a more plot-driven figure) in the 1825 sequel *Gulliver's Last Voyage*, in which the protagonist declares in closing that he remains ready 'to set out, on the ensuing spring, in quest of new discoveries' (*Gulliver's Last Voyage*, 79). Hodgart's *New Voyage* opens immediately with a bleak post-*Travels* update: 'My Reconcilement to the Yahoo-kind in general, which I hinted at the End of my last Book of Travels might at length prove possible, did not come about' (*New Voyage*, 11). Gulliver instead finds renewed joy on his 'safe Return' to Houyhnhnm-Land, seven years to the day later (20). Under a new master, the Houyhnhnms are 'displeased' with the old Yahoo's return because, we learn through lengthy discourse, he had inadvertently caused the downfall of civil society in his absence (71). Finally back in England, Gulliver becomes more depressed than ever: 'My Wife and my Children now found my Gloom and Spleen so impossible to tolerate, that they left my House for ever' (90). In this continued revisiting, as it were, Hodgart out-Swifts Swift for bleakness. Previously loyal characters abandon the story (if not the story template).

Ventriloquizing Swift's Gulliver, Conrad Peregrinus's (Kurt Friedlaender) *A Voyage to Springistan* (1972) takes the protagonist on a fifth voyage to an unknown country north of India. Newness competes with familiarity and familiarity with inversion. The Springistanians bleat like sheep ('*Baa, baa*') and yet appear to be humans.[11] Risible figures to Gulliver, they read as inverted Houyhnhnms. Or rather, they are Wellsian species divided into two groupings: Springists, who have 'powerful Thighs and diminutive Heads' and are 'the Rulers', and Trabists, who can barely 'walk or trot', and are subservient (13). As ever, Gulliver draws parallels with his own society, but in a mid-twentieth-century continuation such parallels strike ever closer to home, not least of all Kikua's chilling 'Speaking-Fit' about 'a final Solution': 'kill[ing] all its *black-haired* Inhabitants and coloniz[ing] the Country' (52). As in the periodical Gulliveriana of the eighteenth century, Friedlaender exploits the author-explorer's voyaging into unfamiliar lands to elicit the political realities of a time-bound readership. (In the Author's Postscript, Friedlaender reveals the manuscript had been completed in early 1945, then published in a small print run in Sweden three years later but rejected by German publishers in the post-war years, and then finally translated into English.) Swift's Gulliver would have lived contently among the Houyhnhnms, despite his own moral shortcomings; among the Springistanians he instead feels 'the compleat Incompatibility of their moral Principles' (82). They are, in short, too '*Yahoo*-like'. Despite the repetition with a difference, as adaptation theorists would recognize it, Gulliver's worldview has decisively changed. Back home in London, he hopes 'to enjoy the Rest of my Days in my little Garden at *Redriff*, and, as far as my Health permits, to occupy my self in perfecting the History of my Travels' (122). Perfecting implies completion. The voyaging has finally ended. Or rather, further fifth voyages were yet to come. On 12 July 1724, after several years in London, Gulliver set sail for Madagascar in Brady's *Voyage to Inishneefa*. Really, he finds an allegorical version of Ireland, then part of the Great Kingdom of Nartibnia (an anagram of Britannia). The fifth voyages at once revisited and extended Swift's fantastical world-building principally to provide pointed political commentary on the secondary authors' modern-day purviews: Hodgart's experiences as a visiting English professor at Cornell in the 1960s, Brady's as a visiting medical professor at Trinity College Dublin and Saint Patrick's Hospital, and Friedlaender's as a former German soldier during the rise of Nazism. Refitted to the authors' own environments, these examples exemplify the importance of authorship in Matthew Freeman's historicized model of transmedia storytelling, along with character-building and world-building.

Mrs Gulliver

An alternative type of revisiting as extension re-views (and reviews, in a critical sense) the original plot from the perspective of Gulliver's wife, Mary. A spate of these refocalizations appeared in the late 1990s: John Kessel's 'Gulliver at Home' (1997), Karen Joy Fowler's 'The Travails' (1999) and Alison Fell's *The Mistress of Lilliput or The Pursuit* (1999). Before this, we find Davy King's 'The Woman Gulliver Left Behind' (1978) and, more recently, Lauren Chater's *Gulliver's Wife* (2020). As a loose collective of minor-character elaborations, these works will be the focus of the present and subsequent sections. While the broader genre of minor-character elaboration has extensive precedents, as Jeremy Rosen has shown, it emerged most distinctly in the 1960s and has become increasingly popular in the literary marketplace over the past three decades.[12] The recuperative feminist paradigm that features prominently in this mode of writing remains most closely associated with Jean Rhys's *Wide Sargasso Sea* (1966), an extended critique of Charlotte Brontë's portrayal of Edward Rochester's first wife, Bertha (Antoinette Mason), in *Jane Eyre* (1847). Shakespeare's Gertrude and Ophelia, among many others, have gained powerful voices in more recent novels. We therefore might compare the modern Marys against the benchmark of the repurposed Bertha and other maligned female characters. Or, to historicize the genre more narrowly, we might analyse the 1990s Mary Gulliver fictions in the context of a boom in feminist amplifications that appeared around that time, such as Marina Warner's influential reimagining of *The Tempest* (1611), *Indigo* (1992), in which Prospero's daughter Miranda takes a central role. Most closely analogous to our present case study would be Sena Jeter Naslund's *Ahab's Wife, or The Star-Gazer* (1999), in which tangential references to the wife and child left in Nantucket by Captain Ahab in Herman Melville's *Moby-Dick* (1851) expand into a 650-page novel.

In the immediate context of a transfictional character study, we will instead follow Mary Gulliver across different texts expressly to extend the boundaries of world-building and character-building beyond the central figure and related core properties. Such an approach helps ground the genre as it has been (and could be further) practised today and thereby solves, locally, Rosen's concerns for the inherent openness of minor-character elaboration. As Rosen concedes, the genre's 'relatively stable center' rests on the overt appropriation of recognizable characters, as well as plots and settings that we might presume can be tracked.[13] Tracking different versions of a specific character also provides sufficient evidence required to test Rosen's assumption that the 'basic structure' of the genre requires taking 'a typological minor character and expanding upon that structure, *elaborating* it to produce the referential sense of a full, imaginary person'. Rosen continues: 'minor-character elaborations perform in fiction the mental work that generates realist characters'.[14] The new Mary Gullivers do tend to be realistic, within the limitations of the historical purview in which their stories are set. Sometimes they have surreal tendencies, in keeping with late-twentieth- and early-twenty-first-century literary trends. Sometimes their realism becomes heightened by the unreality that surrounds them, including Lady Mary, the sentient doll with whom Mrs Gulliver shares narratorial duties in *The Mistress*. To account for the staunchly destabilising perspectives from which *The Mistress* and *Gulliver's Wife* are narrated, in formalist terms, we might buttress Rosenian realism with Christian Moraru's distinction between counterwriting and underwriting in contemporary literature.[15]

Counterwriting entails rupture, even full-on dissent: one finds this most compellingly expressed in the persistent critique of Lemuel Gulliver's unabashed neglect of his family. Underwriting more deferentially endorses the host text, expanding its established world-building within implied parameters or else carefully demarcated alternative universes. Of the writers considered in this category, Fell and Chater most blatantly mingle both approaches. And each develops complex tonal shifts in order to understand a character that hardly existed in Swift's *Travels* and which therefore can only become a palimpsest of distinct, non-definitive reimaginings.

So far, these engagements have grounded Mary in a familiar but metafictional approximation of eighteenth-century English society. Within the much larger category of creative responses to and expansions of *Travels* produced in the past three centuries across the globe, the eponymous lead character – or a clonish namesake of Lemuel – has been taken on multiple further voyages, sometimes beyond the stars, centuries into the future. Some replace him with an entirely new character, whether an invented son or a modern imitator. Mary Gulliver refocalizations have instead kept the new lead in her own century; this conforms to the emphasis placed on historical fiction in Rosen's framework, as well as a humanist view of character that relies on biographical plausibility. Fell takes us back to the site of the first voyage, filling in implied gaps in the captain's memoirs from Mary's perspective. Chater, more recently, contrasts Mary's life independent of and with her conniving husband. Expanding the domestic plot, Chater also switches the true romantic interest to Richard Sympson. In the 1735 revision of *Travels*, Swift had confined that additional character, Sympson, to the paratextual matter that, chronologically speaking, came after Gulliver's recorded adventures. Under the cover of *Gulliver's Wife*, Chater actually splices two minor-character elaborations together by rerouting us towards modern novelistic practices (multiple plots, time jumps and more). That is, Mary and Sympson become characters subjected to romantic tendencies and other human-like matters; this adjusted dynamic not only expands their original functions (as an at-home wife and an apologetic print agent, respectively) but radically retrofits them for a different formal setting (the modern novel rather than the original prose satire, or even the children's adventure story, among other early and persistent types of reworking). This is counterwriting in action. There is also underwriting: Mary, and to an extent Lemuel, despite his newly diminished role, gets more rounded out in Fell's and Chater's novels than the eponymous author-explorer of the original *Travels*.

Within Rosen's schema of minor-character elaboration, conversion should equate to being 'demonstrably transformed' yet recognizable, not 'merely extended' – or, what adaptation theorists call repetition with variation.[16] Mary Gulliver provides an extreme case with which to test this framework. Some authors have given her extra children or grandchildren, as well as additional love interests, or changed her biographical particulars (like her place of birth). And yet, as the named wife of Gulliver, even when liberated from him, she remains a nominally subsidiary character in a teleological sense. In other words, Mary is all but absent in the source text and yet was constructed within its boundaries. We solve the contradiction through doubleness: modified characters can remain functions of a canonical work and yet act as if they have an autonomous existence. Put another way, plausible continuations of Mrs Gulliver do not have a firm template with which to adhere, but, within concerted transmedia storytelling, there are still expectations with character-building and world-building that must be upheld. In *Travels*, Lemuel only refers to Mary in passing as 'my Wife' (on nineteen occasions). A faint paranarrative can nevertheless be salvaged from such asides. By the third voyage we detect marital conflict in the casual remark that the 'only' difficulty Lemuel faces in undertaking the latest journey entails securing his wife's consent.[17] For each voyage, the narratorial imperative demanded Gulliver's wanderlust over domestic dutifulness: 'I stayed but two Months with my Wife and Family; for my insatiable Desire of seeing foreign Countries would suffer me to continue no longer' (*GT*, 112). In moments of despair Gulliver can engage our empathy by alluding to familial woes: 'I slept about two Hours, and dreamed I was at home with my Wife and Children, which aggravated my Sorrows when I awaked and found my self alone in a vast Room' (*GT*, 132). More often, the explorer's family services the comedy: 'My Wife ran out to embrace me, but I stooped lower than her Knees, thinking she could otherwise never be able to reach my Mouth' (*GT*, 213). And finally, after living with the Houyhnhnms he so greatly admired, Lemuel rejects his kin and kind: 'During the first Year I could not endure my Wife or Children in my Presence, the very Smell of them was intolerable' (*GT*, 434). Here the satire darkens into a misanthropic comment on the hypocrisies of civilized society. As we shall see, each of the works by King, Kessel, Fowler, Fell and Chater latches onto specific aspects of Swift's paranarrative of

Mary's life in England, either by expanding on the farcical elements of the limited interactions with her transformed husband or exacerbating the emotional neglect felt by someone in her position.

Whereas the periodical and book-form new voyages tended to adhere to Swift's basic template of the lead character, the Mary Gulliver works that have appeared in recent years more patently adapt the wider cast of characters or repurpose their dynamics. With the more guarded exception of Fowler's 'The Travails', each short story or novel in this mode signals the prominence of Lemuel Gulliver in its title, seemingly to reduce him to a different type of husband, explicitly a well-meaning and thence tragic or (more commonly) a selfish, villainous one. To differing degrees, the new texts quote or at least heavily paraphrase from *Travels*, though they adopt different positions on the status of the original. For some of the Marys, their husband's book proved immensely popular; for others, the book did not yet exist and therefore could be corrected in real time. King's 1978 first-person short story, 'The Woman Gulliver Left Behind', begins as a lament from an abandoned wife but grows into an angry critique of an unreliable husband. Mary uses Lemuel's words against him, quoting from and then commenting on *Travels*. She wears the label of 'female Yahoo' with ironic honour, and plans her own travels, having also taken up the pen. While set in the same historical period and locale as Swift's original, the diction and tone sound modern. This inaugurates a comical, casually flippant mood around King's Mary. Her dawning sense of self is tongue-in-cheek rather than retaliatory: 'I was a fleeting appearance, occasionally glimpsed, very much a bit-part, an unimportant extra in a cast of thousands'.[18] Her husband's failings, initially, seem farcical more than callous: 'I was left literally holding the baby. It was my lot to explain to the kiddies why their daddy never came home in the evenings' (2). Scenes replayed from *Travels* seem stupid: 'He bent down & hugged my knees', after the return from Lilliput (6). As the story progresses her situation is more than inconvenient, it's illogical: 'I lived in quiet domestic reclusion – a widowed mother – apart from interludes of ecstatic reunion with my absentee husband' (5). As a lover, she candidly criticises Lemuel: 'If anything, his travels made him less keen on sex, (so much so that since his final return he refuses to touch me)' (8). Gulliver's returns lack comfort, at best: 'in a sense he *had* died, for he was no longer the old Lemuel I knew' (10). An ad-hoc character in *Travels*, a prose satire,

Gulliver haunts the new text even while he has been shunted from this facet of the story: this is transfictional character-building in action.

No longer lovers, the Gullivers become rival authors. 'He's given *his* side of the story', Mary reports (11). 'It's bound to be a bestseller & I can't help feeling a certain sense of pride in his achievement'. But, she argues, the book will make Gulliver famous 'on the strength of deserting me & the kids, while I, the abandoned wife, who faced my responsibilities without complaint (till now), get hardly a mention & no praise'. Discounting the wonders recounted in *Travels*, King's Mary fixates on an equally persistent theme of her husband's story: 'He talks about female "lewdness, coquetry, censure & scandal" & "the caprices of womankind"'. 'Presumably in his estimation', she notes, 'I am one of the "ranting, lewd, expensive wives" he refers to'. Having appropriated his misinformed words in scare quotes, her response can be definitive: 'I have to set the record straight'. This is dissent that relies on the host text even while it openly challenges it. As an aspiring author in her own right, Mary admits to her shortcomings: 'It's a pity that what I've been able to put into words is clumsily-expressed & deficient in the satirical perspicacity that he displays' (12). She believes in the power of the writing cure, if nothing else: 'this commentary is not so much a way of getting my own back as an attempt to come to terms with my experience, to sort matters out in my own mind'. Unlike her husband, she hopes to help others: 'If any of this ever gets further than my locked drawer, perhaps my little excursion into the world of letters will serve as a warning to young ladies with illusions about wedded bliss'. As a formerly minor character, she seizes self-control by relinquishing her reputation as the wife of the celebrated author-explorer: 'So goodbye Mrs Gulliver! Godspeed Mary Burton! This female Yahoo intends to do some travelling of her own' (12–13). Ironically, of course, she remains tied to the world discovered – or created – by her estranged husband. The short story cuts off before the travels begin and therefore before any proper counterwriting can ensue. Judged against Rosen's criteria of a minor-character elaboration, in which modified characters should be demonstrably transformed yet familiar, this Mary appears to be stuck in an unfulfilled sequel masquerading as a revision.

Another first-person short story from Mary's perspective appeared in John Kessel's 1997 collection *The Pure Product*: 'Gulliver at Home'. Rather than address unmarried women, this Mary addresses her (new) granddaughter, Eliza, daughter of the Betty mentioned in both Swift's original and King's refocalization. Despite the ominous tone at the outset

– 'No, Eliza, I did not wish your grandfather dead' – Kessel's Mary insists 'I love him'.[19] The new Mary also quotes (even more extensively) from her husband's book, seemingly in approving admonishment of herself: '"Seven months," he says, "were a sufficient time to correct every vice and folly to which Yahoos are subject"'. And the newer Mary expresses greater sexual interest in her 'stallion' of a husband (330). The attraction seems mutual: 'Whenever Lemuel returned from these voyages he wanted me, and I do not hesitate to say, I him' (336). This version of Gulliver, it turns out, has honest, familial motives: 'Lemuel hoped to improve our fortune by doctoring to sailors' (332). The youngest child hero-worships his father: 'When other of the townschildren mocked Lemuel, calling him a madman, Johnny fought them' (335). Such a Gulliver would be unrecognizable to readers solely of *Travels*, but it makes sense within the remit of a more clearly signalled narratological refocalization or, in terms of transtextual authorship, disruptive counterwriting. In these sorts of adaptive works, stronger emphasis can be placed on world-building and even minor-character-building, particularly where the central figure has been widely established across diverse cultural environments over a long period of time.

Gulliver's prior words are used against him in the new story, however, including the pompous boast made on his behalf by Richard Sympson in the publisher's notice prefixed to the first and subsequent editions of *Travels*. 'It's as true as if Mr. Gulliver had said it', Mr Trent jeers in the local shop one day, causing wide laughter (337). In this instance, Gulliver the author inadvertently affects Gulliver the character at home. The tragicofarcical actions of *Travels* seem yet more ludicrous from Mary's point of view in the modern reading context, without Gulliver's detailed account of life among the Houyhnhnms: 'Sarah was staring at a man who had entered on all fours, peering up, his head canted to the side, so that his long hair brushed the ground' (337). Mary remains empathetic, happy to go from 'widow to wife in a single instant'. On other occasions she freely articulates different emotions in a manner denied to us in Swift's monological original: 'I was angry, and I wept' (339). Increasingly, the 'young stallion' loses interest in his wife: 'He shudders at my touch' (340). Refusing to blame Gulliver for his irrepressible wanderlust, Mary blames circumstances instead: 'As a young man his heart was full of hope, but his heart has been beaten closed' (341). Like King's Mary, Kessel's Mary acknowledges the success of her husband's *Travels* ('It is all they speak of in London' [342]). But, unlike her more immediate literary forebear, she keeps her misgivings to herself and Eliza. Providing comfort for the broken traveller is all she has. Post-*Travels*, has that become Mary's character function? Not quite.

Inspired by Kessel's story, as the author telegraphs beneath the new story's title, Karen Joy Fowler's 'The Travails' (1999) gives yet more voice to Mary's frustrations. In other words, Fowler's text appears at the outset to be an elaboration of Kessel's expansion. Formally, however, the new text reveals noticeable differences. Kessel's Mary addresses her granddaughter, not Lemuel. When discussing her husband's life and experiences she acts as if he is not well-known yet: 'The third of five sons, Lemuel hailed from Nottinghamshire, where his father held a small estate' (331). Her audience is really the casual reader of Swift's *Travels*, a point made clearer by the end, where Mary concedes that 'His book has been a great success' (342). 'The Travails' instead comprises eight intimate letters signed by Mary to her husband ('Dear Lemuel').[20] Written across a sixteen-year period, from 28 September 1699 to 13 November 1715, the letters correspond with Lemuel's adventures overseas. (By his own claim, in *Travels*, Lemuel had begun his initial voyage on 4 May 1699 and was shipwrecked on the coast of Lilliput by 5 November. He finally arrived home, after intermittent returns, on 5 December 1715.[21]) The letters capture some of Mary's shifting moods over such an extensive period. Initially she is full of love and hope: Mrs Nardac 'thinks you will not come Home this time and she wishes me to know she thinks this. But I know otherwise!' (85). Seven years later she feels emotionally estranged: 'We no longer seem to fit together, you and I' (89). Across the letters, her feelings fluctuate, as they do in the real world. Nine years after that, Mary still expresses affection for her husband, despite his absenteeism: 'So much Time has passed since I had any Word of you, I fear the Worst' (93). This is not to suggest that 'The Travails' merely speaks back to *Travels* in highlighting more emphatically the emotional fallout experienced by the neglected housewife, a vital feature of feminist minor-character elaborations since at least the 1960s.[22] Fowler's text operates in a culture of personhood.

Expanding the paranarrative of the domestic life of the Gullivers in *Travels*, Fowler's epistolary short story describes in meaningful detail the now complex relationships of the canonical children, Betty and Johnny. Kessel also addressed the fallout of the feckless voyager's actions on the children left behind, but such fleshing out centred solely on Lemuel's reputation (Johnny 'worshipped him as a hero' [Kessel, 'Gulliver at Home', 335]). Fowler instead gifts them independent lives, if not quite agency. Some of the detail, particularly in the beginning, highlights their decorative functions as children of the period: 'Johnny is growing out of all his Clothes, and Betty and I are kept forever sewing' (Fowler, 'The Travails' [85]). But they grow into young adulthood across the text. 'Betty has a Beau in Mrs. Balnibarb's middle boy, William', a farmer's son whom Mary describes as clean and polite (89). Betty does not speak, but her body betrays her youthful inexperience: 'She colours if his Name is spoken but makes no effort in his Presence to delight him' (90). The courtship evidently proves successful: in less than two years, and within two pages of the text, they are engaged. That relationship also proves violent, however, as Mary infers from bruises on her daughter's wrists and neck. There is a telling dramatic irony in the fact that the only words spoken by Betty are on the first page, as an infant – '"There is Papa", she said, pointing to a Crumb of Bread' (84). Betty has an enhanced paranarrative in the new expansion, but it becomes a grim one suited to some of the harsher tones of the host text. Meanwhile, Fowler's Mary fears Johnny will copy his father, a common enough trope in Gulliverian imitations since Desfontaines's *Le Nouveau Gulliver, ou Voyage de Jean Gulliver, fils du capitaine Gulliver* (1730) had captivated European readers. 'I do request that you discourage Johnny from going to Sea', she writes to Lemuel. 'I fear your Stories have had the opposite Effect' (90).

A new character created in the margins, Betty's own daughter, Anne, may also be a victim of domestic abuse. A once exuberant child, she now 'hides in the Stables, preferring Beasts to People' in what amounts to a dark homage to her increasingly misanthropic grandfather at the denouement of his own memoirs (93). This Mary, too, inadvertently mimics Lemuel's creeping misanthropy in what amounts to an ingenious instance of repetition with disturbingly little variation: 'We are a wicked Race, we People, and it is better to be acquainted with as few of us as possible' (94). Having gained these insights without leaving London, she renders the lessons of her husband's arduous voyages redundant, though we lack the fantastical details. 'Mrs. Biddle said that you have such Stories to tell us', she wrote to her husband back in 1701, seemingly never to hear more about them (87). In sum, Fowler's Mary fulfils the functions of a post-textual commentator on a well-known prose satire and yet exhibits realistic character development over the same time span. In keeping with other feminist minor-character elaborations of the 1990s, she critiques the male protagonist of an established work. On her own terms, this version of Mary also feels complex emotions as a concerned wife, mother and grandmother and even emulates her husband's life lessons. The epistolary format departs from the memoirish pamphleteering of *Travels* but at turns redoes and expands the original in subtle ways. Blatantly modified in form, and to a surprisingly restricted degree in characterization, this short story intuitively strikes the right balance between demonstrable transformation and familiarity, a hallmark of the minor-character elaboration as distinct from the mere extension.

Home and abroad

Comprising snippets from Mary Gulliver's own travel diaries as she tries to rescue her lost husband, and free indirect discourse from a sentient doll named Lady Mary, as well as a mingling of eighteenth-century metafictionality with modern hypertextuality, Alison Fell's *The Mistress of Lilliput or The Pursuit* (1999) radically rethought the structure of minor-character elaboration. The first part of the novel retells Swift's story from a relatively unfamiliar vantage point, the Gullivers' domestic life, in which Lemuel typically has a far more fleeting role to play. A well-established serial character associated with unique fantastical worlds, neither Gulliver the explorer nor his adventures require much expansion in the present setting. With great economy of expression, Fell therefore describes Gulliver lost at sea for some months and then brings him back, much changed, within a matter of paragraphs. Returning home 'on a December day in the year 1715 a ragged stranger', Gulliver finds 'a wife in whose faithful heart he reigned supreme, and whose ardency, moreover, was perfectly undiluted!'[23] Lemuel, though, speaks strangely and with whinnying sounds before collapsing. Unable to stomach the 'odious smell of a *Yahoo*', he has reached his lowest point, as readers of the original *Travels* will recognize (44). Barely fifty-two pages into a 351-page novel, the second part can begin: a continuation that takes us beyond Swift's text. Gulliver absconds yet again here, at once reinscribing the wanderlust built into the primary character template and creating space for the new lead figure to take on a different role. The book's dual title had pre-empted two seemingly contradictory, if related, storylines – *The Mistress of Lilliput* or *The Pursuit* – and we will now witness Mary's choice in action.

If Lemuel Gulliver's story has become most widely known as 'the tale of derring-do', the narrator observes, 'then we stay-at-homes had also been exposed, if not to mortal danger, at least to the risks which are faced by any ordinary Londoner' (55). We might expect to continue the account of Mary's life at home, notwithstanding the change in location signalled by the first part of the novel's title; instead, the narrator 'surrenders' (its word) the narration to 'the lady herself': 'It is to this manuscript' – a travel memoir – 'I now refer you' (61). *The Pursuit* it is. This memoir begins on 6 January 1718, shortly after Gulliver's canonical timeline ends. Weeks (and chapters) pass before we land in Lilliput ('the island of midgets made famous by Mr. Gulliver himself' [96]). The 'well-read' reader has the dramatic advantage over Mary, the narrator reveals, as her husband's book remained in manuscript form, 'hidden in a manger of straw, dung-smeared, and much nibbled by cockroaches'. Ingeniously, then, *The Mistress* signals that this is no mere extension. It modifies while it elaborates. It is autonomous yet inextricably linked to the original. Even Mary's biographical particulars are inexplicably changed; a hosier's daughter from London in the host text, this Mary is Scottish. Ostensibly, we retrace the first author-explorer's steps as though in a sequel – but not quite. The doll-narrator, Lady Mary, can 'fill in' the uninitiated reader of the published *Travels* through lengthy asides in self-referential parentheses ('Here the reader who is familiar with the *Travels* will note that the Lilliputians had abandoned their bows and arrows for superior powder and shot...' [98]). Swift's Gulliver, whom Lionel Basney had dubbed a roaming camera suited to prose satire, has been surpassed by a nonhuman character with unusual levels of narratorial omniscience that extends beyond the present book. Here we witness a subtle reworking of the remit of a plausible extension of *Travels*: the established human characters remain shaped by regularity while the narrative voice has been dispersed beyond a singular and fallible explorer-turned-jobbing author (and rendered banally supernatural).

The major adjustment in narrative voice does not override the established world-building. If anything, it better consolidates it. Implicit in the doll's account is not merely a redoing of Gulliver's prior adventures, but, from the Lilliputians' perspective, a linear expansion: Mary now faced 'dangers far graver than those that were ever faced here by her husband', in light of their subsequent advances in military technology. In turn, as the doll-narrator surmises, Mary's body poses different threats to the Lilliputians than Lemuel's: 'If Mr. Gulliver, with the best will in the world, had flooded the Empress's Palace with his discharge of urine, what landslips of sewage might not his wife let loose upon the capital, and with what deluges of blood inundate it at her monthly time?'

(104). While Lemuel's body, in Swift's telling, incited laughter and awe, Mary's lay prone to invasion by self-proclaimed adventurers: 'The cave-mouth which now confronted him was tall and narrow, surmounted by a bulbous pillar, flanked by winged buttresses, and with a floor irregularly rutted and slippery from subterranean streams' (139). The secondary narrator becomes part of the foreign landscape first explored by her husband. Here, repetition wars with familiarity in a curiously intimate demonstration of embodied difference for the Gullivers. Modification can dramatize (in)equality. Like Gulliver among the Brobdingnagian ladies at court in Swift's *Travels*, the Lilliputian explorer's titillation turns to horror when facing the giant female form: 'when he saw the infernal colours of the place, its pinks and purples, crimsons and carmines, he thought he had been swallowed up by the mouth of Hell itself'. A tension arises in Mary's revised characterization, between that of a female body as textual property and a neo-eighteenth-century woman seeking agency.[24]

Offsetting this formal conflict, the narrator flits between human-like empathy and a rejection of such qualities 'too human for a doll to comprehend' (132). It can understand rage but lacks the appropriate means to experience it: 'Reader, if I had had heckles to rise they would have stood up straight at this juncture' (209). If the direct address to the reader were not sufficient, elsewhere the doll becomes more Gulliver-like than any other character, including Mrs Gulliver. This ironic development becomes most palpable when the narrator expresses a loathing for women: 'Thus my dear mistress was dear no longer, any more than women were the gentler sex' (221). As a taleteller, too, the doll keeps reminding us of the materiality of the story as it unfolds, not unlike Swift's Gulliver: 'should I fail in my resolve you have my permit to strike me from the page' (231). Fell's Mary, meanwhile, becomes a reflective character rather than the figural author-explorer we have long associated with her husband's role. Having abandoned her travel diary, she strives to bring Gulliver back into action after finding him on the hospital island named Ogé. Despite the brand-new setting and the extended timeline, the eventual reunion of the Gullivers offers the closest point at which Fell's novel recalls the shape and tone of the original *Travels* (if we include within it Pope's appended Lilliputian poems of 1727). Mary seeks Lemuel's embrace, but he rejects her. By now, though, he has gained greater self-awareness off the page: 'After the shipwreck I was not myself, I fear, for several months' (323). Despite her arduous journey to find her lost husband, and in doing so, validate the romantic quest genre, Mary departs on her own terms: 'I would rather be a foolish fleshly woman than a perfect paragon, for such a one you seem to seek' (334). A book-length paranarrative that spurns a straightforward redoing of Gulliver's prior voyages, *The Mistress* nevertheless interrogates the fallout of the wanderlust that drove the first author-explorer away from home. Here we see the power of creative engagements as commentaries on canonical texts beyond mere dissent. Or, if considered in terms of concerted transmedia storytelling, such engagements reveal the robustness of the most familiar core templates amid substantial formal and generic changes.

As in Fell's feminist refocalization, Mary receives full attention in Lauren Chater's *Gulliver's Wife* (2020). A plausible continuation of Swift's prototype from a modern perspective, Lemuel has become a shell of his former self. However, *Travels* has not yet been published in this world, though some set pieces are replayed and even condensed into throwaway rants: 'What she learned from his strange ramblings was this: cast away with no hope of rescue, he was taken in by a race of tiny people'.[25] And other characters allude to Gulliver's claims ('Your husband, the storyteller' [11]). Addressed as 'Widow Gulliver' at the outset, Mary considers her husband to be dead and buried: 'She'd watched the men carry his empty coffin into the family crypt' (5, 11). This acquired widowhood dramatizes the contradiction of liberation in minor-character elaborations. Characters should be modified, not merely extended, but they cannot be wholly changed. Widow Gulliver is Mrs Gulliver by any other name. (Besides, widowhood is a misnomer – her husband turns up alive.) Other minor characters gain promotion, such as Gulliver's cousin, Richard Sympson, formerly a print agent but now Mary's true love interest. 'She should have married Richard, who might have given her what she still wants', she realizes, towards the end of the novel (324). Modification here equates to making different life choices within an established world, a neat character-based counterpart to the adaptative imperative for repetition with variation. Eschewing the waning intimacy of the Gullivers seen in other refocalizations Chater instead removes their sexual compatibility from the outset: 'the hot spear she had anticipated revealed to be nothing more than a flaccid disappointment' (24). Bodily, Mary's drunken, opium-addicted husband is all but gone, 'an actor, wearing her husband's visage' (33). No longer the lead protagonist, Gulliver has become a husk of an eighteenth-century character.

As a taleteller, Lemuel still retains his power to enchant, to his children at least: 'When Pa returned from sea, her mother's stories faded from Bess's mind [. . .] How could her lessons compete with his, or with the shells he brought back, the words he'd gleaned from other places and cultures?' (132). The largely implicit characterization of Swift's Mary haunts Chater's Mary, who is similarly unable to liberate herself from the author-explorer's proven taletelling. It takes new but clued-in characters such as Casper to see through Lemuel: 'You know they have a saying about him, down at the inn? "As true a thing as if Captain Gulliver said it." He grins. "Did he really see a monster? Not everyone is convinced that he did"' (134). Paradoxically, Casper has alluded to the publisher's preface that had appeared in the printed *Travels* since 1726. Or, to fix the paradox in-universe, perhaps such flippancy lends credence to the misplaced claims made by Swift's Sympson long after the fact. (Such an example of belated retrofitting supports my broader claim throughout this study that transmedia storytelling need not be systematic or concerted to be effective.) Mary has other truth-telling concerns, namely, who is the mysterious Piet Willems, and what is his relationship with her estranged husband? And will Willems confirm or contradict Gulliver's bizarre stories of miniature people? Corporeally and emotionally absent even when he resides in London, in the family home, Gulliver nevertheless imposes himself on Mary's sense of self: 'Like the chair sitting incongruously in her parlour, it's as if her life has been erased by his return' (294). Even Lemuel's children wish him away from the story – and from existence. As Johnny admits, 'I wished he would disappear and Uncle Richard was my father' (362–63). Unwittingly, Gulliver obliges. At the end of the novel he embarks on what we presume is the canonical voyage to Brobdingnag. Laputa and Houyhnhnm-Land lay beyond that, and so this refocalized novel will eventually sync with Swift's prose satire, embedding beneath the surface of the expanded story a seething feminist counternarrative. Chater's Gulliver is feckless, to put it mildly: a selfish father and a deceptive husband, his addictive personality does not fully square with the creeping puritanism of Swift's character template. Viewed in the now-expanded purview of Mary Gulliver fictions, he nevertheless fulfils the role now expected of him: not an author-explorer challenging the tenets underpinning civilized society so much as a narrative impediment to be overcome. Minor-character elaborations do not just extend prior works, reverentially or otherwise;

they modify them anew for their purposes, and in order to retain a new internal integrity in terms of plot and character dynamics.

Extensions of character in the broadest sense often stabilize a literary sequel that is focused on major or at least familiar properties and settings. The blatant malleability of minor-character elaborations, by contrast, not only allows for but demands the modification of lesser-known or archetypal characters. Form and genre are especially prone to adjustments in this mode of writing. *Oh, Gulliver! Mrs Gulliver and the Secret of Size* (2023), the first volume in Erga Netz's projected series recentred on the slightly renamed Mary Burton-Gulliver, extends the trope of a distanced husband and wife in what is essentially a retracing of the original first voyage in Mary's own words told through a mixture of retrospective diary entries and present reflection. First-person pontification becomes pillow-talk reportage. Mary reveals herself to be the true author of the final chapter of Swift's *Travels* in a letter wittily addressed to Richard Sympson Junior, the son of the publishing agent attached to the framing narrative of the host text. By this point, on 28 October 1749, as stated in the signature, Gulliver had been dead for four years. Completing but then expanding on her late husband's travel memoirs, just over fifty years after the ill-fated first voyage, the 'old, sick, and lonely woman' (her words) will find solace.[26] Such a premise also frees up the actual author, Erga Netz, to flit freely between the familiar ('He found that his arms and legs were strongly fastened on each side to the ground' [51], a reference to the initial landing in Lilliput) and the newly concocted ('Silently weeping, I envisioned him growing up to become a big lad, fighting and kicking' [116], as she observes of their dead infant son George). Another type of revisiting as extension attends to other familiar – but unfamilial – characters. The post-*Travels* story of Gulliver's 'little nurse' from Brobdingnag makes up Leo Sonderegger's *Glumdalclitch* (2000), where she grows into womanhood, marries Harlbruug (a new character), creates a Gulliverian museum, and is saved from the villainous Skraagnok (yet another new character) by a crew of English sailors who have retraced Gulliver's steps. (By implication, the Gulliver that Glumdalclitch knew has died.) A post-Gulliver Lilliput and places populated with relocated Lilliputians have long featured prominently in children's Gulliveriana, most memorably in Henry Winterfeld's *Castaways in Lilliput* (1960) and T. H. White's *Mistress Masham's Repose* (1946), where Maria finds them exiled on the lakes of Malplaquet.[27] Later still, Jamie finds them in Andrew Dalton's homage to White, *The Temples of Malplaquet* (2005).

Gulliver does make an appearance in Sam Gayton's *Lilliput* (2013), as a malevolent giant who imprisons the heroine. Usually, nominally condensed versions of *Travels* for children render Gulliver as gentle and sketch him in pastel colours. At each extreme we find incompatible but entirely plausible iterations of Swift's prototype attuned to the needs of contrary creative environments.

Other types of domesticated Gulliver have emerged in modern children's literature. Carter Crocker's *Last of the Gullivers* (2012) reconfigures Swift's character into a Proppian mentor to a troubled twelve-year-old American named Michael Pine. No mere plot guide, in fact, Crocker's Gulliver has a magical quality that belies his everyday appearance ('a man came in, tall, bent, silver-haired, old as earth').[28] This Gulliver appears to retain some cognition of the former adventures, too, just as the modern Lilliputians invoke memories of their ancestors: 'Great Ghost of Bolgolam!', exclaims one, amid an attack by urination from Michael (41). Really, 'Lem Gulliver' is a nested codename. Quinbus Flestrin is 'what they've called all the Gullivers', Lem reveals, when he takes the boy to see the little people of Lesser Lilliput at the end of his garden in Moss-on-Stone (50). Fittingly, for a study of cultural afterlives, the 'original Lemuel Gulliver' had helped write the Lilliputian constitution on 20 March 1720. One of the three eternal principles enshrined there is: '*no Journey has an End*' (59). Also fittingly, chapter twenty-two ('A New Chapter') excerpts passages from a manuscript in the original Gulliver's hand, 'Part Five. A Voyage Back to Lilliput' (181). The discovery that the first Quinbus Flestrin had helped some Lilliputians escape their war-torn home and resettle with him in Moss-on-Stone induces existential panic among the Lesser Lilliputians: 'Are we *not* the only ones? Are we part of a larger race?' (186). Some actions, including wars, can simply take place in the garden of the current incumbent of the role of Gulliver. Ironically, the nominal Gulliver abandons Michael for an off-page mission of his own for most of the book: 'I can't say when, or if, I'll be back' (95). A complex variation of the Gulliver-less Gulliveriana, *Last of the Gullivers* removes Lem Gulliver in order to create original plots in a new, if reminiscent, version of Lilliput. Collectively, these different types of engagement with the source material stretch the boundaries of continuity built into transfictional and transmedial storytelling. Not merely uncoalescing versions of a singular character, Gulliver has become a transmedia type – *a Gulliver*.

Gulliver's clones

When we consider the full range of Gulliveriana from the eighteenth century to the present, one of the most persistent forms of engagement concerns not a period-appropriate Lemuel Gulliver but fictional affiliates, whether nominal offspring or time-forwarded travellers who share his name and other characteristics. Some are self-proclaimed direct descendants, such as Philip Hippophil (a great-grandson on the father's side) in Walter Copland Perry's *The Revolt of the Horses* (1898), a war-torn and relocated extension of the story of the Houyhnhnms. An American relative (a great-great-great grandson on the mother's side), the titular author-explorer of *Gulliver Joi* (1852), undertook 'marvelous adventures' in Kailoo, Hydrogenia and Ejario with the belief that the 'love of adventure is hereditary'.[29] Émile Bouchery's *Les Petits-Neveux de Gulliver* (1845) centres on the grandnephews of the author-explorer, who apparently even predicted that La Chambaudière would have yet more wonderful tales to tell, in the latter's words ('c'est moi, dont les voyages seraient bien autrement merveilleux que les siens').[30] Another Francophonic descendant of Lemuel Gulliver, Patrick Guill'Vaër discovered the last living Lilliputian on a mysterious island in Edmond Édouard-Bauer's science fiction story for the Parisian periodical *Je sais tout* in 1921. Wanderlust was in the blood of an Edwardian descendant of a lovechild Gulliver had conceived with an inhabitant of Callimago, an incident omitted from *Travels* on the grounds of moral decency.[31] Callimagians do not tend to leave their idyllic island, we learn, but the unnamed narrator nevertheless voyages to Isotaria. Indirectly, Swift's character template has been revalidated in unfathomed environments.

Literary relations can expand the core world-building under the auspices of self-appointed authority. *A Fable Founded upon Fact, Translated from a Manuscript, Found in an Old Castle, May 10th, 1784* (1784), a verse satire, was similarly based on a manuscript found in an unnamed castle apparently written by an unnamed great-grandson of Gulliver. Another great-grandson named Lemuel Gulliver chances upon an unpublished poem that mentions Laputa. He 'edited' it for publication in 1813 as *The Eo-nauts, or The Spirit of Delusion*. Verigull Gulliver, a grandson, struggled to complete a five-page fragment of his own travel memoir in 1832.[32] In a transmedial context this was still a remarkable achievement: his father, namely the son of Lemuel, had feared ridicule from the public and even kept the original *Travels* out of Verigull's hands.

(This is a neat variation of the persistent trope of secondary explorers inexplicably claiming to not know the name or work of the first Lemuel Gulliver.) The most famous familial author-explorer appeared early, in Pierre-François Guyot Desfontaines's *Le Nouveau Gulliver, ou Voyage de Jean Gulliver, fils du capitaine Gulliver* (1730), and enjoyed immense success. Dutch, German and Italian translations followed a year later and ran to several editions. John Lockman rendered the book into English as *The Travels of Mr. John Gulliver, Son to Capt. Lemuel Gulliver* (1731). By this point, Desfontaines's loose and often digressive translation of the original *Travels*, as *Les Voyages de Gulliver* (1727), had already gained a keen readership across Europe.[33] Lemuel Gulliver Jr is also the pseudonymous author of *Modern Gulliver's Travels* (1796), where he finds Lilliput almost a century after his father had discovered it.

Desfontaines's narrator is apparently the same John mentioned in *Travels* as the son of Mary and Lemuel before the latter undertook his ill-fated voyage in 1696 (though he becomes Jean in the French and Joan in the Dutch). Less plausibly, the younger Gulliver of *Modern Gulliver's Travels* is the illegitimate issue of a Blefuscudian nun. Conceived between 1703 and 1705, if we stick with the dates established in *Travels*, he lived to write his autobiography well into his nineties. (A precedent for time-forwarded clones had now been set, long before the rise of media convergence culture.) The French editor's preface insists on the originality of *Le Nouveau Gulliver* while relying on the readers' prior experience with *Travels*: 'as the public have made the philosophical, and bold ideas of Capt. *Lemuel Gulliver* familiar to them; they would be less surpriz'd at those of *John Gulliver* his son [. . .] for tho' the fictions are very different, there yet is a kind of analogy between them'.[34] Inadvertently or not, the editor invites comparisons around absurd juxtaposition, subverted binaries and other techniques common to both texts. The Letalispons, 'a people, who return to the bloom of youth at a certain age, and enjoy a long life', are anti-Struldbruggs.[35] He may find different worlds, but John Gulliver believes himself to be a carbon copy of the first Gulliver: 'I can say that I take very much after my father, not only with regard to the exterior qualities, but also those of my mind'.[36] By contrast, the half-Blefuscudian Lemuel Jr knows very little about his reputed biological father other than what he gleans from manuscripts given to him by a man he considers to be his truest role model, Father Rambellius. Bio-textual influences from within battle with socialized ones, and they further undermine the personhood definition of literary character as practised in this period.

Yet another Gulliver the Younger 'retraces' (his word) the original's steps in *Voyage to Locuta* (1818), though he opts to proceed 'still farther', just beyond Laputa, to explore another island in a similar setting – in adaptation theory this is repetition with a difference.[37] In transmedia storytelling, it is expansive intertextuality. Some nominal descendants have less interest in Swift's world-building. By 1979 Lemuel Jr had found innumerable new worlds, as in Esmé Dodderidge's science fiction retelling, *The New Gulliver; or, The Adventures of Lemuel Gulliver Jr in Capovolta*, though this offspring is a namesake only. Barry Pain's Lemuel Jr appears to have little familial connection with Swift's Gulliver, despite his name, particularly if we account for the anachronistic references to the Factory Acts, steamships and telegraphs in *The New Gulliver and Other Stories* (1913). Pain, a New Humorist, nevertheless cleverly splices the absurdism of Laputa with the austerity of Houyhnhnm-Land on the Island of Thule, thereby recapturing the spirit of the original while rejecting its formal features. Colin Milne makes a more explicit connection at the outset of *So This Is Glasgow!* (1938), a witty inverse of *Travels* in which the modern-day Lemuel Swift Gulliver, from Tasmania, revisits (and comments on) the home country of his 'famous ancestor'.[38] While these notional namesakes do not have to adhere to Swift's character template, or even exhibit some common characteristics, they nevertheless endorse the personality, habits or actions of the long-established Lemuel Gulliver.

Expanding our set of clones to include non-Gullivers, we find an early example in *A Trip to the Moon* (1728). Murtagh McDermot, the authorial pseudonym, dedicates the work to the 'Worthy, Daring, Adventurous, Thrice-renown'd, and Victorious Captain Lemuel Gulliver', and displays a similar mix of aptitude and ignorance as he recounts his fantastical voyages.[39] This is repetition masquerading as difference, a tangential expansion rather than a furthering of the original. In the final forty-odd pages of *A Voyage to Cacklogallinia* (1727), Samuel Brunt similarly journeys to the moon, an obvious departure from *Travels* but another endorsement of the early trend for lunar Gulliveriana. However, the bulk of *Cacklogallinia* parallels Gulliver's earthbound voyages, not least of all its avian utopia of sorts, which superficially resembles Houyhnhnm-Land. Its principal figure, Captain Brunt, whom the Cacklogallians dub *probusomo* ('Monster of Nature'), straightforwardly recalls the Brobdingnagian depiction of Gulliver as a *lusus naturae*.[40] Both author-explorers have an overly idealized vision of England, demonstrate advanced language-learning skills, and view their respective hosts, Cacklogallians and Lilliputians, as bickering societies in decline. Some other character connections in the period seem forced, as in Baron Munchausen's claim to be Gulliver's appointed heir in a revised edition of Rudolf Erich Raspe's *Singular Travels* (1785–87).[41] Evidently, the borrowed fame worked: the new version rapidly ran to eight editions as *Gulliver Revived*. Transmedia world-building need not always focus on enhancing or extending the original template; sometimes it can just be exploitative.

Non-Gullivers kept cropping up well into the next century. William Munro's *Daniel Thomson: The Scottish Gulliver* (1892) is the 'Scottish Gulliver' in name only; or, rather, he fits a loose Gulliverian archetype rather than into any sort of approximation of Swift's properties. A more substantial work from the late Victorian period, *The Adventures of Gulliver Redivivus* (1881) by Joseph Orme, immediately signals, in the opening sentence if not the title, who the actual hero is: the non-Gulliverian Christopher Columbus Smythe. Some characters have had the name Gulliver thrust upon them, such as young Omar in Michael Morpurgo's *Boy Giant* (2019), whom the gleeful Lilliputians dub the Son of Gulliver when he crashes on their coast ('What "Gulliver" meant I had no idea').[42] In addition to Gulliver's nominal descendants and para-Gullivers with no explicit connection, a third grouping comprises far-flung figures who share Gulliver's name and wanderlust. Among the most famous such works in this area are Frigyes Karinthy's *Voyage to Faremido* (1916) and *Capillaria* (1921), as they are commonly known in English, and Sándor Szathmári's *Voyage to Kazohinia* (1941).[43] *Faremido* has been labelled as a fifth voyage, and its Gulliver ostensibly remembers his experiences in Lilliput, Brobdingnag, Laputa and Houyhnhnm-Land. But the year is 1914 and World War the occupation. A sequel to the sequel, *Capillaria* pushes Karinthy's Gulliver into further fantastical worlds. Szathmári, meanwhile, moves his Gulliver to 1935 with little need for explanatory justification. Justus Franz Wittkop's *Gullivers letzte Reise: die Insel der Vergänglichen* (*Gulliver's Last Voyage: The Island of the Mortals* [1941]) introduces into the Gulliverian world an unknown idyll facing warfare and revolution and whose inhabitants have cruelly limited lifespans of just thirty days. An adventure story written by a former soldier who later fled to England towards the end of the Second World War, it cannot help but be a political allegory of war-torn Europe.[44] In a 1936 novel, *Pyatoe puteshestvie Gullivera* (*Gulliver's Fifth Voyage*), M. Yu Kozyrev describes Gulliver's perilous sojourn in 'Yuberalliya', a pun on fascist Germany (Über alles) and the Soviet Union (Überall) – understandably, it went unpublished until 1991.[45] Not quite exemplifying the concertedness of transmedia storytelling, such examples nevertheless demonstrate some looser ways in which familiar literary properties can be refitted to new environments.

Set in the context of protests against the Vietnam War, a 1968 novel titled *Schule der Planeten* (*School of the Planets*) by the Swiss author Felix Gasbarra takes Lemuel Gulliver and Jonathan Swift (now a fictional character) on an interstellar voyage to the land of the Yahoo-like Mnus and the Houyhnhnm-like Mecs.[46] Swift also interacts with Dr Gulliver in the ninth volume of Simon Hawke's *Time Wars* series, *The Lilliput Legion* (1989). When Swift introduces Dr Gulliver to his real-life peers Joseph Addison and Richard Steele in an eighteenth-century tavern in this novel, we are primed to re-hear his story. Farcically, though, the drunken sailor 'grunted and passed out, striking his forehead on the wooden table with a resounding thud'.[47] 'Brief, but effective', Steele retorts. Passionately defended by Swift, this Gulliver endures ridicule among his contemporaries. Soon enough, Steiger, a mysterious young man from the future, seeks him out to record his words: '"You . . . you *believe* me?" Gulliver said, astonished' (6). As a character, Hawke's Gulliver has been all but discarded by the eighteenth-century intelligentsia. In the twenty-seventh century, Gulliver the author still matters, especially as an accidental authority on the Lilliputian warriors who threaten the lives of millions. Until the end of the novel, the Temporal Intelligence Agency insist on wiping Gulliver's knowledge of the future to which he has been brought before returning him home and denying him any further voyages. 'For your own good, you'd damn well better make sure he *never* hears of this', Andre tells Gulliver, with his amanuensis, Dr Swift, in mind (114). Gulliver's original journey to Lilliput, it transpires, actually entailed crossing into a parallel universe. And that retconned knowledge is already too dangerous. Dallying with enforced closure, Hawkes's use of science fiction world-building at once respects Swift's boundaries, in narratological terms, and problematizes them from a reader's perspective.

Using the term 'clone' figuratively throughout this chapter, we might note that human cloning exists as a motif elsewhere in modern Gulliveriana: Ariazad's (Varoujan Kazanjian) *Gulliver in Cloneland: The Fifth Travel of Gulliver* (2000). Like the Hungarian-made Gullivers, this narrator draws on established experience; unlike them, he remains in his own century, though the science belongs to ours. Gulliver cloning often keeps radical reboots in line with the general idea of *Travels* without restricting their adopted milieux. Michael Ryan's *Gulliver* (1993) at turns reinscribes or outright rejects the original. In that book's fourth and final voyage, the narrator – now a twenty-second-century spaceship's surgeon – lands in Ecologia, where intelligent dogs, pigs and horses marvel at the talking human. Treated like an inferior creature, though, this Gulliver refuses to stay. In *The Lilliput Legion*, Hawke had wrenched Lemuel Gulliver from his own time and place while challenging his fictionality: 'You're talking about a novel by Jonathan Swift, for God's sake!', insists an incredulous Dr Darkness (120). Ryan's Gulliver seems oblivious to the highly publicized life of his forebear, even while he follows (or subverts) the broad outlines of the original voyages. Adam Roberts's *Swiftly: A Novel* (2008) jettisons the four-voyage structure entirely, as well as the setting and general style of *Travels*. Like *Last of the Gullivers* and suchlike engagements, it is an extension, a refocalization and a reimagining all at once.

Written in the first person, Edward M. Lerner's 'My Fifth and Most Exotic Voyage' (2017) flings the author-explorer into Chicago in the year 2022. Here he is more a fictional character than a person, as the bemused moderns inform him:

> My face became hot. 'Lemuel Gulliver, sir, *is* my name'.
>
> 'It could be a great coincidence, I suppose'. He seemed dubious. 'A famous book written at about your time has the title of *Gulliver's Travels*'.
>
> About my time? 'I wrote *Travels into Several Remote Nations of the World*. Without my leave, the editor changed the title'.
>
> Doctor Kelly removed his spectacles to polish the lenses with the end of his cravat. 'Actually, Jonathan Swift wrote it. It's a satire'.[48]

Amid relentless denials of his existence, a crisis of identity overwhelms the narrator: 'Lemuel Gulliver was a man of action. Whomsoever I might be, I knew not any other way to act' (19). A Gulliverian archetype of the fantastical voyager, this figure soon becomes a modern writer, having discovered that marvellous modern invention, the ballpoint pen ('a tapered metallic tip terminating in a tiny metallic ball'). So comprehensive is his prior knowledge of *Travels*, the pseudo-Gulliver ('Lem') ponders whether he might actually be Swift instead; but the experts note they look unalike, based on historical paintings and records. Lem's final solution to the puzzle is more readily accepted: he has come from an alternative reality, a mainstay of modern transmedia storytelling. In the confines of the story, such a trope fits the genre, namely, a science fiction tinkering with the origins of *Travels*. Such a trope also heightens the collapse of the author-explorer into his component functions as expressed across multiple reworkings of the source material framed in other genres across many years and in different fora, whether chapbook adventures or periodical satires, among others. In adventure stories, Gulliver primarily serves as an agent of plot. In satire, Gulliver the author can keep commentating on updated social or political concerns.

Spaced out

The Space Age, loosely meaning the second half of the twentieth century, freely adopted Gulliver and his *Travels*. Centred on Lieutenant Gulliver (sometimes Gullivar) Jones, an archetype of the bold voyager beyond the stars, Edwin L. Arnold's *Gulliver of Mars* (1905) belatedly found a cult following among science fiction readers after it was reissued in 1964. A 1965 animated film, *Garibā no Uchū Ryokō* (*Gulliver's Travels Beyond the Moon*), features a wizened Professor Gulliver, now a reclusive rocket scientist. Two of the most popular of all science fiction franchises, *Doctor Who* and *Star Trek*, instead relied on an 'authentic', eighteenth-century Lemuel Gulliver. A five-part *Doctor Who* serial directed by David Maloney and written by Peter Ling, *The Mind Robber* first aired on British television between 14 September and 12 October 1968. The second Doctor (played by Patrick Troughton) and his companions Jamie (Frazer Hines) and Zoe (Wendy Padbury) arrive in The Land of Fiction, a pocket universe in which a prolific but now wearied English writer from 1926 has begun to appropriate characters from Earth stories to appease the indefatigable Master Brain computer.[49] First billed as merely a 'stranger' in the second episode, Bernard Horsfall appeared in the guise of one such character, 'Gulliver', in the remaining series.[50] As a fictional construct, Ling's Gulliver lacks autonomy – he speaks only in phrasing lifted from *Travels*. This includes distinctive diction, such as 'Grildrig' and 'Splacknuck', as well as key biographical particulars, in his first encounter with the Doctor. And yet, the Doctor does not recognize the identity of the stranger until the third episode. Even though the Master of the Land of Fiction narrates for us throughout the story, Ling's Gulliver operates as a sort of supplementary narrator, as he states his actions ('I was ready to defend his life'). As a character, he often refuses to partake in new action, such as helping the Doctor and the companions fend off robots, presumably because it would corrupt the fixed boundaries of Swift's source text.

In the belated novelization of *The Mind Robber* (1986), Ling stresses the strange familiarity of the character: 'Whoever this man might be, he had a frank, humorous expression; he did not appear to be a villain. And – wonder of wonders – he spoke English, even if his phraseology was a little old-fashioned'.[51] While we might think of adaptation as a process of assimilative normalization, this example represents a more confrontational strategy of appropriative dispossession in which established literary properties have been flagrantly adopted but alienated. If anything, the Doctor has assumed the Gulliverian role of a stranger judged harshly against the indigenous rules. The Master has 'articles of impeachment against you, for treason and other capital crimes', Gulliver informs the Doctor. The Doctor, like Swift's Gulliver, considers this absurd: 'Treason? Oh, really! How can I be a traitor when I don't even know where I am or what I'm doing here' (48). Ling's Gulliver, though, reminds us of and perhaps accentuates his own foreignness in Swift's remote nations: 'I cannot tell', he answers to the Doctor's straightforward query, 'What is the name of this extraordinary place?' This Gulliver falls into fictional limbo, neither in Lilliput or other Swiftian nations nor fully on a fifth voyage. Gulliver again meets the Doctor, now reunited with the companions Zoe and Jamie, a few pages later. The Doctor wishes to flee. Gulliver, however, sees no reason to 'escape' (the Doctor's word): 'I looked upon myself to be fully settled for life' (63). Unlike Swift's book-born Gulliver, Ling's clone feels no threat, even when an army of mechanical soldiers attacks the group. He lacks fear or other human emotions often gifted to characters with approximated personhood.

Later, the Doctor realizes, the soldiers 'don't live in *his* world – so he can't see them' (65). Even later, Gulliver reveals that he assumed the group were hiding from Yahoos, that 'cursed race of inferior creatures' met in the original fourth voyage (113). Again, if judged as an agent within the story, this Gulliver seems redundant. As Jamie notes, 'I've never seen any Yahoos, and you've never seen any White Robots, so we don't know what we're both talking about'. And the Doctor soon disregards Gulliver's advice: 'Who says I won't see the Master? It's what I came to do!' (116).

Ling's Gulliver fulfils a plot function only inadvertently when Zoe follows him across a beam of light, triggering an alarm. Lacking full corporeality, Gulliver cannot affect it directly. And he cannot take an active role in new action:

> The man in the tricorne hat gazed out into the distance, past the columns of soldiers, without a sign of recognition. The troops stamped into attention, forming up around him, but he gave them neither a word nor a glance. Instead, he stretched his arms, flexing his muscles and yawned. (64)

Transported to a different reality, indeed a burgeoning transmedia franchise (the Whoniverse), the man in the tricorne hat seems neither dead nor alive. A textual ghost, this Gulliver exists beyond the bodily restrictiveness of Lilliput or the perpetual violence of Brobdingnag. He mouths the words of the original – often ingeniously turning monologue into conversation – but he has a different spirit. Curiously, then, by strictly adhering to the particulars of Swift's book-born Gulliver, this provides a potent example of how overly reverential intertextuality can short-circuit the otherwise endless possibilities associated with authorship, world-building and character-building in transmedia storytelling.

Despite the Doctor's frequent characterization of him as one of the most famous of eighteenth-century travellers, Gulliver has become an anti-traveller. Lacking the existential restlessness of Swift's Gulliver, Ling's clone functions as an embodied interlocutor who at turns furthers exposition and embodies the metafictional elements of the fantastical environment. As a narrative agent, he frustrates Zoe. At the denouement of the story the Doctor grapples with the Master, who has now revealed his plan to free himself from authorial imprisonment on the planet at the expense of his replacements. Zoe appeals to Gulliver for help, but he stays loyal to his adoptive Creator, the Master of the Land of Fiction, who is himself the puppet of a computer mainframe. 'Alas, we obey our creator', Gulliver says without irony (139). Instead, Cyrano de Bergerac and D'Artagnan, and other conjured or concocted characters, fight on behalf of the Doctor and the Master. Such action only further heightens the curious characterless function of Ling's Gulliver. This characterlessness is intensified further still when the second Doctor meets Gulliver again in a follow-up flash fiction penned by Marc Platt in 1992.[52] Unable to locate his recorder, a defining accoutrement of this version of the multi-personality character, the Doctor mentally re-enters the Land of Fiction. However, when 'Gulliver' suddenly quotes new dialogue not attributable to Swift, the Doctor realizes that this is in fact the Time Lord Goth in masquerade. The textual ghost turns ghostwriter again.

Gulliver appeared in another popular science fiction franchise, *Star Trek*, throughout the 1990s, in a frequently reissued novel set in The Next Generation era, *Gulliver's Fugitives* (1990) by Keith Sharee.[53] While searching for the USS Huxley, a starship missing for over ten years, the Enterprise crew stumble across a forgotten colony of humans on a planet called Rampart, a world where fiction, speculation and the imagination are outlawed. A survey team beams onboard the Enterprise to search for contraband materials, and suddenly the crewmembers find themselves in the middle of a civil war between a band of rebels, the Dissenters, and the planet's mind police. Gulliver appears late in the story, but his impact is felt early on. In the 2340s, two decades prior to the present, an elementary schoolgirl named Amoret discovers a single illustrated page from *Gulliver's Travels*. The image happens to be an iconic one: 'a man tied onto a kind of sled and surrounded by a busy swarm of people no bigger than his finger'.[54] Inspired by the imagery of this contraband, Amoret grew up to become a Dissenter. Always carrying the tattered page with her, she offers it to the Starfleet officer Deanna Troi, to whom she stresses its personal value: 'It's the only piece of genuine classic fiction I've ever owned' (66). 'I've spent all my life trying to write the rest of the story', she continues. 'Someone has to keep it alive': we might infer that she hopes to complete the story as written, filling in material known to Earth readers in 1990 but lost to Rampartians by the twenty-fourth century. Or perhaps it will inspire yet more stories. A relic of human creativity for Amoret, the page now holds conflicting connotations: tragedy, in its association with the Dissenter's impending execution, but also hope, 'an avatar of something immeasurably greater, something that could live on after the page was gone'. An arresting officer stuffs the page into a metal cylinder hung by his side and, with a puff of smoke, destroys the artefact. As abrupt as the act is, this is not the end of Gulliver's afterlife here.

Condemned to death alongside the rest of the Enterprise's party (Captain Picard, Riker and Data), five short chapters from the end of the book, Troi fades in and out of consciousness. Suddenly, a great hole opens in the roof, and a giant human hand reaches in. As the owner of the hand becomes more visible, Troi recognizes him from Amoret's burned page: 'The giant was Gulliver himself, in the flesh' (232). Like the weaponized body of Swift's Gulliver among the Lilliputians, put into service against the Blefuscudians, this looming figure crushes the enemy with ease. The twenty-fourth-century clone shares the original's monstrous glee: 'The giant seemed amused by the angry little mite'. All of this has been conjured out of Troi's mind in a visceral hallucination. Presumably, then, she had read more of *Travels* than the word-and-image scrap found by Amoret – or at least consumed a literary or visual portrayal of Gulliver in Lilliput at some unknown point. In other words, Troi represents the casual consumer of Gulliveriana well into the future. Whether a bookish character or a post-book figure, Gulliver has survived at least eight centuries after his birth. And while Gulliver's presence in the *Star Trek* novel may be merely a figment of a character's empathic imagination, he temporarily serves a significant purpose in the plot as the rescuer. Troi eventually realizes that the crew remain incarcerated, and the scene had been a flight of wish fulfilment: 'No Gulliver had come to rescue them' (242). Indeed, in the vision, the CS (Cephalic Security) had seemingly achieved what the Blefuscudians could not: they felled him with shots from a truck-mounted radiation cannon: 'Gulliver collapsed [. . .] The earth shuddered for several seconds, and then all was still' (234). Sharee kills off Gulliver in a vision within what appears to be an extra voyage (on Rampart) or, in effect, an adjusted redoing of the original's first voyage. Although ranging across different formats (novels, periodical essays, short stories and TV serials) and genres (political satire, feminist refocalization, science fiction and more), Gulliver's last voyages did not necessarily take him to new places. Familiar and alien all at once, such voyaging relied on but was not restricted by Swift's characterization, plotting or world-building.

3 IMAGING GULLIVER

Lemuel Gulliver's image has been widely disseminated around the world through illustrated editions of *Travels*, comics and graphic novels, live-action and animated films, stage plays and puppet shows, standalone prints and paintings, postcards, card games and other entertainment ephemera, and even statues and murals.[1] Put another way, Gulliver has haunted bookshops and libraries, public and home cinemas, theatres, toy shops, galleries and museums, parks and other civic spaces for 300 years and counting. Such dispersal implies that a recognizable figure occupies these diverse environments. In practice, the pluralism built into the book-born Gulliver, within and across the early editions of his own *Travels*, only multiplies further across transmedia storytelling and material culture alike. Gulliver emotes bemusement, amusement, cheeriness, pensiveness, contemplativeness, alarm, exacerbation or disinterest, sometimes statically and usually with little regard for plots old or new, in the most commonly available images.[2] Some pictorial Gulliveriana parallels and often extends Swift's character-building, world-building and authorship. Just as novelistic extensions have, from the outset of the title character's afterlife, become part of the Gulliver story as though created through posthumous collaboration, so imagistic reworkings bear the stamps of other creatives. Since 1838, many artists have imitated what David S. Lenfest refers to as J. J. Grandville's fantastic and comical grotesque style, though few have so fully committed to the accretive pictorial narrative of an ageing, increasingly tragic Gulliver built up over more than four hundred pieces.[3] Thomas Morten designed a similar number of plates in 1865, and, like Granville's, these were reprinted more than a dozen times well into the next century.[4] Not merely depicting individual scenes, Morten foregrounded the 'progress' of Gulliver from haughty colonialist to disillusioned creature. On a smaller scale, Johann Sebastian Müller's plates for John Hawkesworth's 1754 edition of *Travels* initially present an unfeasibly boyish Gulliver in the first image, seemingly to leave us more affected by the haunted older man fending off Yahoos in the fourth and final one.[5] For a 1930 illustrated *Travels* Rex Whistler replicated scenes in highly elaborate decorated frames.[6]

More often than not, Gulliver has been portrayed as an eighteenth-century male with light or perhaps sunburnt skin, though his hair colour may range from bright yellow to jet black, and he has been aged up or down, thinned out or pumped up. Increasingly there have been notable exceptions to the core template across different media. Mae Munuo, a woman of colour, recently took on the title role of a cognate character (Grace Gulliver) in Jaz Woodcock-Stewart's stage adaptation for Unicorn Theatre in March 2022. For all the plasticity of Gulliver's appearance, however limited in terms of race or gender so far, a shared assumption among artists insists on a semblance of anthropocentric realism. As a quick testament to this curious investment in the personhood of Gulliver, observers had complained that the character presented in Charles R. Leslie's 1835 painting for Lord Egremont, *Gulliver's Introduction to the Queen of Brobdingnag*, was not a human being but 'a puppet made of wax and wire'.[7] Nevertheless, the competing visual traditions of the fleshed-out and figurine Gullivers, I wish to show, have become equally valid though equally inconsistent. This seeming contradiction between recognition and revision further indicates that Gulliver is best understood within a transmedia purview, even if he preceded the emergence of media convergence culture. In the present chapter we will consider a selection of images in different formal contexts and so expand our understanding of the narratological tension between the author and the character. The first section, 'What does Gulliver look like?', begins with the conflicting portraiture of Lemuel Gulliver found in the front matter of the first (and many subsequent) editions of *Travels*. Then we will consider early visual reworkings, namely artworks in widely disseminated translations such as Pierre-François Guyot Desfontaines's *Les Voyages de Gulliver* (1727) and popular abridgements like Francis Newbery's *The Adventures of Captain Gulliver* (1772). After that, we turn to modern illustrations in which kinetic iterations of Gulliver as a figure of action and adventure displace unduly (and dully) realistic ones, typically through cartoonish or symbolic suggestiveness. Indicative works here, respectively, include Chris Riddell's drawings for Martin Jenkins's *Jonathan Swift's Gulliver* (2004) and Kokor's (Alain Koch) three-volume hardback comic *Les Voyages du Docteur Gulliver* (2006–9).

Rather than depicting a full-bodied Gulliver, many artists and illustrators have captured mere parts of him. This involves one of the earliest of all creative engagements with *Travels*, William Hogarth's satirical print *The Punishment Inflicted on Lemuel Gulliver* (1726), where we glimpse Gulliver's behind, as well as modern print advertisements. 'Classic comics', the second section of this chapter, focuses on comic-book depictions of Gulliver from the 1930s to the present day, principally works produced for major staples of the industry such as Gilberton's *Classics Illustrated* and Marvel Comics. So far, I have prioritized the textual, narratologic (and sometimes semiotic) approach to transmedia storytelling, in Paolo Bertetti's terms. We now bring in the visual and discursive coding of sequential art, and this includes giving attention to the layout and transitions on the page.[8] The next section, 'Adapted and updated', extends this formalist approach with some additional reworkings of *Travels* in graphic novel form, such as Cynthia Martin and Donald Lemke's *Jonathan Swift's Gulliver's Travels* (2008), along with individual volumes for Salariya's Graffex in 2009 (scripted by John Malam with artwork by Penko Gelev) and Kalyani Navyug Media's Campfire in 2010 (scripted by Lewis Helfand and illustrated by Vinod Kumar). After this we turn to a reworked *Travels* set in the 1990s, a graphic novel centred on a clueless descendant of Lemuel Gulliver, Martin Rowson's *Gulliver's Travels: Adapted & Updated* (2012). Alan Moore refits the eighteenth-century author-explorer for a largely para-Victorian collective of public domain characters in *The League of Extraordinary Gentlemen* (1999–2021), where he draws equally on Gulliver's separate functions as an author and an explorer. The next chapter will expand the focus to include performative media (film, television, video games and plays). Considered collectively, the range of Gullivers imaged between the 1720s and the 2020s, from his own portraits in *Travels* to cameos in twenty-first-century graphic novels, reveals the fuller potency of the serial character within different media environments.

What does Gulliver look like?

Within the diverse body of visual Gulliveriana accreted over three centuries across different media we might identify two broad approaches: one that prioritizes the humanness of Gulliver the character palpably affected by the unfamiliar worlds in which he finds himself and one that treats him as a warm puppet subject to the whims of the surreal nations. Each approach responds to contrary facets of Swift's prototype, chiefly the restless voyager and the domesticated 'living doll', to adopt John Traugott's phrasing.[9] These are not always mutually exclusive categories. Removing or otherwise amputating the protagonist's body can heighten the psychological disarray suggested by the imagery. Other characters or creatures might gain equal or greater billing so that Gulliver's heroism can be enhanced or undermined as required. Where Cynthia Martin's buccaneering Gulliver swooshes wasps to death with his sword in her illustration for Donald Lemke's *Jonathan Swift's Gulliver's Travels* (2008), Arthur Rackham's emaciated voyager, dressed in a loose shirt and slippers, barely fended them off in 1909.[10] Against the more kinetic showings, the figurine tradition began in earnest with Benjamin Motte Jr's 1727 duodecimo edition of Swift's *Travels* and continued with what was in effect the first major children's version of the story, Francis Newbery's *The Adventures of Captain Gulliver* (1772). In the first Motte plate (**Figure 1**), three Gullivers can be seen in different states after being captured in Lilliput. While the on-page plurality aids a pictorial narrative, from initial capture to life in the unfamiliar capital, the factory line of figures codifies the dehumanization of the character. Quite simply, there are too many bodies to register as a singular man. At the bottom of the page, where he looms largest, an inert Gulliver lies open-eyed and open-mouthed, with his feet pointing in an unnatural position for a human body. The large claw-like hand in the centre adds to the puppet-like look. In the middle of the image, another Gulliver is casually wheeled away, unfazed by the sharp end of the half-pike up his nose (and, unlike Swift's Gulliver, seemingly not capable of sneezing in response). At the top, he now stands upright, with his hands awkwardly jutting out to the sides as though held up by strings. Many of the woodcuts included in the Newbery abridgement instead concentrate on individual objects (a comb, a pistol and a watch, among other things).[11] Placed within this visual lexicon of literal objects, Gulliver looks like a propped-up puppet when seen tied to the beach in Lilliput – a reading endorsed by the vacant stare on his face as much as the improbable lack of alarm.

In other images within Newbery's *Adventures*, Gulliver looks like a hairless, even featureless doll, such as when he is pictured upside down in the jaws of a Brobdingnagian dog or (in an earlier image) in the mouth of a child, or even (in a yet earlier image) when dangled by a boy or carelessly displayed in the palm of the farmer. There is a semblance of movement in the picture of the miniature explorer fending off a rat (**Figure 2**), but here the impracticable stance looks more figurine than

FIGURE 1. Illustration of Lemuel Gulliver in Lilliput: *Travels into Several Remote Nations of the World* (London: Printed for Benj. Motte, 1727).

performative. Newbery would have had financial priorities in mind, particularly within the confines of the tiny trigesimo-secundo format adopted for the revised *Adventures* in 1776, so we must not put too much stock in the aesthetic choices, let alone the artistry, of these specific images. Other abridgers chose to present an ornately coloured, fleshy

Gulliver, as in a small chapbook published in Glasgow during the early 1800s (**Figure 3**). But many kept illustrations out altogether, particularly in Britain.[12] For readers of early Dutch, French, Italian and German translations, Frans van Bleyswyck had already established a youthful Gulliver slender in form and impeccably dressed, in the first illustrated *Travels, Reibeschryving na verscheyde afgelegene Natien de Wereld* (1727), and its many European successors.[13] Gulliver's unlikely youthfulness has always been a common trait in illustrated books, as well as the comics that have followed in recent decades. For all the action of Van Bleyswyck's full-page prints, however, there is still something ineffably puppet-like about the lackadaisical and large-handed giant in Lilliput. Now open-eyed, the prostrate hero's puppetness is intensified within a similar image in the other widely circulated illustrations first found in Desfontaines's duodecimo *Les Voyages de Gulliver* (1727); and he became increasingly doll-like, as a juxtaposition with the 1762 version shows (**Figures 4** and **5**). In 1872 *Travels* became the first foreign literary work to be translated into modern Chinese; since then, it has been issued in no fewer than 1,400 editions, including diverse variations for children.[14] The first illustrated Chinese version was published in *Tapestry Portrait Novel* (绣像小说), in 1903, adorned with intricate woodcuts focused on Gulliver strapped to the Lilliputian shores and other major narrative motifs.[15]

Modern illustrators continue to eschew photorealism, seemingly to instil Gulliver with a more exaggeratedly kinetic appearance, rather than convey a deranged and increasingly beaten-down sailor or the sullen Gulliver that had initiated the writing up of *Travels*. A subtle exception to this rule, Chris Riddell's lavish drawings for Martin Jenkins's *Jonathan Swift's Gulliver* (2004) flit between scatological slapstick and the macabre.[16] Gulliver there appears at turns unkempt and clownish, evidently affected by the events in which he finds himself but blasé about his surroundings too. Kokor (Alain Koch), the illustrator of the three-volume hardback comic *Les Voyages du Docteur Gulliver* (2006–9), favoured suggestive line strokes with bold blocks of colour. Thanks to strategic shading and subtle palette adjustments throughout, Kokor's Gulliver shifts between gentleness and distress within single transitions between panels. For Bertrand Galic's 2020 adaptation of the third canonical voyage, *Les Voyages de Gulliver: De Laputa au Japon*, Paul Echegoyen intricately sketched a low-key Gulliver now wary of Captain Robinson's new offer ('me promettez-vous que nous ne croiserons ni géants . . . ni créatures s'apparentant, de près ou de loin, aux Lilliputiens?').[17] With rattish pirates,

FIGURE 2. Gulliver fighting a Brobdingnagian rat: *The Adventures of Captain Gulliver* (London: [F. Newbery], 1776 [1772]).

alienish immortals and harlequin-like Laputans set against absurdist backdrops, the fantastical voyager becomes banal, even grounded, in the all-too-human if un-Swiftian longing to return home. As we shall see in subsequent sections of the present chapter, comics and illustrated books reinscribe, unwittingly or otherwise, the figurine qualities of the early woodcuts – though they tend to imbue the figurine Gulliver with more life – or the artful emotiveness of Grandville and others. Within the most colourful and kitsch of artworks an undertone of Gulliver's deep derangement can usually be detected.

The nominal lead character does not need a face or an entire body to make his presence felt on the illustrated page. We glimpse little more than his gargantuan bottom in one of the earliest visual reworkings, William Hogarth's *The Punishment Inflicted on Lemuel Gulliver* (1726), but he still dominates the satirical scene amid the blunt mockery of recognizable government figures.[18] By implication, the giant hands that we see tying twenty-one tiny humans to the hills in Grey Jakarta's 2009 advertisement for Scott's Emulsion belong to Lemuel Gulliver, who, seemingly a habitual consumer of the dietary supplement, has finally outsmarted

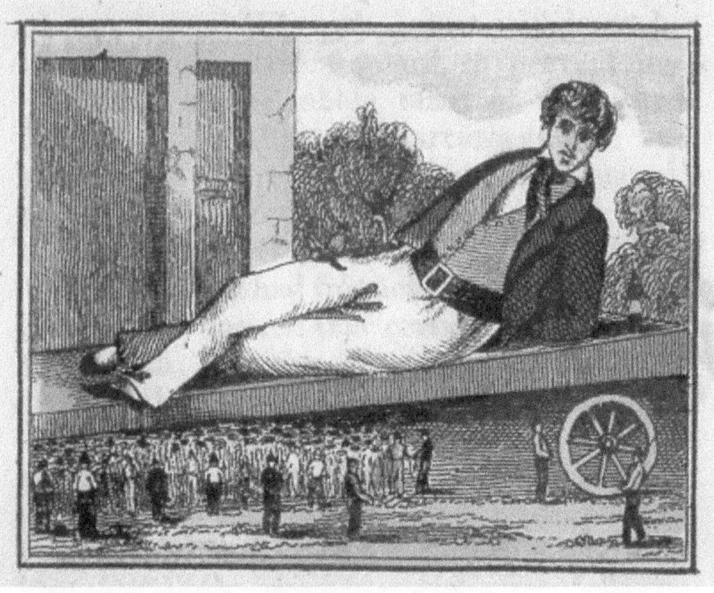

FIGURE 3. Gulliver in action: *Travels* (early 1800s). Courtesy of University of Glasgow Archives & Special Collections, Wylie collection, Bh13-*c*.28.

the Lilliputians.[19] To dissipate his outsized presence, some artists simply replace Gulliver with a child actor, with whom he may not necessarily share a name, or with a cartoon celebrity such as Mickey Mouse in *Gulliver Mickey* (1934), Betty Boop (a nominal great-great-granddaughter) in *Miss Gulliver's Travels* (1935) and Gerónimo Stilton in *I viaggi di Gulliver* (2012, 2019), or controversial political figures from Napoleon Bonaparte to Adolf Hitler, down to Donald Trump.[20] In an illustrated book series for schoolchildren, Thomas Kingsley Troupe and Xavier Bonet's *Midnight Library* (2019), in which appointed Pages fall into fictional worlds at the witching hour, Jordan Young ('Girl-Mountain') finds herself stuck on the Lilliputian shores in place of her fictional forebear. Frequently mentioned but never seen, the original Gulliver benignly overshadows the new adventure: 'When the Man-Mountain visited us, he always consulted the silver oracle.'[21] Gulliver quietly haunts marketing imagery in such a way too. A male fashion model usurping the adventurer's life in Lilliput fronted Moncler's summer clothing range in 2016 under the direction of Annie Leibovitz. (Shortly before this, a Gulliver-like model had broken free of her Lilliputian ties in the 'Don't touch my Breil!' television

FIGURE 4. Gulliver in Lilliput: Pierre-François Guyot Desfontaines, *Les Voyages de Gulliver* (Paris: J. Guérin, 1727).

campaign run by the Leo Burnett Milan agency for Breil watches.[22]) Long before that, in the 1870s, Gulliver ironically endorsed spool cotton strong enough to immobilize a giant. Some advertising agencies go so far as to use insentient characters such as a tethered egg (for A. G. Edwards's Nest Egg campaign) or motor vehicles (such as Volkswagen's Touareg),

FIGURE 5. Gulliver in Lilliput: Desfontaines, *Les Voyages de Gulliver* (Paris, 1762).

among other things. Not all Gulliveriana needs a Gulliver: the general principle applies to pictorial engagements too.

Within some illustrated books Gulliver can look like two entirely different people. *The Great Illustrated Classics* volume published under the Baronet Books brand in 1995 features on the cover Joseph Miralles's carefully painted image of the protagonist dragging the Blefuscudian fleet ashore. Inside we find 103 individual line drawings of him by Pablo Marcos, in varying levels of detail as required by the scenes. Miralles's Gulliver appears fleshier, older. Marcos's has the increasingly conventional appearance of a dashing young adventurer. Precedent for this confusion was set by Swift himself. After all, the original author endorsed at least two noticeably different character portraits and therefore tacitly encouraged the lack of uniformity. Really, there are three different men called Lemuel Gulliver in the frontispiece portraits (one in 1726, across two slightly different states, and two in 1735).[23] Not yet forty years old when he undertook his initial journey, by the time *Travels* appeared in print, in 1726, Gulliver looked like a weathered, broken man in John Sturt's official portrait (**Figure 6**). Thick lines beneath his large, etched-in eyes, thinning hair and clumped-up clothing bear this out. And yet he lacks a quill pen, let alone nautical equipment. In other words, the Gulliverian motifs are not to be found where we would most expect them. Lemuel Gulliver would have been around sixty-five years of age at the time and seventy-four when the revised version of *Travels* appeared with a new portrait in 1735. However, the text around the 1726 portrait in early copies of the Motte edition states he was fifty-eight. As that was Jonathan Swift's age at the time, readers might have inferred a clue to the true authorship of the book. The 1735 versions (expressly in the octavo format) further accentuate the connection between author and character, even though they were kept separate when they appeared together in the four-volume *Works of J. S., D.D., D.S.P.D.* (1735), a metatext ('the Author's Works') (**Figures 7–9**).[24] However, the men, now facing in the same direction, share facial similarities (in the eyebrows, eyes, nose, mouth and chin), though Gulliver looks slimmer and dressed for adventure. Even the new oval frame and plinth mimic that seen in George Vertue's sketch of Swift in *Works*, as though the portraits could feasibly hang together on a wall among other images of real people.

Against the authorial gamesmanship of the official portraits, an alternative type of interpretation could focus on their enhanced codification of Gulliver as a character. This reading might entail viewing Gulliver as an avatar alongside other fictional agents, such as Hythlodaeus from Thomas More's *Utopia* (1516), or Panurge from François Rabelais's *Pantagruel* (1532), or actual people, like Isaac Newton, then the President of the Royal Society, the Dutch minister Philippus Baldaeus or Swift's Scriblerian collaborator, John Arbuthnot.[25] Alternatively again, in

FIGURE 6. Frontispiece portrait of Lemuel Gulliver: *Travels into Several Remote Nations of the World* (London: Printed for Benj. Motte, 1726).

serial terms, we might consider the role the portraits take in capturing Gulliver's life within and beyond the book. As David Womersley notes, the 1735 duodecimo edition adopts a harsher image that better fits the narrative of someone who had endured the hardships of the fourth voyage.[26] Peter Wagner invites us to consider not just the drawn face of

FIGURE 7. Frontispiece portrait of Jonathan Swift: *The Works of J.S., D.D., D.S.P.D.* (Dublin: G. Faulkner, 1735) (Vol. I).

Gulliver but the words and images printed alongside it. 'Both epigraph and pedestal', he writes, 'elevate Gulliver to the position of an important man'.[27] Such elevation is fake. Grant Holly observes of the 1735 portrait that, despite its mimetic context, it 'is not a portrait, pure and simple'.[28] In the first place, he clarifies, 'it is the engraving of a portrait, which implies that it is a representation of a representation, a double translation which,

FIGURE 8. Frontispiece portrait of Gulliver: *The Works of J.S., D.D., D.S.P.D.* (Dublin: G. Faulkner, 1735) [duodecimo edition].

though it still achieves the illusion of a three-dimensional object in a two-dimensional space, presents itself much more openly as a mapping, the product of the conventional cuts and striations of a style of engraving'. In the second place, he continues, 'there is no such person as "Lemuel Gulliver"'. And in an expansive reading context that takes stock of other publications, we should not ignore the metafictional, Crusoean

FIGURE 9. Frontispiece portrait of Gulliver: *The Works of J.S., D.D., D.S.P.D.* (Dublin: G. Faulkner, 1735) [octavo edition].

impression of Gulliver that fronted Samuel Richardson's *Travels into Several Remote Nations of the World. Vol. III* (1727; hereafter *Volume III*), a plagiaristic extension masquerading as an official continuation. The full-body shot of the fantastical voyager captures a steely-eyed, if shabby, hero poised for action in a further strange nation. Janine Barchas, Grant Holly and Peter Wagner have rightly highlighted the flagrantly counterfeit qualities of the official frontispiece portraits within an oscillating author-character nexus (though they exclude Richardson's *Volume III*). In my interpretation the different portraits collectively inscribe an unfettered fictional afterlife for the character.

Ontologically, Gulliver is neither alive nor dead, though he has always had a material presence beyond the words attributed to him. A black-and-white (or otherwise two-tone) likeness of an author within a masonry frame, which may have a Greek or Latin inscription alongside or beneath it, the frontispiece portrait that emerged in English book production during the seventeenth century carried memorial connotations. That author may be in the pomp of life when the book was published, but usually the image will be a more youthful or otherwise idealized rendering. More commonly, as was the case with Jonathan Swift and Eliza Haywood in the eighteenth century, the authorial portrait appeared in collected works, which, by definition, came towards the end of the writer's life or just beyond it. Gulliver may well have further adventures lined up: the 1735 octavo portrait suggests he remains primed for such, and the fulsome body image in *Volume III* compounds this impression. Perhaps Swift sought to confine his creation to the book on which his image has been stamped. Closing the book hides from view the frontispiece portrait, thereby laying Gulliver to rest in his papery coffin. But coffins can be opened; enter the adapters. The title page of Johann Heinrich Waser's 1761 German translation of *Travels* features an ornate vignette portrait of Gulliver by Salomon Gessner.[29] Such reverential treatments of the author-explorer ultimately proved to be somewhat rare, though the practice has resurfaced in a modern medium. Some recent graphic novels and comics adaptations of *Travels* contain character portraits – as distinct from authorial ones – in which other characters, including generic character types, join the lead protagonist on a gallery wall. Rather than memorialize Gulliver per se, such illustrated cast lists essentially operate as study aids that prepare the reader for the story about to unfold. The 1943 *Classics Illustrated* retelling opens with an establishing image of a prostrate Gulliver in his giant form, with youthful, auburn locks. At the back of the book a framed portrait of Swift in period-appropriate dress dramatizes the distance between the author and his chief character. Such a distance becomes yet starker in the 1976 *Marvel Classics Comics* version (originally published in 1974 by Pendulum Press), which presents a large black-and-white caricature of Swift's head and shoulders on the inside cover facing towards the large, full-sized body of Gulliver striking a movie-poster stance, flanked by alternative iterations of Gulliver, along with Glumdalclitch, two Houyhnhnms, and various thematic objects.

Often a full-length Gulliver fronts the introductory section of books within this format, in a pose more reminiscent of Robinson Crusoe in the original publication of the 1719 novel that bore his name (or Richardson's fraudulent *Volume III*).[30] A striking example of this type can be found in Campfire's 2010 graphic novel written by Lewis Helfand and drawn by Vinod Kumar, in which practically the entirety of Gulliver looms over the reader, and encircled heads of the supporting cast surround him. In a 2013 manga – translated from Japanese into French in 2017 – Kiyokazu Chiba adopts the trope of an enlarged, movie-poster Gulliver in his opening cast of characters, though he more subtly depicts the contrasting sizes by not tilting the angle so much but rather draws our attention to a large, booted foot stretching into the foreground. Chiba's cover image – which is to say the back cover, as mangas are read back to front – ingeniously confronts the challenge of scale by showing a large Gulliver holding a smaller Gulliver holding a yet smaller Gulliver. Perhaps the strangest illustrated cast of characters list occurs at the outset of the 2008 Stone Arch graphic novel, by the writer Donald Lemke and the artist Cynthia Martin, where a jarringly diminutive Gulliver stands idly alongside Glumdalclitch and other key members of the Lilliputian and Brobdingnagian episodes. This is not to say that Gulliver the author has been removed from the author-character-reader nexus in this modern print context. Some comics and graphic novels place writerly iconography on the cover and throughout, and some catch Gulliver in the act of composition. Or, in the case of Chiba's manga, Gulliver reads relevant books expressly in preparation for the first voyage not yet taken. But, as we shall now see, comics creators tend to present the more persistent tension in visual Gulliveriana, between characterization and figuration, within the framework of sequential art.

Classic comics

The first major English-language comic book version of *Gulliver's Travels* appeared in issue no. 16 of Gilberton's *Classics Illustrated* series in December 1943. There had been earlier adaptations in this form. Wheeler-Nicholson's *New Comics* serialized parts of *Travels* in 1936, alongside two major nineteenth-century novels, Charles Dickens's *A Tale of Two Cities* (1859) and H. Rider Haggard's *She* (1887). Gaston Niezab's ogrish Gulliver adorned French-language issues in *Les Merveilleuses Histoires* during the mid-1930s (*Gulliver à Lilliput* [no. 9] and *Gulliver chez les Géants* [no. 10]). But, with a large catalogue and distribution network, *Classics Illustrated* (originally known as *Classic Comics*) dominated the marketplace between 1941 and 1971 – and spawned global imitations. The artist of the *Classic Comics Gulliver's Travels*, Lillian Chestney Zuckerberg (hereafter Chestney), established a fantastical, colourful take on the material that proved influential for years to come (**Figure 10**).[31] The comics historian William B. Jones Jr instead criticizes the scripter, Daniel Kushner, who, he says, 'entirely missed the "savage indignation" of Swift's satire'.[32] If judged in terms of the series' chief stated criterion, to draw readers back to the works of the 'World's Greatest Authors', such criticism may be warranted.[33] The one-page 'Life of Jonathan Swift' at the back of the comic does refer to the original book as a 'savage commentary' on eighteenth-century Europe; a contemporary commentator assumed whoever wrote the brief biography had not read the comic, which, whether true or not, at least indicates the lingering emphasis on literary fidelity in this critical purview.[34] Considered in the realm of a broader-ranging and long-bedded transtextual and transmedial afterlife, however, Chestney and Kushner's Gulliver does resemble the characterization expressed in the juvenile retellings reaching as far back as Newbery's third-person reorientation of *Travels* in 1772. After all, as a testament to its own market success, the comic went through fourteen printings by the winter of 1969. If anyone had concerns about fidelity solely to Swift (as a great author), it did not harm sales.

The full-page advertisement on the inside back cover of the 1943 version of the comic claims each title in the series 'contains a complete adaptation'.[35] This comic does not travel beyond Lilliput, however. It is a complete adaptation of a culturally accepted abridgement of *Travels*, we might say. In any case, this issue fulfils the series' prioritization of adventure above all else. They dispense with Gulliver's background information, and he heads to sea as early as the first panel. That perilous first journey, and the inevitable shipwreck demanded by the genre, takes up the opening four pages. Spotted by a startled Lilliputian, as the caption attests, Gulliver enters the world of Lilliput as late as page five and remains in restraints for the next seven pages. Within that sequence, a single panel mimics the rapid turns in which Swift's Gulliver expresses

FIGURE 10. Lemuel Gulliver in action: *Gulliver's Travels: Classics Illustrated*, adapted by Daniel Kushner and illustrated by Lillian Chestney Zuckerberg (New York: Gilberton Company, 1965 [1943]).

terror at and then terrifies his captors: 'For a moment he is stunned, then he shouts . . . And in terror the Lilliputians scurry away' (8, bottom panel). The switch to third-person narration conflates the reactions of Gulliver and the captors, though the perpetual scream drawn onto the giant's face and the relative blurriness of the small figures keep the attention on the chief character. Notably, though, many other characters come to the fore in this comic, in keeping with the enhanced interest in adventure above other narratological elements built into Swift's original properties. Every protagonist needs at least one antagonist; here, Gulliver battles political intrigue more persistently than the arrows that scarcely scratched his face at the top of the eighth page. Among traditional square and rectangular boxes, circular and semi-circular panels resembling telescopes and portholes spotlight the sneering faces of Admiral Bolgolam and other conspirators.[36] Against such shots, Gulliver leaps and runs from panel to panel. The kinetic if pallid-faced hero becomes undone by whispering villains wearing archetypal dress. Adventure ebbs into political drama. As an adventure-cum-political tale, the comic's narrative seems strategically ill-matched to its kitsch colouring.[37] And the relentless busyness of the pages contrasts comparable issues in the series, such as Henry C. Kiefer's *20,000 Leagues Under the Sea* (1948), which was based on Jules Verne's similarly named *Twenty Thousand Leagues Under the Seas* (1870). No longer a narrator, Gulliver gets relegated to figurehood, that is, he becomes an agent around which plot happens. Despite the physical prominence of Gulliver throughout the comic, including bits of him jutting out of frame, Chestney and Kushner essentially reduce him to a plot device. We glimpse Gulliver the writer, such as when his large hand signs a scroll under duress. In general, the few caption boxes shaped as manuscripts to mimic the bookish aesthetic of *Travels* provide exposition in the third person. This is the story of Lilliputian politics and warfare. Swift is the great author here, not Gulliver.

Less than two years after Gilberton dropped *Gulliver's Travels* from the official *Classics Illustrated* reorder list, Dell Publishing, a rival company in New York, produced their own version in 1956 under the auspices of *Dell Junior Treasury*. According to Jones, their script 'stuck much closer to the original than Kushner's Swiftian improvisations.'[38] Trained in the style of European comics, the unnamed Italian-born artist Alberto Giolitti did the illustration, which, Jones adds, offered a more 'realistic representation' than seen in the 1943 comic. This entailed placing novelistic text beneath each individual panel and deploying word balloons and sound effects at strategic points. Certainly, Dell pitched the comic as a faithful adaptation of Swift's prose satire, which they define in the prefatory matter as 'a humorous cartoon-in-words of the courts, statesmen and parties that he knew'.[39] As in the *Classics Illustrated* version and many of the comics that have followed over the past eight decades, Giolitti opens on Gulliver's ill-fated sea journey rather than his prior life. (As a serial character, he needs limited biographical introduction.) Notably, we have first-person narration, a return to Swift's original mode of delivery but a rejection of the Newbery abridgement and its imitations, which had gained wide readerships over many decades. Indeed, the Dell comic ingeniously dramatizes the distinct but interrelated elements of Swift's hybrid character, the author-explorer: the text carries throughout the comic the singular voice of the reflective narrator while the word balloons convey the immediacy of the events as they affect the explorer in real time. The author is often serious, even pompous: 'I, Lemuel Gulliver, was among the six men who managed to lower a boat' (1, bottom panel). The explorer is at turn courageous or carefree. Unlike his longsuffering predecessors, Giolitti's muscular Gulliver jerks his hand free of the ample ropes within three panels. His hand veers into another panel, simultaneously repelling and grabbing the tiny assailants. Comedy comes in the form of Gulliver's colossal sneezes, and the violence posed by the Lilliputian captors becomes little more than farcical – 'One rascal [. . .] barely missed his target!' (9, bottom right).

A distinctly middle-aged man in appearance, Dell's Gulliver nevertheless assumes the role of a boy in Toyland. Although stern in features and in the narrative voice conveyed across the text, he dances a jig and strolls throughout the miniature scenery with his hands on his hips. He faces little sustained threat. Even his attack on the Blefuscudian fleet has acquired a playfulness: 'wah-hoooooo!', he yells, with arms raised out of the water (17, bottom panel). In the final stage of the comic, Gulliver departs Lilliput untroubled. Happily taken onboard the *Antelope* without experiencing the mental disarray suffered by Swift's prototype, the Dell Gulliver swaps stories with Captain Biddle (Biddel in the source material). Presented with a Lilliputian cow, Biddle dubs it a 'clever *mechanical toy!*', though its subsequent actions convince him otherwise (29, middle left). Again in contravention of Swift's misanthropic original but in keeping with the internal logic of the adventure comedy presented here, Gulliver happily reunites with his family. His wife turns his only remaining souvenir, a Lilliputian coverlet, into a quilt. Domestic order has been restored and the political intrigues of the *Classics Illustrated* version averted. Under the branding of Thriller Comics, the British publisher Fleetway adapted *Travels* shortly before Dell, in 1952. Written by Peter O'Donnell and drawn by Selby Donnison, this version flattens out the author-explorer; intermittent text provides exposition in the third person, while a greater use of word balloons conveys Gulliver's reactions in situ. Having endured short-lived fairytale threats in Lilliput (and Brobdingnag too), nevertheless, their hero similarly finds solace with his adoring family (if only 'for a while!').[40] Handsome and light-hearted, the Thriller Gulliver still carries the ultimately debilitating wanderlust built into Swift's character template, whether readers of this specific comic were aware or not. Considered in terms of transmedia storytelling, however unsystematic and belated, such a shift in critical focus indicates yet again the flexibility of Swift's world-building, character-building and authorship (to revisit Matthew Freeman's transmedia model). When refitted into different creative environments, Gulliver's storylines can be full of adventures of varying levels of menace (including none at all). Secondary characters can fulfil different functions, not least of all Gulliver's wife, Mary. As discussed in the previous chapter of the present study, the barely visible presence of Mrs Gulliver in *Travels* has incited a disparate array of treatments in subsequent textual and pictorial adaptations, from the sexually frustrated woman in Pope's early Lilliputian poems to the nurturing housewife in Giolitti's comic. Authorial (or editorial) adjustments to the host text typically entail shifting the generic framework, or other formal elements, to differing degrees of severity. In visual narrative media such as comics, this often equates to an adventure story by accentuating the unlikely heroism of Gulliver, downplaying his misanthropy and providing closure.

Effortless playfulness had been a stronger keynote of an earlier comic-book Gulliver, whose strip straddled issues twelve and thirteen in the third volume of *Treasure Chest of Fun & Facts* (1948), which was produced by an American Catholic publisher, George A. Pflaum, and distributed to schools for educational purposes. A yet more heavily condensed (five-page) retelling than seen in the other comics so far, the strip begins with Gulliver already a feature of Lilliput. At turns, he positions himself as the object of play ('The King's huntsmen used my feet as barriers') and the subject ('I put them in my pocket').[41] And sometimes the play is mutual: 'I fashioned a platform for military exercises with my handkerchief'. Earlier in the decade, in 1942, Novelty Press had serialized their own adaptation of *Travels* under the Target Comics brand. On the cover of the third volume (no. 10), Gulliver holds a microscope over a copy of a *Target* comic, out of which leap miniature cowboys and heroes, among other unrelated characters. Gulliver has taken on the role of the astonished Brobdingnagian scientists who peer over him in perhaps one of the most familiar Gulliverian book illustrations of all. But his gentle smile, along with the childlike figures that nonchalantly appear under his gaze, points towards the exuberant tone of the serial and, in the broadest terms, the emergent comics tradition in Gulliveriana. Gulliver also cameoed in other comic serials, as in the eighth issue of the Quality Comics' *Kid Eternity* crimefighter series produced between 1946 and 1949. Summoned into the present day in 'Zero the Midget' (1948), a rugged fortysomething Gulliver gleefully helps the young hero track miniaturized villains. Released almost half a century later, in 1995, a '3D Color Classics' version of *Travels* was produced for inclusion in fast-food combos aimed at children in one of America's largest restaurant chains, Wendy's. Outwardly they followed the pattern of the *Classics Illustrated* issue. Immediately plunged into a violent shipwreck scene, the Wendy's Gulliver experiences bemusement and then shock on the Lilliputian beach. Even though the image of Gulliver strapped down by little figures is undoubtedly the most recognizable of them all, here it is splashed across the breadth of two pages – and augmented with ChromaDepth™ using the attached 3D glasses – to joyous effect. Shock has been permanently etched on his face, as though he has no trace memory of the scene. Handsome and sensible, as the foreword has it, this serial Gulliver seems entirely new and yet utterly familiar. To the Lilliputians he must declare – anew and yet for the first time – his identity ('My name is Gulliver') and assure them of his character ('I am *not* a monster').[42]

Old tricks still work. Like Swift's self-congratulatory Man Mountain, the Wendy's Gulliver pretends to eat someone, to the alarm of bystanders: 'The giant . . . *ate* that man!' (7, top right). Couched within fast-food ephemera, this comic represents (and simultaneously re-presents) a traditional Gulliver for a young target audience with differing degrees of knowledge of, let alone predetermined interest in, the Man Mountain. Eighteenth-century editions of *Travels* for children find a late capitalist corollary here, in the most surprising but ultimately appropriate of venues. Some old actions need to be reworked for the intended audience: instead of urinating on the empress's palace, he spits out the fire. While this comic nostalgically retraces prior works in the form, a new love interest has been found, the young and beautiful (and unmarried) Empress Shelfin

Mully Ully Gue, and a love rival (Prince Otto of Blefuscu). Apparently not bothered by the love rival – or the enemy fleet, for that matter – a grinning Gulliver cheerily returns home. This and other comics took advantage of the source material's cultural saturation, subbing out actions as they needed, introducing new characters and plots, or simply replaying old favourites. Given his transmedial ubiquity, Gulliver could be easily absorbed into existing cartoon franchises too. Bastei's *Gulliver*, a thirty-six-part comic serial in German, appeared between 1979 and 1981 as a commercial tie-in with the Hanna-Barbera cartoons centred on the author-explorer. Gulliver, now dressed in modern garb and joined by a canine sidekick, is the headline act, with smaller strips for cartoon icons such as Scooby-Doo and Squiddly Diddly. The general plotlines in their Lilliput follow the usual patterns, but numerous new threats and opportunities enter this Gulliver's realm. Largely retooled for slapstick, the German serial strikes enduring and novel childlike notes of adventure.

Marvel reinvigorated the literary comics mantle abandoned by *Classics Illustrated* at the outset of the 1970s. A reprint from a 1974 Pendulum Press production of *Gulliver's Travels* appeared as issue no. 6 under the *Marvel Classics Comics* banner in 1976. This was scripted by John Norwood Fago and illustrated by E. R. Cruz. Formally, the comic departs markedly from the established *Classics Illustrated* treatment. The earlier comic had combined third-person captions with minimal first-person speech bubbles; the latter sticks with first-person captions threaded in the small white spaces around the pictures. Cruz removes boxes completely, giving the narrative a progress-style structure: the reader's eye usually shifts across the page, top to bottom and often left to right, taking in renderings of Gulliver posed in chains on the Lilliputian shores or otherwise poised for activity (**Figure 11**). This Gulliver is an unflinching man of action rather than a mere figure of wonder. Even in Brobdingnag he retains a fleshy appearance. At his smallest he takes on the monocoloured blobbishness prevalent in illustrated books and comics, but here his gestures and general demeanour resist the figurine features of the predecessors in this format. In the *Classics Illustrated* version of *Travels*, Chestney had mingled the more conventional panel structure with telescope-like circles. Far from boxing Gulliver in, though, that structure allowed the hero to punch through into adjacent images as he wished. Fighting his restraints, among other things, Chestney's Gulliver sought autonomy. Cruz's Gulliver takes a firmer presence in the story – indeed, the artist often displays his muscular body – and yet, the

FIGURE 11. Gulliver in action: *Gulliver's Travels: Marvel Classics Comics*, adapted by John Norwood Fago and illustrated by E. R. Cruz (New York: Marvel Comics, 1976).

four worlds in which he finds himself receive their own attention. The Pendulum Gulliver tells his story in the past tense, dissipating any real danger while retaining an adventurous spirit. Generally feeling content along the way, this Gulliver is an author drawn to curiosity. Signing his name in cursive ('Captain Gulliver'), he hopes to impart Houyhnhnm wisdom to his family, and 'my reader' must leave him to a simple life in a definitive conclusion ('The End').[43] The *Classics Illustrated* Gulliver had seemed more restless, hinting at lingering disquiet: 'it will take me weeks to get used to moving among people my own size!', he declared, onboard a ship to which he may well return.[44] As a sequential art form, the comic book has long proven ideally suited to Gulliver's versatile personality since either or both facets of his functions as an author and explorer can be foregrounded.

The Spanish publisher Editorial Bruguera had their own 'Illustrated Classics' series, *Joyas Literarias Juveniles* (distributed in English under the King Classics brand), in which *Gulliver's Travels* appeared as issue no. 22 in 1978. Attributed to Anne Mueser (the adapter), this was scripted by Antonio Vidal Sales and drawn by Alfonso Cerón Núñez (interior art) and Antonio Bernal (the cover). Cerón uses panels in a notably more regimented manner, along with captions and speech bubbles. Curiously, the captions commingle both first-person and third-person voices, and the verb tenses are not consistent. Many of the third-person captions nevertheless explain or advance the plot. This means the conflation of voices undermines rather than reinforces Gulliver's authority as a storyteller. The lack of bookish imagery, let alone the by-now-familiar transmedia image of the protagonist writing his travel memoirs, consolidates the can-do adventurism of the tale by default. 'I want to be a sailor!', this youngish Gulliver announces (in a thought bubble) in the first panel, where he dejectedly sits cross-legged, head in hand.[45] During the Golden Age of Indian comics, the late 1970s to the mid-90s, Manoj Comics devoted an issue to *Travels* (*Gulliver Bono ke Desh me*). This work was also available in English as *Gulliver in the Country of Dwarfs* and was reissued by HardPress as recently as 2019 (despite the title, the comic adapts the first two voyages). Within nine panels, over three pages, the Manoj Gulliver finds himself in an instantly recognizable spot: bound to the Lilliputian beach and beset by tiny humans brandishing arms. Initially bemused – by the foreignness of their language more than anything – Gulliver grows bored. Catching hold of one of 'those strange creatures' – the caption marks out their foreignness, not Gulliver's – the Man

Mountain turns into a benevolent liberator before the page is finished: 'Run away son! You are free!'[46] Intimidating but without harming them, Gulliver soon convinces the 'Blefuscians' (Blefuscudians) to enter peace talks with the Lilliputians. As in Swift's source text, jealous courtiers nevertheless conspire against the giant, who departs. Immediately he gains passage on an English ship heading to India. Stopping at 'one of the African's islands' on the way, Gulliver finds himself in the next strange adventure – among 'mountain-like men' with predominately bluish-grey or light brown skin (17, bottom left; 19, bottom right). Giant cats and rats threaten the hero, yet again, though he dispatches them with ease. A miniature marvel, the Manoj Gulliver wows the queen and faces few dangers in the court. Even then, the wasps with which he jousts offer him and others ample amusement. Accidentally lost at sea one day, Gulliver is quickly rescued by the same English ship that had transported him so seamlessly from one nation to the other. Like many Western retellings of *Travels* for children, the Manoj Comics version prioritizes action over satire and the figurine over the characterful. Read in those terms, the comics consolidate one major aspect of Gulliver's characterization, the imperilled adventurer, through different formal and semiotic strategies.

For decades Gulliver has been brought into established comic book stables either as part of an established catalogue of adaptations from 'the classics' or as an old-fashioned traveller cameoing in the adventures of others. The *Classics Illustrated* team claimed they were offering a complete adaptation of the source material. This is partly correct: rather than rework Swift's *Travels*, they creatively engage with the chapbook tradition of abridged 'adventures' or the visual Gulliverian culture-text that has built up around Swift's properties more broadly. Relatedly, the comics historian William B. Jones Jr has criticised the scripter, Daniel Kushner, for misreading Swift's savage indignation. Again, this is partly correct: Kushner and other adapters in various media have instead responded to different facets of Gulliver's cultural afterlife. The main comics tradition in Gulliveriana, from the 1940s to the 1990s, favoured a highly active, playful adventurer in situ and largely downplayed the mental tortures experienced by the author-explorer. Pendulum's muscular Gulliver was a partial exception: as well as an agent of plot, he is also an author driven by a semblance of curiosity rather than gut-wrenching wanderlust or period politics. Dell's chiselled, if childlike, Gulliver provided a more common model: relegated to figurehood, he does not narrate his fantastical voyages. Such patterns in comic book characterization are complicated by the commercial needs and established aesthetic frameworks of the production teams. Glibly put, Gulliver is not necessarily a high-prestige character. But neither is he a convenient one. As a hybridised author-explorer whose body (and perception) undergoes drastic changes amid disparate remote nations, he poses a creative challenge in terms of both sequential narrative and visual representation. Commissioned as part of Russ Kick's *The Graphic Canon*, a three-volume anthology of comics adaptations from a literary treasure-trove running from *The Epic of Gilgamesh* (*c.* 2100–1200 BCE) to David Foster Wallace's *Infinite Jest* (1996), Gareth Hinds's 2003 'Gulliver's Travels; Part II: A Voyage to Brobdingnag' might be the closest we can come to a 'true' collaboration between an original author and a comics artist (in Kick's words).[47] The editor's requirement of the adapters was clear: 'Any approach, any medium, any style' are permitted but 'I wasn't interested in a workman-like, note-by-note transcription of the original work'. Against Chestney's cleaner style under the influence of illustrated children's editions, Hinds favoured a grubbier look and thereby accentuated the gritty realities of Gulliver's misadventures in the second of the canonical remote nations.

Opening with a large metatextual representation of a tatty but readable copy of *Travels* that cribs the author-explorer's first-person narration to set the scene, Hinds simultaneously grounds his contribution in the source material and re-establishes Gulliver as a serial character.[48] The story itself moves more rapidly through the original beats: parted from a fleeing crew, Gulliver is captured by a giant and shortly sold to the royal family. At court he endures some of the same hardships as his book-born counterpart, as well as the care of his nine-year-old nurse, Glumdalclitch. The little nurse had taken a stronger role in Gulliver's life in *Travels*, though her affective emotional turmoil when separated from him has been largely ignored by adapters. Hinds similarly reduces Glumdalclitch's role while instead retaining the lengthy and less visual intellectual discussions between Gulliver and the incredulous king. While Hinds does revisit the farce and threat of this voyage favoured by other adapters, not least of all fighting off rats and wasps, as well as the kidnapping of Gulliver by the court monkey, there is an unusually high emphasis placed on the political satire. This includes Gulliver's infamous defence of military weapons, which shocks the peaceful giant to the extent that he exiles the miniature marvel. Text-heavy on the page but still replete with well-chosen, often disgusting or otherwise discomfiting pictorial set pieces, this commissioned work addresses head-on the creative challenges posed by the source material. This entails substituting long descriptions with action and reaction shots, removing multiple scenes (most notably, the exhausting performances in taverns that almost kill Gulliver), downplaying specific characters (such as the benevolent farmer and his wife, their daughter Glumdalclitch, the jealous court dwarf and the flirtatious queen), and reducing (somewhat ingeniously) some of Gulliver's most pompous speeches ('blah blah "legislative" blahblah "judicial" blah blah . . .' [455]). And the ending flattens out the final sequence of the original account of the second voyage in *Travels*, where a deranged Gulliver frightens his rescuers. While foregrounding Gulliver as an author-explorer, put another way, Hinds strategically undermines Swift's character-building (by unwriting specific speeches) and authorship (by dissipating the emotional turmoil built up over multiple book chapters). Highly diverse in form and focalisation, in sum, sequential artworks produced over recent decades evince but also extend beyond the structural tensions built into Swift's characterization and the retooling that immediately followed in abridgements and illustrations.

Adapted and updated

Although not explicitly named or numbered within a series, Donald Lemke and Cynthia Martin's *Jonathan Swift's Gulliver's Travels* (2008) mimics the serial structure of the *Classics Illustrated* stable and thereby invites comparison. At the back of the book we find a similar two-page advertisement for other volumes, including a list of standard source texts, namely popular Victorian novels ranging across action, science fiction, horror and other genres, such as Robert Louis Stevenson's *Treasure Island* (1883), H. G. Wells's *The Time Machine* (1895) and Bram Stoker's *Dracula* (1897). The endorsement on the back cover, attributed to *School Library Journal*, echoes the educative ethos of *Classics Illustrated*: to provide 'a gateway to otherwise daunting works of literature'.[49] The illustrations on the covers present the iconic imagery associated with Swift's prose satire. In the main panel on the front cover of the word-and-image reworking of *Travels*, a handsome man heaves ropes while towering over adoring miniature people. To the right, he is fastened to the ground, while, in separate frames, small soldiers gaze at his oversized objects, and a bare-chested giant lurches towards the viewer. In isolation, the images give little indication of the main story, and so the uninitiated reader will have to piece them together as they work through the graphic novel. Considered within a transmedia purview such imagery will be understood differently, depending on the diverse cultural environments already traversed by readers or viewers, whether textual or visual, narrative or non-narrative, or comprehensive or fragmented. For the initiated consumer who has engaged with any number of Gulliverian works, in other words, the adaptative principle instantly appears: in the broadest terms, this is a heroic, Odyssean Gulliver. The summary on the inside leaf drives the message home: 'His adventures could be the greatest tales ever told, if he survives long enough to tell them'. As this iteration of Gulliver does survive sufficiently enough for the tale to be read, the book becomes a story of voyage and return. With a small adjustment in focus within a visual format, the long-accreted Gulliverian world-building and character-building have been plausibly refitted for a populist, if non-Swiftian, genre that crosses media with relative ease: the epic adventure.

In the context of a transmedia character study, this graphic novel also furthers our discussion of the bifurcation of Gulliver into a character and a figure, as a mindful enactor of plot and a sentient object around which the plot happens. Told in the first person through captions and thought bubbles, the plot follows Swift's *Travels* but abridges heavily or turns long intellectual monologues into dialogical exchanges focused on exposition. This is not to say the action moves too swiftly. On the contrary, the artist spends more time with certain set pieces than usual in pictorial representations of the material. Gulliver's pre-voyaging life, including his education, has been entirely cut – a common enough approach in the comics tradition. (Taking a different tack in 2007, Jun Wang's *Manga Literary Classics* version for Y.kids devotes separate panels to Gulliver's schooling, career, wedding and fatherhood over three large pages.) Within two pages of the opening of Lemke and Martin's graphic novel the author-explorer has become shipwrecked. That iconic first interaction with the Lilliputians now occupies four pages (and ten panels), and this adaptative pattern continues well into the next chapter. Gulliver's position moves around in stark ways, even though his body remains fixed in one place. That is, the point of view transitions from a close-up of his incredulous face before a long shot reveals a prostrate body; and then in profile, he observes a small figure on his chest. In the next panel, at the top of page thirteen, he roars in anger. Immediately beneath this, in another panel that fills the breadth of the page, his head is on the right, facing an army of small people with half-concealed faces and ghost-like bodies. Over the page, the spotlight swivels again as Gulliver, lying with his head now pointing to the right, struggles for freedom. Facing a flurry of arrow fire over the next three panels, he gives in to 'the creatures' (14, bottom panel). Not until page twenty, more than halfway through the Lilliputian chapters, does Gulliver finally lose his chains. The most iconic static image of a tethered Man Mountain has here become a potent narrative motif through the pliability of comic-book machinery.

Throughout the graphic novel, the Lilliputians personate inhuman figures, painted red from top to bottom at the most extreme. In some panels the narrative attends to their concerns, zooming in on emoting faces. At no point, in this voyage at least, does Gulliver lose his human features. Sometimes the artist represents him through a large foot or even just a boot – a familiar enough image from single-shot marketing campaigns. In the third chapter ('The War with Blefuscu') the body parts receive heightened attention, such as the torso and bare forearms, as Gulliver drags along the toylike ships. Elsewhere, such as when he urinates on the burning palace, bodily actions are discreetly implied with vivid sound effects bestowed in excessive consonants ('zzzzzzzip', 'tsssss' [31]). In the next voyage, 'Land of Giants', Gulliver's men are sketched in green from top to toe and without facial features, since they are not the main focal point. Compounded by inequalities in sizing, however, this styling invariably reveals their toyness in relation to the large-featured giant towering over them. Gulliver himself retains his personlike image, if not his size, on the whole (we briefly glimpse him as a tiny red figure in the hands of the giant in the final panel of page forty-three and the top of page forty-four, before the giant brings him into his household). Even then, his washed-out appearance in a tiny bed held by Glumdalclitch briefly turns him appropriately doll-like. In the next picture, Martin renders Glumdalclitch wholly in pink, while an intricately drawn Gulliver gazes at himself in the mirror. The dollification of Gulliver has been quickly nixed. Grildrig, as Glumdalclitch now dubs him, becomes a character rather than a figure. This emphatic development makes the ensuing episode, in which grinning men force 'this little creature' to perform exhausting tricks, all the more menacing (48, bottom right). Repeating the prior pattern in which Gulliver gains characterful colour when brought into the farmer's household, a new episode at the court begins with a toylike rendering of Gulliver trying to convince the queen of his value. Dismissing the incredulous king's remark that 'It's nothing more than a toy', a now coloured-in Gulliver asserts his worth: 'I am much more than that, your majesty' (52, top right). From this point, Martin's Gulliver alternates between being Grildrig the figure in the presence of Glumdalclitch (denoted with whole wash colouring of blue or light brown) and a self-aware character able to comment on his circumstances: 'I would have lived happily enough in that country if my littleness had not caused several more troublesome accidents' (53). By the end of this graphic novel Gulliver has come full circle; narrowly escaping death at sea, he has been happily reunited with his peers. He picks up the quill to write up the adventure. But further, undefined adventures may await him beyond the book's covers, he concedes. While facing some of the perils of his book-born forebear and the residual prejudices of that character template, this is a hopeful Gulliver who essentially follows the heroic closure favoured in the comics tradition sustained over the previous seven decades.

Travels garnered at least two other graphic fiction imitations of the *Classics Illustrated* variety at around this time. The first, scripted by British writer John Malam with artwork by the Bulgarian artist Penko Gelev for Salariya's Graffex in 2009, offers a more age-appropriate Gulliver.[50] As a consequence of fitting in all four canonical voyages, it moves with stark economy through some of the main plot points built into Swift's prior world-building. Considered within the framework of transmedia storytelling, such an approach neatly conforms to Shane Denson and Ruth Mayer's notion of a serial figure, who, in retellings, needs little introduction or elaborate framing because of their cultural familiarity, even if 'one has never dealt explicitly with the figure before'.[51] Rather than dwell on, let alone expand, the establishing action of the source material, Gelev's Gulliver is shipwrecked, tied and freed within a matter of frames. In Brobdingnag he's discovered and sold within two pages. He traverses the Laputan Academy within two more. And, throughout, footnotes and informational banners arm the reader with everything they need to understand Swift's eighteenth-century language. Stripped back, the experiences nevertheless overwhelm Gulliver, though, like his 2008 predecessor by Lemke and Martin, he ends with a hopeful message. Favouring a painterly style over the filmic appearance of Gelev's rendering, a 2010 graphic novel for Kalyani Navyug Media's Campfire imprint, scripted by Lewis Helfand and illustrated by Vinod Kumar, covers similar ground in wholly different ways. The Campfire Gulliver undertakes all four voyages, yet again, but he reaches a downbeat conclusion more akin to the source text. Both Malam and Helfand, the respective scripters, echo (and modernize) the words of Swift: 'Thus, gentle reader, I have given you a faithful history of my travels for sixteen years and over seven months'.[52] To this Malam simply adds a further, partial verbal echo: 'For the rest of my life I will apply the lessons I learned from the wise and thoughtful Houyhnhnms'.[53] Helfand's Gulliver can hardly endure his family: 'I began last week to permit my wife to sit at dinner with me', another partial echo that relays a different tone in the new creative environment. Kumar's young, blond Gulliver has a striking and prolonged physical presence in his endeavours. Gelev's older Gulliver favours intellectual reflection. Despite their blatant divergences, each rendering recalls the original character template.

Not long after these notionally faithful if divergent pictorial retellings appeared came Martin Rowson's 'adapted & updated' *Travels*. Set in the 1990s, this graphic novel centres on a clonish descendant of Lemuel Gulliver who finds himself in New Lilliput, a dystopian society that prides itself on its technological and cultural advances even while smiley masks have been forced onto the faces of its downtrodden citizens. The narrator of Rowson's *Gulliver's Travels: Adapted & Updated* (2012) does not reveal his name, but he does accidentally retread his antecedent's paths. Like the prototype, he marries Mary Burton, the second daughter of Edmund Burton, hosier, of Newgate-Street – an elaborated character in the spate of novel refocalizations that appeared in the 1990s, here Mary Gulliver remains implausibly like her eighteenth-century counterpart. And, like Swift's main character, the updated version attended Emmanuel College in Cambridge. (In the afterword, Rowson finally reveals his so-called co-author's name: Lionel Gulliver.) Besuited yet dishevelled and unshaven, the new Gulliver finds himself strapped down – again, like his forebear. But such restraints were put in place merely to transport this Man Mountain rather than in fear of him. They have been expecting him, in fact. To their mind this must be the actual Gulliver: 'Welcome back! Dr Gulliver!'[54] Jarringly, at the same time, a colossal statue honours the first Gulliver; the smiley mask it wears makes Swift's Gulliver belatedly complicit in the dire world he had inadvertently set in motion (**Figure 12**). Swift's world-building, put another way, gains a layered satiric embellishment in Rowson's visual update. A particularly powerful political note is struck when we pan out to reveal a homeless man joylessly lifting his mask to eat while the Gulliver statue looms in the background, along with a parody of the Millennium Dome, a budget-busting blight

FIGURE 12. Lionel Gulliver and the statue of Lemuel Gulliver: Martin Rowson, *Gulliver's Travels: Adapted & Updated* (London: Atlantic Books, 2012). Reproduced with the permission of the author.

on the Labour government's list of achievements in the 1990s. The main interest of the first voyage concerns the modern world-building of New Lilliput itself and its Blairite prime minister, the leader of the New Slamecksan party (a parody of Tony Blair's New Labour cabinet). Bored and bemused throughout, the unnamed new Gulliver effectively takes a secondary role, that of a roving camera. His main active function entails bemerding the exploitative Blumflum Dome, albeit accidentally, in a more visually scatological redo of Swift's urination scene. (Tantalisingly, Swift had included that scene on the list of suggested woodcuts sent to, but largely ignored by, the publisher – Rowson simultaneously completes and updates the source text's words and images.[55])

Forced to face his crimes, quite literally, the late-twentieth-century Gulliver prepares to meet a major new antagonist, the mysterious emperor: 'Could he be a creature of my own *dimensions*, who kept Lilliput merely as a kind of *toy*? Or might he be even *bigger*?' (I.33). Amusingly, the Lilliputians need to place him under a microscope to see him, a neo-Swiftian (or, if viewed within the longer history of visual Gulliveriana, Hogarthian) takedown of pompous leaders. The Brobdingnagians whom the new Gulliver meets on the second voyage seem to recognize him too: 'Gowvah!' 'Stupid child!', a woman says to her daughter, Glumdalclitch (a namesake of the little nurse in the original). 'It is not a "Gulliver". "Gulliver" was the name of a particular specimen of this species of vermin which washed up on our shores by accident 300 years ago!' (II.16). The timbre of this speech uncannily echoes the final judgement of the repulsed King of Brobdingnag in the source material. Largely sidelined, or reassigned to the role of absent observer, the new Gulliver continues to represent his maligned species. Rowson's protagonist therefore epitomizes Denson and Mayer's spectral seriality, which describes the peripheral familiarity acquired by fictional characters through repeated adaptation across different media. Pulling on an additional thread in Freeman's tripartite model of transmedia storytelling, authorship, we can also recognize how Rowson modernizes the source material. Now Rowson augments Swift's satire on human hypocrisy with direct and, in a verbal sense, updated rebuke: 'Oh be quiet. You really are a pompous little prick, aren't you?', says the Brobdingnagian 'crone', jabbing a finger at the just about visible man held in the so-called ogress's hands (II.20). Shown wall paintings of his ancestor's time in Brobdingnag, Lionel Gulliver displays the same sort of self-delusions as the original even in an entirely different setting. Noting the image of a great bird taking Lemuel from the giants, the new Gulliver pities the hosts: 'My heart quickened at the thought of the affection in which they must have held him at that time . . .' (II.21). New Gulliver's ignorance is dramatically exposed when, oddly, he admits he did not know his famous ancestor had written a book. A giant copy of that book had, just two pages earlier, taken up a prominent position in a large panel on the page. More than that, throughout the entire graphic novel, Gulliver had regurgitated fragments of that foundational text. Put another way, his words are borrowed without him knowing it. Overfamiliarity and ignorance collapse in a fugue of cultural saturation and authorial injoking.

In the next voyage, the modern Gulliver fails to identify Laputa when it looms into a panel, though the residents recognize him with a quickness not shared by the original inhabitants in *Travels*: 'Dr Gulliver! Please climb the ladder!!' (III.9). And the imagery recycled from the host text means nothing to him, such as the monument of a cucumber, an ironic homage to the ludicrous experiments conducted in the Academy of Lagado. This brings us to the third aspect of Freeman's transmedia model. Counter to the unknown places opened out in the long tradition of book-based extensions of *Travels*, Rowson reconstructs Swift's world-building only for his revised character to refuse it. Even the heavily aged Struldbruggs, some of whom had met the original Gulliver, hold little interest in or for him. Yet again Gulliver has been sidelined by a different figure of fun, an overenthusiastic geneticist who shares a close physical resemblance to the scientist Robert Winston, a familiar face on British television throughout the 1990s. Regardless of form or style, reworkings or extensions of *Travels* have often freely localized their references for their target audiences – graphic novels no less so. The narrative tension between recognition and non-recognition in Rowson's *Gulliver's Travels* culminates in the final voyage, where invited tour groups are only permitted to visit Yahoos and Houyhnhnms in restricted circumstances. Joining Gulliver's group by association, we witness Yahoos subjected to a dulling domestication programme and a dismal waste disposal system before we come to what we understand to be 'the highlight of your trip!', a close encounter with the Houyhnhnms (IV.9). When they hear the name 'Gulliver', however, the Houyhnhnms react with alarm. They blame the long-extinguished Yahoo mutiny on Lemuel Gulliver, much to Lionel's regret: 'Over and again I cursed that earlier Gulliver, thanks to whom I should now never learn any more of the austere wisdom of the HOUYHNHNMS' (IV.14). The source text has literally thwarted the redo, despite the character's uncanny copying of the first Gulliver's deep admiration of the talking horses. Lionel finds another copy of Swift's *Travels* among a large shipment of luxury goods, essentials and raw materials. Unlike the earlier glimpse of the book, rendered on the page as a handsome octavo, this one has a modern, cartoonish cover. Such an image, grimly, sits at odds with the 'hand-tooled yahoo velum' in which it has been bound (IV.15). In the final one-page panel, Lionel commences reading, and presumably he will be disturbed – perhaps irrecoverably so – by the undeniable coincidences of their respective travels.

In Milo Manara's erotic retelling of *Travels* in graphic fiction, *Gullivera* (1996), a female Gulliver had similarly retraced her near-namesake's travels into the four remote nations while reading a copy of Swift's extant book. And yet, like Rowson's Gulliver, Gullivera fails to note the peculiar coincidences with – let alone the blatant departures from – the original. The source text in each case functions both as a nostalgic anchor for the reader at least vaguely familiar with the main details or iconography of *Travels* and as a new plot propellent suited to the medium's horizon of subversive expectations. Alan Moore's *The League of Extraordinary Gentlemen* series (1999–2021) also relies on our collective recognition of Lemuel Gulliver but makes notable adjustments to fit him into a largely para-Victorian collective of public domain characters that comprises Mina Murray, Allan Quatermain and Captain Nemo, among others.[56] Moore's Gulliver must be at least a generation younger than Swift's Gulliver; his dates have evidently been shifted forward so he can interact with other fictional characters of the second half of the eighteenth century, including a new love interest, Fanny Hill. In Moore's sprawling multiverse meet-up, more pertinently, Gulliver takes yet another secondary role – or rather, a belatedly preliminary one: we eventually learn that he was the leader of the second incarnation of the League. We glimpse him briefly in the first volume, as a decrepit man ('L. Gulliver') in a sepia-tone group photograph-like panel from 1787 framed on the wall of the British Museum in 1898. We see that image again, in a reduced form, in 1969, in the third volume. The recycling of motifs had long been a staple of visual Gulliveriana, but here it has become especially self-referential. Drawn by the series' artist (and co-creator) Kevin O'Neill, an unnumbered spinoff, *Black Dossier* (2007), presents Gulliver and his fellowship in a fight with an ogre within a self-contained strip titled *The Life of Orlando*, which is itself published under the auspices of a mock-comic, *The Trump* (22 August 1953, no. 910). 'Returning to Britain in 1740', the ageless Orlando reveals in the caption, 'I stood by them through Brobdingnag's Giant-wars and helped them in their subterranean adventures'.[57] Such adventures have long ceased, we should infer.

In a later strip within *Black Dossier*, a sequel to John Cleland's *Fanny Hill: Or, Memoirs of a Woman of Pleasure* (1749) titled *The New Adventures of Fanny Hill*, Gulliver engages in a sexual relationship with the narrator in 1754 (he has been aged down, presumably to fit generic expectations). Soon after, Gulliver dies off the page, in 1799, and is buried in Lilliput. (In a surreal episode at the back of *Black Dossier*, the giant legs of Gulliver stomp down some stairs across four panels; none of the characters comment upon the posthumous cameo, suggesting this is an additional, incorporeal iteration.) Logistically, then, Moore's Gulliver is already dead throughout the *League* series: his actions are described after the fact, often in photograph-like panels. Indeed, his sons John and Lemuel Jr, among other descendants, have become travellers in their own right. Moore and O'Neill also scatter numerous verbal and visual references to other, much older Gulliverian works, such as the Manouham and Letalispons mentioned in Pierre-François Guyot Desfontaines's *Le Nouveau Gulliver, ou Voyage de Jean Gulliver, fils du capitaine Gulliver* (1730), plus such places as Hunchback Island, Geometer's Island, Greedy Island, and Foolyk. Gulliver expresses an interest in finding Locuta, the subject of Elizabeth Susanna Davenport Graham's 1818 sequel, *Voyage to Locuta*, which 'a son of mine once told me he had found'. Pedantically, we might observe that Graham's character only refers to the original voyager as 'my revered ancestor', not a father; perhaps we should accept that literary kinship by definition defies the rules of biological kinship.[58] Moore nevertheless endorses both the longer, wider Gulliverian literary afterlife and his part in its ongoing perpetuation across different media. As an explorer-turned-author, too, Moore's Gulliver continues to make his presence felt beyond his lifetime. In the second chapter of *The New Traveller's Almanac*, a text-heavy, triple-columned mock-travelogue that appears towards the end of the second volume of *League*, we learn that 'Lemuel Gulliver's margin-notes conjecture that the banished intellectual horses of Abdera may have sired the Houyhnhnms, talking horses the much-travelled Gulliver had previously encountered'.[59] A long section of the almanac's fifth chapter quotes directly from Gulliver's post-*Travels* log: 'Balnibarbi, it distresses me to note, is every bit as hopeless and impoverished as when I saw it last' (37). Moore ingeniously splices the mock-bookish and visually alert strands of Gulliveriana.

Disconnected from his own travel memoirs, Gulliver's established (and new) discoveries informed a larger body of writing on behalf of the League in which Lilliput and Locuta coexist and in which Vairasse's

Sevarambia seems as real as Sussex. Such seemingly deliberate alienation from the source material actually revisits the original Gulliver's expressed duty to the British government, since 'whatever Lands are discovered by a Subject, belong to the Crown', even if he doubts whether it is 'worth the Charge of a Fleet and Army' to conquer Lilliput (*GT*, 438–39). Moore's Gulliver is literally and figuratively an agent of plot. By contrast, Rowson's Gulliver poses a robust challenge to any meaningful distinction we could make between character and figure; though, in fact, other characters pick up the narratorial slack. The long-dead Lemuel Gulliver in Rowson's graphic novel has been turned into a statue, a colossal item to be forcibly adored rather than meaningfully interacted with. And yet, in his absence, that haunting figure shapes both the plot and the societies left in his wake. Present throughout and our main focalizer, Lionel Gulliver instead takes on the vacated role of narratological figure. Plot happens to him and in spite of his unfeasible ignorance of the world in which he finds himself. Even passing reflections on the attraction of the Houyhnhnm worldview, to him, follow that laid out by his ancestor. Killed off in 1799, Moore's Gulliver instead subsists in a tableau of former adventures, a snapshot of action lacking an active figure, or in scholarly echoes subsumed into a larger travelogue. In the third volume of *League* we glimpse another possible Gulliver statue, a large unnamed man in eighteenth-century attire, at the back of a room of curios in the British Museum. Whether carrying a kinetic energy when static or rendered inert, visual Gulliveriana abounds in all sorts of places.

4 GULLIVER REANIMATED

Lemuel Gulliver's prolonged existence across film, television, games and plays evinces the same ontological tension found in the visual Gulliveriana already explored: a figural lead to which plot happens and an author-explorer who shapes and often drives familiar or new, or partly new, narratives. On stage and screen, the nominal protagonist has been aged way up and down, turned into a romantic hero or swashbuckling adventurer, relegated to an advisory role, and even physically merged with painted backdrops. In this chapter we will consider the most famous and some of the most overlooked iterations of Gulliver in performative media, ranging from early pantomimes to silent-era short films through to recent feature-length redoes. The first section, 'Gulliver upstaged', outlines some ingenious ways in which playwrights have dealt with the problem of plausibly bringing the inconsistent body of Swift's Gulliver to the stage. This has often entailed fixating on just one of the strange nations to limit the need for multiple-sized representations. Alternative strategies include pushing the main character to the periphery or removing him altogether, as we find with David Garrick's *Lilliput: A Dramatic Entertainment* (1756) and John O'Keefe's *Friar Bacon; or, Harlequin's Adventure in Lilliput, Brobdingnag, Etc.* (1783), as well as the 'Harlequin' Gullivers that appeared in the first half of the nineteenth century. H. J. Byron's comic opera *The Gaiety Gulliver* (1879) turned Gulliver into a young ne'er-do-well. In their theatrical reworking of *Travels* in 1973, Gerald Frow and Sean Kenny depict the author-explorer as a narrator of past actions only. In 1980, Brian Woolland had two Gullivers on stage. Lou Stein split Gulliver into two separate bodies in 1983. Andrew Bovell freely mingled puppets and human actors in 1992. Peter Rumney relied on an aged-down actor and wooden figures to bring the lead role to life in 2012. Far less reliant on humans, in 2008 the Sergei Obraztsov Puppet Theatre used more than fifty rod and tabletop puppets, including Gulliver's huge leg, to tell their story. Splicing the excess of pantomime Gulliveriana with the self-referential humour of the novelistic extensions,

Farhana Sheikh's 2001 play introduces a frame narrative in which the acting troupe adapt on stage a book they have been reading, that is, the original *Travels*. In terms of engaging with Swift's world-building, or at least the book-based reworkings for children, most productions stay in Lilliput and Brobdingnag. Some playwrights, such as Lawrence Bommer in *Gulliver's Last Travels* (1993), pointedly jump to the final two voyages as though extending the culture-text through relatively less familiar terrain.

Filmmakers have embraced the challenge posed by Gulliver's embodiment, or, put another way, the Man Mountain has always attracted technical innovators. The second section of the present chapter, 'Gulliver's bodies', opens with contextual analyses of the first major cinematic reworkings of *Travels*, Georges Méliès's *Le Voyage de Gulliver à Lilliput et chez les Géants* (1902) and Max and Dave Fleischer's feature-length rotoscoped animation for Paramount Pictures, *Gulliver's Travels* (1939). This will be followed by a comparative focus on live-action Gullivers: Kerwin Mathews in Jack Sher's *The 3 Worlds of Gulliver* (1960), Feroz Khan in Ravikant Nagaich's *Rani aur Lalpari* (1975), Richard Harris in Peter R. Hunt's *Gulliver's Travels* (1977), Andrew Burt in Barry Letts's *Gulliver in Lilliput* (1982), Ted Danson in Charles Sturridge's *Gulliver's Travels* (1996) and Jack Black in Rob Letterman's *Gulliver's Travels* (2010). The third section, 'Animating Gulliver', expands the previous attention given to animated films to include works produced in the second half of the twentieth century up to the present day, such as Hanna-Barbera's seventeen-part cartoon series, *The Adventures of Gulliver* (1968-69), and their feature-length animated movie titled *Gulliver's Travels* (1979). Among animated Gulliveriana we will also trace a notable trend in which the protagonists, whether new or old, return to familiar if fantastical lands, such as a late episode in the short-run anthology series *Journey to the Center of the Earth* (1967) and Ilya Maksimov's *Gulliver Returns* (2021), which was scripted by Michael Ryan, an experienced reworker of *Travels* in novel form. In sum, the live-action and animated films and television series rely on an enduring character but engage with different facets of Swift's authorship and world-building. And that character has been treated in seemingly contrary ways, whether this involves revising his physicality or personality to suit a different generic framework, adjusting his function in the story, or reducing him to a phantom presence quietly haunting the new work. The final section, 'Corpsing', revisits the seemingly pat comparison of Gulliver in Lilliput to the statue of Colossus. We end the main business of this study of transfictional and transmedial storytelling by tracing the persistent rendering of Gulliver in statuary across different platforms, principally graphic novels, video games and print advertisements – as well as actual statues and effigies still littered throughout the world.

For all their manifold aesthetic and thematic divergences, the works examined in the present chapter rely on their consumers' faint to fulsome engagements with the source material in its original, abridged or expanded forms (or a blurring of these variations). As in many of the comics and graphic novels already explored, films usually take Gulliver's pre-existence as read, or they at least reference prior journeys while in the act of retracing them. Within a study of transmedia character, the category of 'reanimated' Gulliveriana also foregrounds the clonish Gullivers who look, sound and act in vastly different ways and yet broadly adhere to a prototype with whom they share a name or familial connection. The more general fantastical voyager template both extends beyond the text-based Gulliver created by Swift and his circle and gets absorbed into the accretive Gulliverian model with which that character type has become most associated in the public domain. It is no coincidence that such a unique public domain character as Lemuel Gulliver has been continually conjured into celluloid existence through trick photography, cel-animation, rotoscoping or 3D rendering. A mainstay of illustrated Gulliveriana, as discussed in the previous chapter, the paper-born giant bound to the Lilliputian shores keeps facing off against horrified, aggressive or otherwise bemused figures on screen as they creep into view as though for the first time. Beyond visual or performative motifs, however, rarely do screenwriters 'adapt' the full plot or other narratorial features of *Travels* in any sustained sense. Rarely do they take the lead character on 'fifth' voyages. Instead, they tend to rework, recontextualize or refocalize select items from the metaphorical Gulliverian museum that has accrued over the past three centuries, often stopping in a newish Lilliput. And, as in the novels and short stories explored in earlier chapters, they tend to repurpose existing character relationships or develop original ones. Following Donald Crafton, we might consider two approaches when analysing reanimated characterization. The first in Crafton's model, figurative performance, is extroverted and relies on 'masklike signs and gestures'.[1] Embodied performance, the second type, mimics the lived experience of real bodies. Such a distinction adds media specificity to the contrast we have been making between the figural Gulliver (a toylike object of the plot) and the personlike everyman (an enactor of the narrative). To animate means to give life to something (from the Latin *animare*). To reanimate denotes giving life again to a perpetual Lemuel Gulliver, a palimpsest of proliferating textual and visual incarnations within specific formal settings. The seriality of the character ensures an expansive afterlife that is reliant on and yet resistant to familiar traits. It is precisely because of this entrenched seriality that the creators of performative media have often been more interested in what Gulliver is or has represented than simply what he has done or can do within the new narrative environments. Even the can-do Gullivers that fronted the twentieth-century studio films face technological restraints as much as they pose technophilic opportunities. In short, how can one bring a plausible Gulliver to the screen or stage?

Gulliver upstaged

Unlike Swift's iteration of the main character, the people or animals that the author-explorer meets in *Travels* have not had their sense of wonder worn down by the ubiquitous wares of the street fairs that brought life to London.[2] Responding to the Man Mountain in the way unsuspecting spectators reacted to monster shows in eighteenth-century England, the Lilliputians collectively convey 'a thousand Marks of Wonder and Astonishment' at the mere sight of him, by his own claim.[3] When he finally rises to walk, 'the Noise and Astonishment of the People [. . .] [were] not to be expressed' (*GT*, 42). Brobdingnagians similarly marvel at the toylike man 'shewn ten Times a Day to the Wonder and Satisfaction of all People' (*GT*, 141). The Laputans 'beheld [Gulliver] with all the Marks and Circumstances of Wonder' (*GT*, 226). Even the sanguine Houyhnhnms cannot hide their astonishment: 'The Horse started a little when he came near me, but soon recovering himself, looked full in my Face with manifest Tokens of Wonder' (*GT*, 336). Facing severe logistical impediments in each of the remote nations and lacking any discernible artistic talent of his own, Swift's Gulliver is both gawped at and the gawper.[4] Lillian Chestney Zuckerberg dramatizes this contrarian equilibrium throughout the *Classics Illustrated* comic previously examined, but crucially, she accentuates the seafaring theme. Amid more conventional frames, she draws circular panels to imply and enforce the act of looking through telescopes and ship portholes. What can – or should – playwrights and their production teams do with such a man on the stage? Should they centre the audiences' attention on Gulliver the character or Gulliver the author-explorer, a shaper of the story, or somehow both? How, if at all, will they translate the monological narration to the stage without stifling the spectacle endemic in the material?

Some playwrights (and some filmmakers) simply did away with Gulliver. Or they have instead foregrounded minor or unknown characters. Some have favoured other narrative elements from the host text, such as the fantastical settings. In *Lilliput: A Dramatic Entertainment* (1756), David Garrick's solutions to the technical challenges of mounting Gulliverian material at the Theatre Royal on Drury Lane were simple but effective – and have persisted. He limited the scope to only the first strange nation, without giving us Gulliver's journey to it, let alone any of his various misadventures there.[5] As a serial character regardless of media specificity, after all, the author-explorer required little to no introduction. Such a bespoke engagement co-exists with the source, then amplifies it. Expanding on a small remark from the sixth chapter of the first voyage in *Travels*, Garrick centred the plot of his Afterpiece around the bizarre rumour that Gulliver had an affair with Lady Flimnap. (The director Barry Letts similarly recalibrated his winnowed version around this improbable relationship in the 1982 BBC series *Gulliver in Lilliput*.) Garrick also kept Gulliver (played by Astley Bransby) off the stage for much of the performance. At the same time, a mock-apology prefixed to the print version of *Lilliput* reminds us that Gulliver is more than a mere literary character and thereby prolongs the personhood conspiracy that followed him just months after the initial publication of *Travels*. A (fictional) man named Jacob Wilkinson, so claims 'W.C.', privately revealed to the dramatist that 'My good Friend the Captain [. . .] protested to me, upon his Death-Bed, that [. . .] he never published but one Falshood, and that was about the Lady *Flimnap*'; that is, Gulliver had omitted the true extent of her passion for him.[6] In the context of the new work, this paratextual claim adds emotional heft to the expansion of Swift's side remark. Considered within the framework of transmedia characterization, the claim fleshes out Gulliver beyond the travel memoirs. Paradoxically, Garrick further imbues Gulliver with actual personhood by giving him a deathbed convention, though the Prologue inadvertently or perhaps ironically stresses the puppet-like function of the performers: 'Puppets not made of Wood, and play'd with Wires, / But Flesh and Blood' (V.309). Serial characters are born to die, however temporarily, and regardless of the particulars of the creative environment.

Without naming Gulliver, John O'Keefe's *Friar Bacon; or, Harlequin's Adventure in Lilliput, Brobdingnag, Etc.*, a pantomime staged at Covent Garden on 23 December 1783, also capitalized on the audience's wider familiarity with Swift's properties. Like Mickey Mouse in Disney's animated film *Gulliver Mickey* (1934), another culturally saturated figure of the time, Harlequin, displaces Lemuel Gulliver from the headline role. The painted scenery of Lilliput, as some reviewers noticed, provided more artistic value to the production anyway.[7] *The Flying Island of Laputa; or, Harlequin Gulliver* (1806), *Harlequin Gulliver; or, The Flying Island* (1817), *Harlequin Gulliver; or, Giants and Dwarfs* (1845) and countless other, now largely lost pantomimes, burlettas and spectacles produced throughout the nineteenth century appear to have prioritized the fantastical world-building of the source text while finding a suitable vehicle for a popular stock character beyond the world of Gulliver.[8] The 1817 *Harlequin Gulliver* ran at least sixty-three times that season and therefore provided London's leading clown, Joseph Grimaldi, a regular opportunity to perform his repertoire of tricks alongside his long-term collaborator Jack Bologna (Gulliver, afterwards Harlequin).[9] The nominal 'Gulliver' of Mary Barnard Horne's one-act entertainment, *Gulliver and the Lilliputians Up to Date* (1889, 1903), bizarrely disavows any connection with his namesake: 'I'm a seafarin' man, but I ain't no connection of Lemuel's as I knows on, barrin' the similarity in the names an' the okkipations'.[10] (A modern man of the late nineteenth century, Samuel Gulliver also hails from Chelsea, Massachusetts; an 'American Gulliver' now more closely associated with onscreen adaptations had been established onstage earlier than might have been presumed.) Such engagements rely on but pointedly disregard the nominal lead, presumably in an attempt to offset cultural saturation. Put another way, they are more interested in Swift's world-building than the character-building.

The world's earliest onstage engagement with *Travels* does away with Gulliver while referencing the debt: 'La pièce que nous allons voir est sans doute tirée de *Gulliver*?'[11] Pierre de Marivaux's *L'Ile de la Raison, ou Les Petits Hommes* (1727) instead centres on eight new characters who find themselves in a Brobdingnagian world. Barely a fortnight later, a rival company (Le Théâtre Italien) produced a popular parody, *L'Isle de la Folie*, in which Gulliver (played by Pierre-François Biancolelli) is 'thrust quite against his will upon a fifth voyage', in William A. Eddy's words.[12] After newly encountering quirky characters, this Gulliver eventually meets the monarchs of the neighbouring islands, la Folie and la Raison, both of whom wish to provide a permanent residency for him. He chooses folly: this essentially became the mantra of theatre-based Gullivers ever since. Graceful Gullivers have nevertheless trod the boards, most notably as portrayed by the dancer Pierre-Jean Aniel, wordlessly, in Jean Coralli's ballet-pantomime for the Porte Saint-Martin Theatre, *Gulliver, ballet-pantomime en deux tableaux* (1826). Pantomime versions steadily appeared from the mid-eighteenth century and well into the next century. Between 1854 and 1885, during the heyday of the stage pantomime in Britain, there were at least fifteen versions of Gulliver's adventures staged around the country.[13] For comparison, there were ninety-seven Robinson Crusoes, eighty-nine Dick Whittingtons, and ninety-five Cinderellas. While *Travels* may not have been the go-to source for playwrights seeking enduring folkloric figures, it did retain public exposure among theatregoers every other year at least.

Some production companies needed to recalibrate the physical and personality quirks of Gulliver for their purposes, as in 'The Grand Christmas Pantomime' billed at the Prince of Wales Theatre in Birmingham during the 1875 season. This Gulliver experiences anew his first engagement with the Lilliputians, now with punning wit suited to the artistic context rather than book-based terror mingled with bemusement:

Emperor.—Man Mountain, why so tall?

Gulliver.—Because I'm pop'lar. Man mole-hill, why so small?[14]

The reverse happens in their land of giants, where the now ogrish farmer threatens to eat Gulliver: 'Why two tom-tits like you we'll put together / And make a pie' (42). Absent for much of the performance, Gulliver takes on the unlikely role of 'pa-in-law' to the new lead character, and a crowd of charming figures flit across the stage in bursts of dialogue and song. Unlike her original namesake, Mrs Gulliver, meanwhile, receives new lines of her own, albeit narrowly fitted to the role of wife. Staged at the Gaiety Theatre in London on Boxing Day in 1879, H. J. Byron's 'comic operatic spectacular extravaganza in prose and verse', *The Gaiety Gulliver*, instead ages down 'Lemuel Gulliver', here an 'extravagant young ne'er-do-well' press-ganged into the navy alongside cartoonish rogues such as Scowlygrowls.[15] Played by Nellie Farren in her early thirties, this Gulliver has not only casually shed the canonical family ('I'm a bachelor, and a gay dog' [192]), he has also been reinvented as a shameless rake fixated on winning Polly: 'None in Plymouth is her equal, / Marriage shall be the sequel' (164). He nevertheless finds himself back in Swift's fantastical worlds, Lilliput and Brobdingnag, though only fleetingly and with little interest in those places already more familiar to the audience than to him.

Attention shifts to a brand-new setting, the Island of Comic Song, a more suitable place for the carolling flirt and his crew, rather than Swift's politicized heterocosm. Passing allusions to Laputa suggest this Gulliver retains some inherited memories of his predecessor's adventures, but the more frequent references to Victorian plays and pastimes suggest we should treat him as a literary clone hacked heavy-handedly out of Swift's prototype and placed in an environment attuned to loyal theatre audiences. Byron's engagement mingles elements of a prequel (in its exploration of Gulliver's bachelorhood), a retelling (in its elliptical return to the original remote nations) and a sequel (in adding another nation and an ensemble cast). According to Heinz Kosok, a 'less flippant' approach to the original author's materials only emerged in the twentieth century.[16] In this schema, Kosok downplays the stylistic demands of pantomimes and other forms of stage extravaganzas, including their scope for intertextual irreverence, and has ignored the overriding commercial context in which such engagements should be placed – he is too deferential to character, in other words. Considered more broadly within the purview of transmedia studies, moreover, an overly deferential approach to the material undermines the realities of the belated dispersal of the Gulliverian template outlined throughout this book. Playwrights in any register still have to deal with the practical problem of what to do with Gulliver. Gerald Frow and Sean Kenny's 1973 *Gulliver's Travels* deploys the author-explorer as a narrator of past actions rather than an enactor of additional ones. Lou Stein split Gulliver into two separate bodies in 1983: the young adventurer and the older man reflecting upon those prior experiences. Brian Woolland used a dual Gulliver in his 1980 staging of *Travels* for the Edinburgh Festival: 'Gulliver One' in England, whom the audience sees reading from a diary or speaking directly to his family (that is, Gulliver the character), and 'Gulliver Two', who writes the same diary on his travels (Gulliver the author-explorer). Performed in Warsaw in 1963, Jerzy Broszkiewicz's two-act play *Dwie Przygody Lemuela Guliwera* (*Two Adventures of Lemuel Gulliver*) centred on one actor playing four parts (a lecturer, Gulliver, the Lilliputian Hulgo and the

Brobdingnagian Glum), using different cages to convey their contrasting sizes.[17]

In addition to character-building and world-building, playwrights have paid homage to Swift's metatextual authorship. Farhana Sheikh's *Gulliver's Travels: A Play* (2001) introduces a frame narrative in which Squire asks Francis and his acting troupe to perform a pantomime version of a book he has found: 'Ah, The Reverend Swift! Splendid story. Big people and little people'.[18] Acknowledged as an established, familiar story here, the entirety of *Travels* gets retold in a condensed format that spurns the sanitation of the children's chapbooks that have long loomed large across the reading nation. Francis, breaking from his Gulliver façade, warns the audience that the ensuing urination scene follows the original closely: 'I can show you the very pages of the book', he declares, before brandishing the evidence (55). Enacting the toylike qualities of Swift's original, Sheikh's Brobdingnagian Gulliver is at turns '*represented by a puppet*' (66) and a full-size man in dollish dress. Other enactments eschew materiality. Invoking Swift's maxim that vision is the art of seeing things invisible (as paraphrased by Francis), Gulliver looks upwards, '*as if into a giant's face*' (65), or down, as though talking to Lilliputians so small they evade the audience's gaze. Rather than choose between Gulliver the author-explorer and Gulliver the action figure, Sheikh disperses Swift's original speeches among different characters (Carmen, Susannah and Gulliver), such as Esther, who observes that Gulliver 'was extremely pressed by the necessities of Nature' (34). Such dispersal undermines the unity of character, which is already problematic with serial figures that have forever crossed contrary forms and genres. Dispersal does not necessarily equate to dilution, in any case; Sheikh augments the material with new songs, poetry and character dynamics, often with populist precedents in mind. Unlike the typical Victorian pantomime and more like the novelistic refocalizations of recent years, this includes foregrounding another speaking Mrs Gulliver, to whom Sheikh's Gulliver has been a devoted husband. Bound anew to the Lilliputian shores, among other redoings, this is a familiar, if recalibrated, version played by a character (Francis) played by an actor (Peter Glancey) rather than a literary namesake or rebooted clone.

Most theatrical productions stick with Lilliput and Brobdingnag, which necessitates some fundamental scene setting, regardless of the cultural oversaturation of those voyages. Some playwrights, such as Lawrence Bommer in *Gulliver's Last Travels* (1993), jump to the final two voyages and, in so doing, rely on a familiar character operating in slightly less familiar territory – we might call this an in-house sequel. Put another way, these sorts of piecemeal engagements demonstrate the opportunity a widely known story can still provide for playwrights, namely, finding new but established purviews. Other opportunities emerge out of the technical challenge of representing Swift's unique properties on the stage. Andrew Bovell's spectacular adaptation for The Playhouse in Melbourne in 1992 combined oversized and miniature puppets designed by Philip Millar with human actors to recreate the starkly shifting dimensions of Gulliver's worlds. As in the comics and graphic novels already explored, Bovell's Gulliver is at turns a flesh-and-blood man (played by Andrew McFarlane) and a toylike figure (**Figure 13**). This contrary combination presents not only an elegant solution to the problem of plausibly staging *Travels* but also represents a fitting exacerbation of the Brobdingnagian king's flippant assumptions about Swift's original character, namely, that he can be nothing more than a senseless object. A steady stream of productions has continued this trend of mingling physical theatre with fantastical puppetry, as we find in a 2010 adaptation for the Mermaid Arts Centre in County Wicklow by Wonderland's Alice Coghlan and Conall Morrison's 2013 riotous rendering for Ireland's National Youth Theatre.

FIGURE 13. Gulliver as Grildrig (photograph © Jeff Busby): Andrew Bovell, *Gulliver's Travels* (1992), The Playhouse, Victorian Arts Centre, Melbourne.

Peter Rumney's 2012 version for Curve in Leicester features an aged-down actor (Chris Jack) and wooden figures joined together in bringing the lead role to life. The Sergei Obraztsov Puppet Theatre's human-light production used more than fifty rod and tabletop puppets, including the largest in their collection – Gulliver's huge leg – in 2008.[19] Considered collectively, such examples prove that distinct theatrical reworkings of *Travels* can respond to, and often extend, different facets of Swift's authorship, character-building and world-building (to reiterate the central tenets of Freeman's model of transmedia storytelling). Together they also offer elegant solutions to the problem of mounting on stage a character that logically must be either strictly figurative (or gestural, in Crafton's model) or embodied in mimicry of real people. Instead, they flit between incompatible renderings to accentuate Gulliver's implausible body.

Other playwrights have focused on modernizing or otherwise recontextualizing the worlds in which they placed the central figure. Most recently, Lulu Raczka's 2022 reimagining for Unicorn Theatre uses tabletop sets, video projection and diorama-like scenes with painted figurines to capture the dizzy scaling of the world of Grace Gulliver and the people she encounters. (This Gulliver is a modern young girl seeking escapism from a stifling life with a chronically ill mother.) Other stage-based clones include the central figure in Lonnie Carter's Gulliverian quartet of 1990s stage epics, 'Lemuel Louis Gullivah' (later Gulliver), a Black everyman dealing with racial segregation and other national crises in twentieth-century America. Humphrey Carpenter's Gulliver is a harassed NHS doctor dealing with contemporary issues in vaguely Swiftian locations in a 1995 version. Partially renaming the eponymous lead, Bill Dare's BBC radio series *Brian Gulliver's Travels* (2011–12) and his 2013 novelization take 'Gulliver' to unfathomed fantastical places to engage, satirically, with contemporary concerns. In Dan Coleman's *Gulliver Returns* (2018), a Dawn State Theatre Company production staged in Edinburgh and throughout the UK, a contemporary man named Adam (played by Jack Bence) identifies so intensely with his reading experience of *Travels* that he insists his wife, Lil (Cathy Conneff), call him Lemuel Gulliver. Weaving in adapted elements of *Travels*, the new story allegorizes bereavement and acute mental distress in a modern yet evergreen context. Often harlequinized, aged down, or simply recast, different Gullivers have long been conjured onto the theatrical stage by using puppet models, forced perspective and other low-tech strategies or new media gimmickry. In moving pictures, too, Gulliver has always appealed to technophilic artistry, from Georges Méliès's early twentieth-century trick photography through to 1960s rotoscoping, through to 3D renderings in the 2010s. But, as in every other media explored so far, the author-explorer has not always been the star of the show.

Gulliver's bodies

Of the extant live-action and animated Gulliverian movies produced that I have been able to source, most have been adaptations – typically in heavily abridged form – of Swift's prose satire. The Man Mountain version of the character dominates this filmography, though the diminutive iteration imperilled in Brobdingnag has also helmed a diverse range of outputs, from a Spanish silent film, *Gulliver en el país de los gigantes* (1903), to the equally bluntly titled *Gulliver az óriások országában* (*Gulliver in the Country of Giants*), András Rajnai's second adaptation of *Travels* for Hungarian television, in 1980, up to the present day.[20] As a rule, actors for the large studio productions have portrayed Gulliver as heroic, whether romantic (Kerwin Mathews) or ironic (Jack Black), while cartoons from around the world largely favour Gulliver the fearless adventurer. Just as large parts of the long theatrical history of *Travels* remain irrecoverable, particularly the harlequinades of the nineteenth century, some playscripts and playbills aside, so any study of its film history will have to acknowledge the many lost or unmade works. According to Bruno Edera, the Canadian filmmaker and animator George Dunning had been working on two unrealized projects after *Yellow Submarine* (1968), the highly acclaimed animated jukebox musical fantasy adventure comedy film inspired by the music of The Beatles: *Le Morte d'Arthur* and *Gulliver's Travels*.[21] Such loss, put another way, reveals something about the messiness of much Gulliveriana exhibited in our virtual museum of famous and recovered works, that it can be heavily reliant on convenience and even opportunism. Equally, opportunities are not always convenient. During the Golden Age of Hollywood, Will H. Hays suggested the Modern Picture Association should promote 'better pictures' that would appeal to an educated and increasingly prosperous class of spectator. For this process he favoured literary adaptations. Some of the films he claimed would imminently appear in 1934 – but did not – include adaptations of Oliver Goldsmith's *She Stoops to Conquer* (1773) and Jane Austen's *Pride and Prejudice* (1813), as well as *Gulliver's Travels*.[22] Would the 1934 *Travels* have followed the entirety of the original text? Would it have transposed Swiftian satire to the big screen or refitted the book to a new genre? Would there have been supplementary characters or plotlines? Who would have taken the title role? To what extent would the artistic choices made in the unmade *Travels* have changed the course of Gulliver's afterlife in the public imagination?

Studio executives rely on financial success. Moviemakers may crave the same, though typically they will be at least equally interested in artistic value. Neither group necessarily prioritizes the cultural reception of a literary work, however. In other words, sometimes source materials for adaptations are not so much valued assets but repositories of pre-existing items open to experimental engagement on the secondary author's terms. Almost exclusively set in Lilliput alone and often jettisoning Swift's first-person narration, commercial family movies have habitually followed the reframed abridgements that flourished in the eighteenth and nineteenth centuries and which remain with us.[23] The biggest commercial productions of *Travels* that have appeared so far (in 1939, 1960, 1996 and 2010) share two qualities, as Katie Lanning recognizes: reliance on the latest audiovisual technology and an emphasis on spectacle rather than plot.[24] Max Fleischer considered Swift's text ideally suited to his plans for creating just the second feature-length colour cartoon, in 1939, preceded only by Disney's *Snow White and the Seven Dwarfs* (1937). Before both came a silent German black-and-white animation, *The Adventures of Prince Achmed* (1926).[25] That said, the producers of each Gulliver studio film have considered it necessary to adjust the main genre in which the central plotline has been couched, usually by adding a love interest or antagonist. In each case Gulliver becomes a distinctive kind of hero. While a consideration of technological aspects might distract us from our focus here, namely the figure of Gulliver, in many vital ways the visual medium allows for specific iterations of the lead character to be reanimated. The sight gags of Jack Black's Gulliver rendered in comically oversized 3D projection for the 2010 *Gulliver's Travels* add to his easy slacker charm. Fundamentally a vexed taleteller in Swift's vision, Gulliver was also a carefree sorcerer in the earliest onscreen versions.

Discounting nominal engagements such as the Gulliver-less *Cheese Mites, or Lilliputians in a London Restaurant* (1901), as well as shorts currently lost, I would credit Georges Méliès with the first major cinematic reworking of *Travels*: *Le Voyage de Gulliver à Lilliput et chez les Géants* (1902), which was released in the United States as *Gulliver's Travels Among the Lilliputians and the Giants* and in Britain as *Gulliver's Travels—In the land of the Lilliputians and the Giants*. In the extant four-minute short, the nominal figurehead takes on the dual roles of director and lead actor. Working against the living-statue trope that he often favoured in his other fantastical films, here Méliès populates the screen with busy bodies.[26] The source material provided ideal fodder for the filmmaker's bold innovations so early in the history of the medium, such as the use of multiple exposures and forced perspective to depict the differences of scale between Gulliver and the Lilliputians and Brobdingnagians. To create a semblance of apparently seamless action, Méliès used substitution splices and careful exposure design to merge the disparate elements.[27] Not merely a technophilic vehicle, however, Méliès's interpretation capitalized on the innate farce of the exchange between the at times oversized and miniaturized hero and the villagers with whom he shares filmic space. The latter actors play it straight, avoiding eye contact with the audience and sticking to their roles (as workers feeding the giant or as court clowns teasing the miniature man). The giant harlequin-like Gulliver, by contrast, vamps to the camera, inviting viewers to laugh at the spectacle. Wholly benign and banal, the Gulliverian world contrasts the later transformations of the diminutive kings and queens who dance into life from a pack of playing cards in *Le Menuet lilliputien*, or *The Lilliputian Minuet* (1905), under the guidance of the conjuror, or the marionettes who become humans and attack the puppeteer in *L'Anarchie chez Guignol* (*Punch and Judy* [1906]). In appearance the 1902 version of Gulliver has become heavily bearded and rendered grotesque: Méliès is at once puppet-master and puppet, human and monocled monster, and, above all, the showman and the show (**Figure 14**).[28] Or, in Crafton's adapted model of reanimated characterization, he is simultaneously figurative (gestural) and embodied (personlike). Amid an array of technological innovations, Méliès also demonstrates the endless iterability of Swift's variegated prototype within and beyond media specificity. This is not to suggest that the filmmaker wanted to participate in a belated, concerted dispersal of Gulliver; on the contrary, the character serves the technophilic filmmaker.

As a character, Gulliver looked set to gain a yet more looming onscreen presence in a smash hit animated musical produced by Max and Dave Fleischer more than three decades later.[29] As part of their promotional strategy for *Gulliver's Travels* (1939), Paramount Pictures

arranged for a thirty-foot figure of Lemuel Gulliver to feature in Macy's Thanksgiving Day Parade in New York City, flanked by men and women in military uniform. Static in stature but spectacular nevertheless, the effigy that popped up in the parade shares more than might be obvious with the cel-animation iteration associated with it.[30] In a tie-in game produced by Pepys, moreover, Gulliver features prominently across its packaging and forty-four cards.[31] Aside from a brief glimpse of him as he staggers to the beach after the shipwreck at the outset of the film and the partial discovery of his body by an alarmed Lilliputian shortly after, the Fleischers' Gulliver only appears most substantially roughly a third of the way into the seventy-six-minute movie (**Figure 15**). From the rediscovery of the body to the point when Gulliver finally opens his eyes, a twenty-minute sequence in which the Lilliputians tie the giant while he sleeps, the camera rolls across the supine body. Equal, if not more, focus is put on the ingenious devices the tiny figures use to trap oversized limbs. Aside from some initial exhalation, primarily to alert the unsuspecting villagers as comically as possible, Gulliver's body has essentially become an obtrusive corpse. Amid heavy hammering and slapstick bickering, he does not flinch. The high number of drawings needed to produce an animated figure might suggest this is a practical

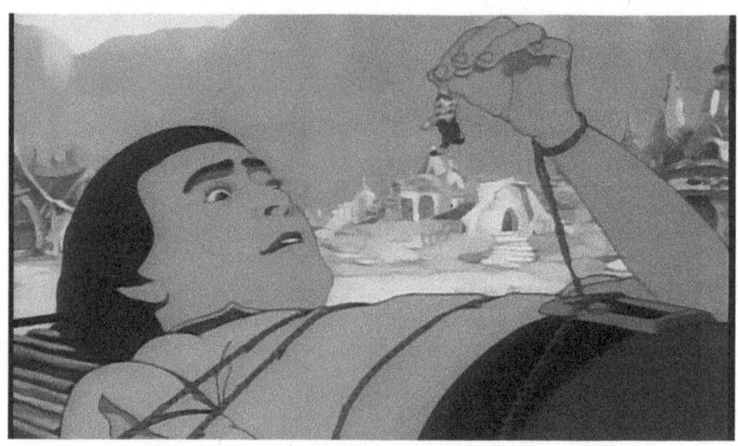

FIGURE 15. *Gulliver's Travels*, directed by Dave Fleischer (Paramount Pictures 1939).

issue. But the time and labour allocated to the Lilliputians indicate it is more of a narratological concern. Eventually awakened by the noise, but far less perturbed than Swift's original in a comparable scene, this Gulliver suddenly bursts into action. Within minutes of opening his eyes, in fact, the hungry monster becomes the saviour of Lilliput against a sudden attack from the Blefuscudians. Returned to the perspective of Gabby and other Lilliputians, the 1939 version displaces Gulliver the author-explorer but does not lose his militarized body. Suppressed as a narratological agent, the former protagonist can nevertheless still partly underwrite Swift's world-building within a quite literally new medium.

The rotoscoped animation of the Fleischers' Gulliver (modelled on the movements of one of the animators, Nelson Demorest, and, in later scenes, the voice actor Sam Parker) intensified the masklike, figurative performance of the multiple-bodied character, in Crafton's terms.[32] Bearing a striking resemblance to the rotoscoped Gulliver, Kerwin Mathews has become the most familiar face of the character in terms of embodied performances on screen (**Figure 16**). Beyond the screen, Mathews also appeared as Gulliver on the covers and in the preliminary pages of Dell Publishing's 1960 tie-in comic in their long-running *Four Color* anthology series, *The 3 Worlds of Gulliver* (no. 1158), and in promotional materials. The coiffured American actor had hardly reached his early thirties when he appeared in Jack Sher's film, *The 3 Worlds of Gulliver* (also 1960), not long after gaining global recognition as Sinbad the Sailor in a profitable

fantasy adventure film.[33] Sher wanted the high-profile comedian Jack Lemmon to play Gulliver, but Columbia Pictures favoured a dramatic actor; this suggests a conflicted vision for the adaptation's tone. Or rather, practical matters took precedence. According to the film's producer, Charles H. Schneer, Mathews 'was one of the few American actors who could play a classical role, and would look right in a period costume.'[34] More to the point, I would add, the actor had gained invaluable experience working on a production heavily reliant on Dynamation, the full-colour widescreen stop-motion technique developed by Ray Harryhausen. In many shots, Mathews moves deftly across the screen as he fends off giant alligators and other new physical threats. In other scenes he reacts with suitable astonishment mingled with heroic calm when placed in unusual environs. Paradoxically, he is both toylike in his actions and yet an embodied character in appearance. Also, he is Gulliver-like in his emotional response but post-Gulliverian, or specifically Raspean, in his deeds (that is, fighting large alligators directly recalls Baron Munchausen's paranarrative of fantastical adventure popularized in English as *Gulliver Revived* since the late eighteenth century).

Under Peter R. Hunt's direction, the 1977 *Gulliver's Travels* aggravated this paradox of toylike personhood by placing a live-action actor alongside cartoonish figures. One of the most famous set pieces in this particular film sees the ruggedly fortysomething Richard Harris roped to the Lilliputian beach, with nine clumps of his light brown hair tied down. Zooming in on the hair, and therefore the face, in contrast with the kinetic body of Mathews, allows a more striking distinction to be drawn (quite literally) between the familiar human face and the cartoonish Lilliputians who surround it. Shortly before this, Feroz Khan also embodied Gulliver on screen, wearing period dress combined with then-modern flared trousers, in a joyous cameo in *Rani aur Lalpari* (*Rani and the Red Fairy*), a 1975 Hindi-language children's fantasy film directed by Ravikant Nagaich. In that film, a young girl named Rani endures increasing cruelty when left with her relatives. Daydreaming Gulliver into existence provides her with fantastical relief. In an upbeat song delivered by Manna Dey, 'Ajab Kahani Gulliver Ki', Khan's Gulliver becomes shipwrecked on the Lilliputian shores – a common enough manifestation of the story. But the interaction with the elites among the small people remains highly cordial. The Lilliputians merely regard him with curiosity rather than violent defensiveness, and he, in turn, views them with scarcely perturbed wonder rather than the anger and arrogance expressed by the original author-explorer. Even Gulliver's genocidal violence against the rivalrous Blefuscudian fleet at most turns into a duck-pond-like dabbling followed by a cheery wave. Amid the childlike fantasy, most of the scene actually explores Gulliver's flirtation with a Lilliputian lady. If we consider the film within the wider remit of Gulliverian adaptations, in which accreted materials have become part of the multivalent culture-text, this is not as misplaced as it might superficially appear. Early book-based Gulliveriana had expanded on the sexual hint in *Travels*, as we saw in the first chapter of the present study.

A more earnest, if no less carefree, televisual series titled *Gulliver in Lilliput* (1982), directed by Barry Letts for the BBC, also recentres on a coy romance between the eponymous lead (played by Andrew Burt) and Lady Flimnap (Elisabeth Slade). The title sequence of each of the four episodes in the series sees Gulliver at a writing desk and reading aloud to the viewer, and in the endings of each he moves against static brownish and white pictures. Such a bookish aesthetic implies the internal prominence of an author-explorer. Jarringly, though, the show itself reduces Gulliver to a subject – an unheroic, middle-aged mariner at that. Lady Flimnap takes over some narratorial function, such as when she explains the political act of rope-dancing to Gulliver (and only indirectly to us). She also saves Gulliver from death by execution, a plot point originally given to Reldresal in *Travels*. Largely nonchalant about his experiences in Lilliput, this iteration of Gulliver nevertheless remains a sight of wonder to those he meets. 'It's a monster! A giant!', declare the Lilliputians who discover him.[35] Lady Flimnap quickly falls in love with the accidental invader and becomes visibly disappointed when Gulliver casually reveals towards the end of the series that he has a wife and two children, even if he is 'no family man'. Iconic scenes get replayed as though for the first time, including the urination on the palace. This version, in sum, transposes familiar material to a different medium with a peculiar mixture of plot irreverence and character fidelity. Filmmakers, like playwrights, face the burden of what to do with Gulliver. In servicing their own plots and character-building, do they favour Gulliver the author-explorer or Gulliver the action figure? Does the celluloid Gulliver narrate Swift's scripted words in an abridged or otherwise altered form, perhaps over his tandem performance on screen, or should he undertake entirely new experiences? Does the spatio-temporal separation of voiceover and onscreen action make him two characters or one? Should filmmakers stick to the original source material – if so, how closely? – or engage with the accretive, multimedia world of Gulliveriana that has long permeated global culture?

For modern audiences, Gulliver dons the face of Ted Danson, who took the role in the 1996 television series for Channel 4, or perhaps Jack Black, the lead actor in the most recent big studio release, *Gulliver's Travels* (2010). Established stars in their own right, Danson and Black found in Gulliver a handy vehicle for their respective period-drama aspirations and slacker slapstick. In keeping with the decades-worth of Hollywood treatments, each actor plays the role with their American accents, though Danson favours a transatlantic inflection. Danson finds himself in a period-appropriate England, whereas Black leaves contemporary America for a Lilliput of indeterminate historical specificity and a comical mishmash of modern and ye olde English. Other actor-focused productions have similarly latched on to the creative possibilities of a vaguely Gulliverian world. *Jajantaram Mamantaram* (2003), a live-action retelling, provided a star vehicle for Jaaved Jaaferi in Bollywood, where Gulliver has been displaced by a completely different character. Having initially mistaken Aditya Pandit for a cruel giant, thumb-sized people enlist his help against a more potent threat, a shape-shifting monster named Jhamunda. The 1996 and 2010 Gullivers remain author-explorers, but their literary aspirations do not match the prototype. A low-ranking bachelor, Black's Gulliver turns to travel writing to land the girl of his dreams. Danson's Gulliver feels compelled to write out his story on the cell walls in order to prove his sanity, even while the act unsettles his claims further.[36] In terms of characterization, though, Danson re-enacts numerous actions, such as impulsively extinguishing the fire at the empress's apartment by urinating upon it (an act usually replaced or cut entirely in adaptations across different media).

In a critical account of the 1996 version, a television series he ultimately dismisses as 'un-Swiftian', Alan D. Chalmers singles out Danson for praise. The Californian actor, he says, looks in various scenes 'appropriately gullible, or pompous, or zealous, or abject, or bemused'.[37] However, practically everything around the title character has changed: the minor mentor Dr Bates (James Fox) becomes the main love rival, the belligerent Brobdingnagian ruler a queen, the Houyhnhnm master a mistress, and the decaying, depressive Struldbruggs are now youthful fiends who kill for sport.[38] Familiarity with the world of Gulliver has been inverted for the initiated audience member, even while it remains a place of new wonders and terrors for the author-explorer, here iterated as a modernish clone in neo-eighteenth-century garb. Simon Moore's screenplay for the 1996 series also resolves Gulliver's psychological issues and vanquishes his enemies.[39] This is adaptation as completion, superficially at least, and only until understood within the expansive framework of transmedia storytelling. Walking with his wife Mary (Mary Steenburgen) and son Tom (Tom Sturridge) across a verdant English setting, Danson's Gulliver speaks over a panning shot before the final credits: 'I see myself for what I truly am'.[40] While this ending and the altered character dynamics may present an un-Swiftian affront to the source material, in Chalmers's schema, Moore's screenplay persistently embraces the competing iterations of the central figure created by Swift and recalibrated by secondary authors in different print and visual media ever since. He's an ogre ('Let's feed them to the giant'). He's a sentient plague, a spectacle at court, a colossal war hero, a Yahoo, and more. Two new Lilliputians, Clustril (Nicholas Lyndhurst) and Drunlo (Edward Woodward), unwittingly (re)coin an already established nickname: The Man Mountain. Adaptation implies a narrow intertextual relationship between a host text and a secondary work. But a transmedia work both relies on and alienates the host.

In the 2010 version of *Gulliver's Travels* updated for the screen by Joe Stillman and Nicholas Stoller, the eponymous lead has no stated understanding of his eighteenth-century ancestor but instead creates new cognate selves: once when he tells Darcy Silverman (Amanda Peet) that he's a travel writer and again when he rebrands himself as President the Awesome of Manhattan for the Lilliputians.[41] In both instances, Gulliver constructs a past out of other, non-Swiftian narratives, whether plagiarized from travel websites or from blockbuster franchises of the late twentieth and early twenty-first centuries (*Star Wars*, *X-Men*, *Pirates of the Caribbean* and more) and other creative products familiar to anyone outside of Lilliput (such as Edwin Starr's 1970 protest song 'War' and film adaptations of Edmond Rostand's *Cyrano de Bergerac*, a popular 1897 play).[42] Early in the movie, in an unsubtle foreshadowing of his life among the live-action Lilliputians, Jack Black's Gulliver plays with Star Wars action figures and thereby establishes a childlike personality that acknowledges yet exaggerates the naivety of the prototype. Against the detached voyeurism exhibited by the nominal protagonist of most onscreen adaptations of *Travels*, including Kerwin Mathews's swashbuckling adventurer, such an act also belatedly, if inadvertently, glimpses the participatory culture experienced by Victorian theatregoers who invested in souvenir sheets after watching Gulliverian pantomimes. Indeed, 20th Century Fox licensed Burger King to release six tie-in toys in their kids' meals range, among which featured a Roll 'N Bobble Gulliver (grinning in modern clothes and lightly tethered to a short set of wheels). This is more a Jack Black than a Lemuel Gulliver, and the other toys focus on non-canonical narrative motifs suited to modern life, such as Lilliputian basketball. (In another playful, if more manic, move, Ted Danson's Gulliver and his son play with generic toy soldiers after the traumatic first voyage in the 1996 series.) While Black's Gulliver might be best viewed as a nominal clone with little conscious connection to his book-born predecessor, despite having a detailed knowledge of transmedia franchises, he also casually bridges nearly three hundred years' worth of conflicted treatments of the author-explorer as an actant with personhood and a personlike figure to which action happens. Danson's version instead dramatizes this narratological conflict before finding a character-focused, novelistic resolution to his unsettling story.

Animating Gulliver

A live-action film in the *Crayola Kids Adventures* series reissued as an EDUtainment Reading Movie by SFK Media, *Tales of Gulliver's Travels* (1997, 2004) has a title that implies abridgement and therefore indicates direct or indirect participation in the long history of condensed reworkings for younger consumers. Ironically, it was one of the first screen adaptations to take the reanimated Gulliver beyond Brobdingnag. (Unlike other children's versions on the page or stage, Brobdingnag does *not* feature here – but Laputa and Houyhnhnm-Land do.) An early teen played by a stalwart of the mode, Adam Wylie, this Gulliver has been drastically aged down to appeal to the target audience. Played by Georgie Cranford, a similarly youthful Jonathan Swift ('the author') is enlisted to set up the improbable tales. Many twentieth-century cel-animated retellings of *Travels* aimed at family audiences instead displaced the lead character for a new one, such as Disney's Mickey Mouse in 1934. And, according to William Lewin, Popeye the Sailor Man was slated for the 1939 *Gulliver's Travels* before the Fleischer brothers settled on the original protagonist.[43] Not all substitutions were a result of finding vehicles for in-house star characters. One of the most highly acclaimed of all Gulliverian stop-motion animations, Aleksandr Ptushko's *The New Gulliver* (*Новый Гулливер*, or *Novyy Gulliver* [1935]) – using three thousand puppets alongside human actors – turned to a new adventurer, Petya Konstantinov (played by the teenage Vladimir Konstantinov).[44] Gifted a copy of *Travels*, Petya awakens to find himself revisiting the Lilliput about which he had just been reading. Renaming himself Petya Gulliver and donning period costume, he redoes major set pieces of his forebear's first voyage: this is adaptation as homage.[45] The reader takes over the character.

A trend for younger substitutes has continued in filmic Gulliveriana; more often than not, they have been put into modern or future-flung dress. *Gulliver's Travels Beyond the Moon* (*Garibā no Uchū Ryokō* [1965]), a seventy-eight-minute Japanese animated film, is particularly inventive, though the *Monthly Film Bulletin* dismissed the work as derivative in the pejorative rather than strictly legal sense.[46] When considered from a commercial perspective disinterested in literary properties, a different picture emerges. The production of *Gulliver's Travels Beyond the Moon* actually marked a major strategic departure for Toei Animation, who hoped to attract an audience beyond Asia by adapting the formula of animated musical features popularized by Disney, borrowing narrative elements directly from Swift and dark forest settings from Hans Christian Andersen, and using the domestic machinery of the American science fiction cartoon sitcom *The Jetsons* (1962–3). The Toei Animation film is not strictly an adaptation of *Travels*; nor is it an extension. It is a study of a child's imagination that, like *Gulliver Mickey*, relies on a pertinent cultural touchstone. A homeless boy named Ricky (Ted in the Japanese original) sneaks into a movie theatre to watch a version of *Travels*, giving us a glimpse of an established adaptation. Swiftly ejected before he can consume the whole film, Ricky is knocked unconscious by a truck. He awakes to find a talking dog and a sentient clockwork soldier. The ensuing adventures enjoyed by the trio take them to a closed amusement park. There they meet a now elderly rocket scientist living in the forest, Professor Gulliver, a distinctive and hardly plausible rebooting of the original character template. They travel to the Planet of Blue Hope, where the Queen of the Purple Planet and her evil robots have enslaved the inhabitants. Armed with water pistols and water balloons, Ricky and the Professor restore the Planet of Blue Hope to its doll-like owners, who regain life as human beings. The boy wakes up in the street to the reality that the canine companion is an ordinary dog and the soldier just a toy. Ricky, it transpires, might be a bad reader of the initial Gulliverian template, or at least a highly creative one.

Ingeniously, the animators blur the lines between the movie within the movie and the new adventures of Ricky until three minutes in, at which point the camera flips to reveal the cinema audience. Rapt by Gulliver's words on screen, Ricky fulfils the inset film's heroic message ('don't give up hope').[47] Instead of a shipwreck in unknown lands, Ricky and his companions enjoy a carefree fairground ride and a journey into space, the ultimate symbol of American can-doism in the 1960s. Ricky's wish fulfilment is, in effect, Gulliver's wish fulfilment too; put another way, the animation studio completes an implicit incompleteness in the source material. Not merely a loose adaptation, in other words, the animated film enhances the belated concertedness of transmedia storytelling built into and around Swift's world-building. When first called into action, Professor Gulliver condenses – within two quick frames – his travels so far (in Lilliput and Brobdingnag) and refers to a journey not yet taken (an unnamed further voyage, perhaps in glancing acknowledgement of the ever-expanding body of Gulliveriana in which multiple fifth voyages had taken place). At turns ominous and juvenile, the animation merges mid-century science fiction Gulliveriana with the family adventurism previously popularized by the 1939 *Gulliver's Travels*. More satirical than *The 3 Worlds of Gulliver as* mimicked within the cartoon's cinema, it nevertheless champions a key message gleaned from the secondary (post-Swiftian) source material in the inset movie: hope. Arguably the most meta of all filmic engagements with *Travels* and its remediations to have appeared so far, the Toei Animation work also comments on the power of remediation while encoding a specific, if expansive, interpretation of Swift's own materials. Notably, Gulliver unwittingly relinquishes narratorial control to the boy and takes on a different role ill-suited to the first author's prototype of the misanthrope. Most animated films, like their live-action counterparts, depend on a more familiar type of Gulliver, however, or at least a familial one. Another Japanese animation of *Travels* featured in the 1970s anthology series *Manga Sekai Mukashi Banashi* (*Manga Fairy Tales of the World*). There, Gulliver appears in a realistic form (an embodied performance), whereas the Lilliputians are drawn in a largely uniform finger-puppet style (figurative performances).

Shortly before that, Jerry Dexter voiced Gary Gulliver in Hanna-Barbera's seventeen-part cartoon series, *The Adventures of Gulliver* (1968–9). This provides a noteworthy example of a new character taking over the allegorical function of the original. Resembling Kerwin Mathews's American embodiment of the heroic adventurer in *The 3 Worlds of Gulliver* earlier in the decade, Gary retains more than a surname in common with his forefather. He too is tied down on the Lilliputian beach – repeatedly so, Prometheus-like, in each episode's opening and closing credits. As in the pictorial Gulliveriana explored in the previous chapter, the striking image becomes a character motif, even if the central character is not quite the Gulliver we would recognize. For all their stylistic and formal differences, in fact, animated Gulliveriana tends to revisit a small selection of such motifs. Familiarity breeds familiarity among consumers, if not among characters. The tethered giant motif features prominently in a short Croatian animation titled *Guliver* (2009). As the promotional tagline runs: 'Gulliver, standing still in a center of the Universe, is a sign of awe for Lilliputians who approach him slowly to start building their civilization by using his tied body as a back bone. He is still and silent while enduring the burden of negligence the Lilliputians. Until one day the ties brake [*sic*]'.[48] This Gulliver looks alien: mouthless, pupilless, blue-grey-skinned and with long, block-like fingers. We are a long way from the environmental farce of the 1939 cartoon from Fleischer Studios, in which the nominal star became a fantastical and fundamentally gentle element in the garishly painted Lilliputian scenery. Best understood as an adaptation of Mathews's Gulliver, the Hanna-Barbera series latches onto the peril associated with the gimmick of differently sized characters rather than merely decentring the out-of-place original character. While many of their production's elements might seem familiar enough, not least of all the satirized pettiness of Lilliput, the writers rerouted the material to the character-focused genre of voyage and recovery: having lost his father Thomas in the pilot episode, Gary Gulliver spends the series hoping to rescue him. Meanwhile, pirates seek the treasure sought by Thomas in the first place, thereby expanding the remit of adventure at sea beyond discovering strange worlds with little harm to the narrative structures. Within the purview of transmedia studies, we would identify this as an adjustment to what Jan-Noël Thon calls the transmedia character type (the fantastical voyager) rather than the transmedia character template (Lemuel Gulliver).[49]

Hanna-Barbera revisited Swift's properties a decade later, with a feature-length animated movie more directly titled *Gulliver's Travels* (1979). Far more earnest than their prior effort, the new story is narrated by Gulliver (now with a more appropriately English accent). Determined to find success for the sake of his family, this Gulliver is a put-upon everyman (a different, more general transmedia character type). Farcical elements remain and even gain enhanced traction on screen, particularly when he sneezes away a Lilliputian. Aesthetically, the film has been drawn in a more realistic style, and the colour palette was kept bold but comparably muted. Enduring many of the catastrophes faced by Swift's Gulliver, this hero ceases travelling after the second voyage. Happy at home with his wife and three children, he ends the tale with the same sort of emotional satisfaction later adopted at the denouement of the Channel 4 live-action series helmed by Ted Danson ('I was a wealthy man before I ever left'). In 1996, under its *Enchanted Tales* brand, Golden Films presented a more whimsical version of *Travels* that revisited the American can-doism of the 1939 animation. Augmented with classical music and a plush royalism, the story fixates on the Lilliputian court without losing Gulliver's perspective, as per the Fleischers' model. If anything, this version more obviously stresses the importance of Gulliver's particular storytelling abilities. For the benefit of a dejected young child in the opening scene, he opens a 1726 'history', namely his own book, and lifts the boy's spirits. (Most filmic Gulliveriana either ignores the authorial element of the lead character's template or at least underplays it; but the anthological format of *Enchanted Tales* accentuates it as an aspect of collective, canonical, literary folksiness.)

Another trend in animated Gulliveriana concerns the protagonist's return to former lands. Some returns were entirely nominal, even exploitative, as in 'Return of Gulliver', a late episode in the short-run anthology series *Journey to the Center of the Earth* (1967). Despite the title as splashed across the opening credits, Gulliver does not feature. Rather, the series' main characters (Professor Oliver Lindenbrook, his niece Cindy, Alec McEwen, Lars and his duck Gertrude) find themselves in a cave beset by Lilliputians ('those strange little people'), though they do not recognize them by that name, as well as an oafish giant and his dog.[50] Unwilling or unable to make the connection to the source material, the new adventurers nevertheless redo some significant actions of Swift's text and its derivatives. Lars, for one, finds himself strapped to the ground by tiny ropes, though, departing from the experiences of the original, his companions free him with ease. A French series comprising twenty-six episodes, *Saban's Gulliver's Travels* (1992–3) both adapts and extends Swift's original. Lemuel Gulliver remains the chief protagonist (and the narrator of the adventures), but he is joined by a clumsy young assistant, Raphael, as well as Dr Flim, his wife Fosla and their daughter Folia. We revisit familiar scenes (or visit them for the first time, to this Gulliver's mind), including Laputa, while additional ones come into view (the gold city and volcanoes among them). Such returns either capitalize on the Gulliverian brand to tell an extraneous story or engage with and extend the original plot points. Understood within the context of transmedia storytelling rather than adaptation studies, each iteration responds to seemingly contrary but long-established engagements and reengagements with Swift's character-building, world-building and authorship.

A more recent, Ukrainian production scripted by Michael Ryan, who, as the author of *Gulliver* (1993), was already an experienced reworker of *Travels* in novel form, does both: it foregrounds Gulliver's unlikely fame and moves beyond it. More specifically, it engages with an accreted and predominantly cinematic treatment of Gulliver. *Gulliver Returns* (2021) revolves around a lead character who shares the outward features of most onscreen Gullivers: he has an American accent, he has been aged down and turned handsome ('pretty', in his words), he has gained a love interest (Marcy, voiced by Alyson Leigh Rosenfeld) and a sidekick (Squeak the mouse), he revels in benevolent piracy (that is, stealing from the rich), and he is a subject of the story rather than an explorer-turned-author.[51] The main difference between this Gulliver (voiced by Wayne Grayson) and his forebears is, to the bemusement of the new Lilliputians, he is *not* a giant. A prophecy emblazoned on stone long ago indicates that

'Gulliver will return in 40 years' to solve their 'gigantic problems', and, in anticipation, their civic space had been designed to accommodate their saviour's oversized body. To indicate that their Gulliver must be the same 'Man Mountain' that had become part of their (and our) folklore, an opening song had listed the original Gulliver's heroic deeds, not least of all his defeat of the Blefuscudians. Logically, the young man claiming to be Gulliver cannot be the same person; despondent, the ruler can only conclude that he is 'some kind of imposter'. Later in the film, however, the 'imposter' casually refers to his former life among the Houyhnhnms (named but unseen) and his authorial ambitions ('I knew I was a great storyteller'). He also claims to remember the fathers of the Lilliputians he now meets and recalls them being much smaller. To his mind, he has returned to a legitimate Lilliput. He is a serial character, in short.

Confusingly, this young iteration of Gulliver also expresses great delight when reunited with Frelock (voiced by HD Quinn), now a much older man living as a sailor in a boathouse, and his dog Edgar (a brand-new character who could not have lived beyond the forty years of Gulliver's specified absence). The name 'Frelock' had first appeared in Swift's text, but not beyond a signature of two officers tasked with itemising the Man Mountain's belongings (presumably, in this extended reimagining, this officious interaction somehow led to an off-page friendship with at least one of them). The revelation that the laws of time have been rewritten fixes this nest of paradoxes in-universe. Four seasons can pass in a single day in this version of Lilliput. Read as a metacommentary on Gulliver's cultural afterlives, Ryan's screenplay for *Gulliver Returns* personifies the fundamental split in the onscreen characterization of the eponymous lead: Grayson's Gulliver shares with Swift's author-explorer an inner life shaped by and extending beyond his voyages into several remote nations, but, outwardly, he resembles in appearance, demeanour and deeds the handsome, carefree adventurers who took his name on the page, stage and screen. *Gulliver Returns* also plays with the material specificity of the medium: animated film, in which timeless characters are reanimated quite literally from a template – not just the one set by Swift but also the various abridgers, scripters, illustrators and other people who extended the allegorical personage across literary and visual culture. Everything can be rewritten. There are no protected characteristics when it comes to fictional characters in the public domain. Newfound adventures can be undertaken at any time. Indeed, after taking a decisive role in defeating the Blefuscudians (again), young Gulliver, along with Marcy, Squeak and Edgar, sets off for further sea voyages – and perpetual returns ('I'll be back soon'). Serial characters defy closure, though their stories demand it.

Corpsing

Even while their Gulliver flees, the Ukrainian animators commemorate his triumph over his newly acquired antagonist, Generalissimo, in a handsome bronze statue. This is not an anomaly. Few literary characters have been rendered in statuary as often as Lemuel Gulliver, not only in public spaces but within other media (graphic novels, films and video games). Really, the fantastical voyager has always been a statue. Largely limiting his movements during the first voyage in Swift's *Travels*, the Lilliputians briefly turn him into a '*Colossus*, with my Legs as far asunder as I conveniently could' (*GT*, 61-2). Martin Rowson inserts an imposing monument of Gulliver in the backdrop of his bleak revisiting, the 2012 graphic novel *Gulliver's Travels: Adapted & Updated*. Not merely a satirist's homage to the original author, such a rendering also shades irony over J. J. Grandville's absurdly grandiose monument from 1838 (and many subsequent French editions of *Travels*) (**Figure 17**). Displayed at the Allgemeinen Deutschen Gewerbe-Ausstellung in Berlin, in 1844, and the Great Exhibition in London, in 1851, a papier mâché Gulliver now resides in Sonneberg's Deutsches Spielzeugmuseum, Germany's oldest toy museum. Not all Gulliverian statues are large and public. Some are small and made for home use. Victorian toy theatres were sold as printed sheets of characters, sets, props, proscenium arches, orchestras and wings that could be decorated, cut out and assembled. Ostensibly functioning as souvenir replicas for theatregoers, such items did not merely mimic human theatre but created additional means of engagement beyond initial spectatorship.[52] Stage tableaus could be re-enacted or paper characters freed from their primary narratives and from their original identity as named figures. Many of these and related pieces have been lost, but doubtless a serial character like Gulliver would have been an ideal subject for this participatory culture, even if, as in the pantomime tradition, he would likely have become a generic sailor among many others or been displaced by different character types. Industry specialists, J. H. Jameson and William West produced souvenir sheets for their Harlequin Gullivers, though they have all but perished.[53] As a

FIGURE 17. Illustration of Gulliver by J. J. Grandville: *Voyages de Gulliver dans des contrées lointaines* (Paris: H. Fournier aîné, 1838).

totem of entertainment ephemera, Gulliver has nevertheless persisted in the digital age. Gamers take over the function of the explorer in the sixth instalment of the *Bridge to Another World* series (2014–present), titled *Gulliver Syndrome* (2019). In various Gulliverian worlds filled with tokens associated with *Travels*, players of this game seek out the character now literally objectified within a virtual platform.

Some statues mimic the mechanics of life: the most striking example of this would have been the eight-foot automaton located on the Enchanted

Voyage, a Hanna-Barbera-themed boat ride, at Kings Island between 1972 and 1983. Yet other oversized statues have broken down, become hidden or have been left to rot. Edinburgh was once home to Europe's largest concrete sculpture, a 100-foot Gulliver comprising tunnel-like limbs for children to play on. Having fallen into disrepute by 2011, thirty-five years after it was built, the 'Craigmillar Gulliver' was removed (a vestigial image of it still haunts Google Maps). Measuring sixty-seven metres in length and nine metres in height, a partly degraded Gulliver effigy currently adorns a playground in Valencia. Opened near Mount Fuji in 1997 but abandoned within four years, Gulliver's Kingdom had the most corpse-like Gulliver of all, a 147-foot glassy-eyed figure exposed to the open air. Gulliverian statuary continues to appear, nonetheless. Since 2014, the island of Usedom in the Baltic Sea has been home to a twelve-tonne polystyrene-and-plastic Gulliver of Lilliput at a family theme park named in his honour, Gulliver's Welt. Opened in Rotherham in 2020, Gulliver's Valley (the group's fourth Gulliver-themed resort in the UK) features its own eponymous giant mascot. Some larger-than-life sculptures have inadvertently gained afterlives of their own. Such is the case of the massive wooden effigy located in a once-thriving amusement park in Buenos Aires that has latterly become the backdrop in a short coming-of-age movie, *Gulliver* (2015), by filmmaker María Alché (**Figure 18**). Even physical monuments lack true immortality, as the abandoned theme park in Japan and the maligned Craigmillar Gulliver

FIGURE 18. *Gulliver*, directed by María Alché © FiGa Films 2015. All rights reserved.

can attest. As in Alan Moore's *The League of Extraordinary Gentlemen* series, the advertising agency Ogilvy also casually murdered Gulliver – along with Cervantes's Sancho Panza, Lewis Carroll's Alice and Kafka's cockroach – in a print campaign for the 2015 Vilnius Book Fair in Lithuania.[54] Looming in the foreground of the illustration by Augustas Bidlauskas, a toe tag on Gulliver's large left foot turns the most famous narrative motif of all into a morbid sight gag. Casually killed off in a striking visual image on the page among other canonical characters, is this perhaps the most appropriate end for Lemuel Gulliver?

CONCLUSION

Towards the end of *Travels into Several Remote Nations of the World*, in the 1726 and subsequent editions, the explorer-turned-memoirist Lemuel Gulliver complained that other people would visit the places described in 'this Work of mine' and, with their own accounts, make everyone 'forget that ever I was an Author'.[1] He was partly correct. Secondary authors have continuously revisited Lilliput and Brobdingnag, and Laputa and Houyhnhnm-Land to a lesser extent. But they have usually done so in his name, or from the perspective of his wife Mary, son John, or a long line of descendants (as well as unrelated namesakes and copycats). Some people have indeed forgotten that Gulliver was an author. Or, more accurately, in their creative engagements they have instead prioritized Gulliver the character, or else repurposed him as an adventure or romantic hero or an older mentor. Either way, Gulliver's complaint avows his own personhood insofar as it reveals an existential concern for a life beyond *Travels*. This is not quite the full extent of the paradox of a book-bound character demanding a post-book legacy. Unusually for a character of any design, let alone one used as a vehicle for satirical commentary by the original author, Swift's Gulliver had conceptualized his own death, or really, the deaths of his relatives. In a letter added to the 1735 edition, he mentions actual Gullivers buried in the churchyard of St Mary's in Banbury, including another Mary Gulliver, who perished in the week in which *Travels* happened to appear in print.[2] Pulling this Mary, Samuel and other Gullivers into his faux universe, Captain Gulliver fictionalizes real people. By ushering readers towards the churchyard in which he, a textual construct, cannot be buried, Gulliver also creates for himself a perpetual afterlife without end.

Put another way, Gulliver's complaint invited adapters of all kinds into his reality. In the early years, this involved members of Swift's literary circle and further fictional characters, such as the captain's print agent

Richard Sympson (who, long after his appearance in the front matter of *Travels*, has also popped up in modern retellings). Alexander Pope and John Arbuthnot, most notably, quickly produced poems and prose pieces that extended the world of Gulliver in the print marketplace. Enemies got involved too, not least a rival cleric-poet, Jonathan Smedley, who sarcastically spliced the author and the character together as Jonathan Gulliver and the Reverend Captain Gulliver, among other metafictional concoctions. Other early engagements capitalized on the popularity of *Travels*, including a fraudulent third volume, abridgements and loose translations. For many decades to come, yet other people found in Gulliver a convenient, communal avatar that could assist with the satirical takedown of a range of political targets. Some attributed to the philistine explorer many unlikely works, such as poems and street ballads, a treatise on marriage and, most bizarrely of all, a pamphlet on a medical hoax. Surprisingly few writers have attempted to mimic Swift's style closely, even when adopting the ruse of reproducing or paraphrasing 'lost' Gulliveriana. Felix Phantom (a fictional character created by Francisco Solano Constancio at the end of the eighteenth century) claimed to be communing with the aggrieved spirit of the late author-explorer (or a ceaseless ghostwriter, a ghost-as-writer). More commonly, anachronistic 'fifth' voyages kept appearing in both periodicals and book form well into the second half of the twentieth century. Ever since the early days of Gulliver's afterlife, there has been a persistent trend for refocalization, beginning with multiple Lemuel Gullivers Jr and other children, up to various self-proclaimed descendants from around the world, like the French explorer Patrick Guill'Vaër, who discovered the last living Lilliputian, and Lemuel Swift Gulliver, the bemused Tasmanian who found himself in 1930s Glasgow. Throughout the 1990s and into the present decade, the maligned Mrs Gulliver has repeatedly told her side of the story. More generally, Gulliverian refocalization follows one of two approaches: revisiting and rebutting the official record, *Travels*, or displacing the author-explorer to varying degrees of severity.

For all their formal and generic diversity, as demonstrated in Chapters 1 and 2, these sorts of creative engagements did not forget that Gulliver was an author. But they often corrected his version of events, expanded the story without him or otherwise challenged his status as a legitimate explorer. Indeed, as a hybrid figure, an author-explorer, Gulliver has posed both impediments and opportunities to fictional and non-fictional writers, playwrights, filmmakers, animators, artists and other types of creatives. Visual and narrative media engagements with Swift's nominal protagonist have resorted to all kinds of logistical actions, as we saw in Chapters 3 and 4. Typically, this has entailed prioritizing one facet over the other, whether that means re-presenting the character as an adventure hero for children or invoking the author as a perpetual ghostwriter. Some have attempted to convey the full status of the author-explorer hybrid in pictorial reworkings, most successfully in comics and graphic novels, while others have cut him out completely, most conspicuously in certain plays. Throughout this study we have relied on a recognizable character template, that of an eighteenth-century ship's surgeon whose wanderlust drives him on four separate voyages to several remote nations. Clearly, though, this general outline has proven pliable. Physically, Gulliver has predominantly been a light-skinned or ruddy middle-aged Englishman. In visual and narrative media, he has nevertheless been radically aged up and down, thinned out or fattened up, given an American, Transatlantic or other accent, and put into modern dress. Gulliver's personality has also veered from beaten down to blasé and from childlike to misanthropic. Swift actually built such inconsistency into *Travels*, where the chief character is a ravenous ogre to the Lilliputians, a pompous plaything in Brobdingnag and a gentle Yahoo in Houyhnhnm-Land. Across the journeys he is by default a feckless husband and father; he occasionally expresses feelings of homesickness, but only as part of a cyclical voyaging and return. Even the official portraits indicate a lack of singularity in terms of physical appearance and the effects the voyaging has had on his mental well-being. Beyond *Travels*, Gulliver has represented different things to different people. To parliamentary commentators such as Samuel Johnson in the eighteenth century and political poets like Wole Soyinka and Yakov Andreev in the twentieth, Gulliver was a potent avatar. To filmmakers and caricaturists, among others, he has instead been a convenient figure of fun.

Tracing the past three hundred years of Gulliver's afterlife across diverse formal, generic and media contexts has yielded three main conclusions. First, characters who have lived long in the public domain thrive on inconsistency, not just familiarity. Inconsistency is vital in both senses of the word: without it, characters become stuck or, as Thomas Docherty would have it, more dead than alive.[3] Second, we need to shift away from personhood theories of characterization to understand Gulliver and his legacy more fully, notwithstanding the author-explorer's gesturing to experiences beyond *Travels*; more to the point, such metafictional gesturing inaugurates the seriality of his multimedial instantiations. Gulliver is an abstract artefact occupying the middle ground between the material and the mental, and as such, he will not be completed. The third conclusion to be drawn from this survey of disparate creative engagements is that, even if Gulliver does not quite fit the requirement of systematic dispersal associated with modern narrative media, he and others like him can still occupy a prominent position in the historicizing of transmediality, let alone the broader realm of transfictionality. As a case study of early transmedia storytelling, arising well before but extending beyond the age of media convergence, Gulliver reveals how multi-authored character-building has worked in practice. In short, his lengthy cultural afterlife has been driven by divergent treatments of a common character as both personlike and a figure, that is, a shaper of narrative and an entity to which plot happens. The first type had box seats set aside for him at the theatre within months of the publication of his travel memoirs. The second type treats him like a toy that lacks an inner life. Yet another type, focused on Gulliver the author, has endured perhaps the strangest afterlife of all – in addition to 'found' works, he has persistently been pulled into posthumous settings to address new political or social questions long after he could conceivably have lived (meaning he is more undead than dead or alive). Authors and artists have casually gifted a death date to Gulliver – Alan Moore went so far as to give him testicular cancer – but it cannot stick. Like all fictional creations, he is immortal so long as there is an audience to be found. If viewed as an early transmedia character, in any case, Lemuel Gulliver does not fit the standard model of concerted storytelling.[4] Instead, the messy dissemination and amplification of his life and adventures across multiple platforms since the very beginning invite us to reconsider the role canonical literature really takes in our cultural, social and civic lives.

Such messiness begs a key question. With what are secondary authors and artists engaging? On occasion, a creative work will explicitly draw a connection with Swift's *Travels*, not only inviting but demanding an intertextual reading. Comics and films will typically namecheck Swift as a 'great author' or foreground an image of the already published *Travels* in homage to the source. In practice, as Gulliver and related literary properties have been dispersed and remixed across various formats for three centuries, we should refer to *Gulliver's Travels* as a multivalent culture-text rather than a singular book, an accretion of uncountable words and images from the hands and minds of Swift, Pope, Arbuthnot,

William Hogarth, Henry Fielding, David Garrick, Francis Newbery, J. J. Grandville, Georges Méliès, Max Fleischer, Alan Moore, Alison Fell, Asa Hiramatsu and many more creatives. I would go further: creative engagements in the broadest sense often attend to narrative motifs, not character. Advertisements and political cartoons place new bodies – and insentient objects such as eggs, watches and cars – under the ropes that had tethered the Man Mountain to the Lilliputian shore. They are not necessarily relying on the target audience's understanding of the reference, even while they replay such an iconic scene. Throughout this book, following Matthew Freeman's model of transmedia storytelling, I have concentrated on character-building and authorship and, to a lesser extent, world-building. My approach has been largely formalist as I have identified narrative motifs and persistent tropes across competing environments only insofar as they reveal something about communal characterization. Where relevant, I outlined the commercial contexts in which adaptative works have been produced and consumed. Beyond this study, more attention might be applied to audiences, particularly participatory cultures. In arranging the materials, I have relied on archontic selectiveness over canonical restrictiveness – the sheer mass of Gulliveriana, however narrowly defined, makes the alternative an unhelpful task. To gauge unguarded engagements with *Travels*, beyond academia or the classroom, I also used non-academic resources found online and throughout the world (for a full list, see Primary Resources in the Bibliography). As a cultural afterlife is, to reiterate, messy, many perishable items have been lost or have eluded catalogues outright.

What remains in our museum of Gulliveriana can still reveal much about the author-explorer's ongoing appeal to writers and artists working in different forms and genres, both popular and literary alike, and the wider public. Emerging online fanfiction fora, such as Archive of Our Own (AO3) and fanfiction.net, provide convenient platforms for further adventures. A simple search for 'Gulliver' on AO3 yields 1,335 hits – this mainly comprises references to a seagull sailor in Nintendo's sprawling and ever-popular *Animal Crossing* game series. Narrower searches in the character field indicate the true figure of Gulliverian fanfiction hosted there falls closer to sixty pieces. In one story attuned to current social media culture, Gulliver finds yet another new kingdom, Attenation, where one's social status correlates with how much attention you receive.[5] Elsewhere, Gulliver meets Long John Silver, Fanny Hill and other public domain characters. Elsewhere again, the fanfic authors revisit specific adaptations of *Travels*, most often the Fleischer brothers' 1939 feature-length animation, *Gulliver's Travels*. Further cameos in different environments, whether the creative industries or newspapers (or theme parks, playparks and shops), are always likely since a firm precedent was set long ago. Within months of the publication of *Travels*, people claimed to know the fantastical sea captain personally, and further sightings popped up in different parts of the press. Gulliveriads, in which unconnected travellers usurp Swift's lead character, may become more emphatic, nonetheless. This is not to suggest Gulliver can be fully displaced, even where the attention may decisively shift away from him. A forthcoming creative engagement with *Travels*, a six-part reimagining for television tentatively titled *The Gullivers* and written by Tom Bidwell, will focus on 'Gulliver's 21st century wife and children as they embark together on a lifesaving mission'.[6] Considering Swift's work as a culture-text, this means Bidwell is also engaging (directly or indirectly) with the novel-based refocalizations that represent an emerging trend in Gulliveriana. More direct adaptations are coming too, including another six-part production for television, which will be helmed by the showrunner Uberto Pasolini and written by William Ivory.[7] Beyond that, reworkings and mashups in every conceivable format surely lay ahead as we surpass the three hundredth anniversary of the first publication of *Travels*. Book-based and audio abridgements and translations will assuredly keep the author-explorer's words alive, in any case. Beyond *Travels*, the transmedia character type of the fantastical voyager, wherever it goes, will always be underwritten by Lemuel Gulliver. As the mass of materials associated with it attests, that template alone should more accurately and permanently be renamed: *a Gulliver*.

NOTES

Introduction

1 *Daily Journal* (25 May 1727), [no pagination].

2 Michael Treadwell speculates that Swift's university friend Richard Coleire, an English clergyman who survived hardships as a chaplain for the Royal Navy, may have been a model for Gulliver: 'Swift, Richard Coleire, and the Origins of *Gulliver's Travels*', *The Review of English Studies* 34, no. 135 (1983): 304–11.

3 Both quoted in H. Teerink, *A Bibliography of the Writings of Jonathan Swift*, ed. Arthur H. Scouten, 2nd edn (Philadelphia, PA: University of Pennsylvania Press, 1963), 203–4.

4 Quoted in Kathleen Williams, *Jonathan Swift: The Critical Heritage* (London and New York: Routledge, 2009 [1970]), 62–3.

5 For the contemporary reception see Jonathan Swift, *Gulliver's Travels*, ed. Harold Williams (London: First Edition Club, 1926), xxvii–xxxi.

6 Richard Saint-Gelais, 'Transfictionality', in *Routledge Encyclopedia of Narrative Theory*, ed. David Herman, Manfred Jahn and Marie-Laure Ryan (New York: Routledge, 2005), 612–13 (612).

7 Lars Elleström, *Transmedial Narration: Narratives and Stories in Different Media* (Basingstoke and New York: Palgrave Macmillan, 2019), 6.

8 Henry Jenkins, 'Transmedia Storytelling 101', *Pop Junctions* (21 March 2007), http://henryjenkins.org/blog/2007/03/transmedia_storytelling_101.html. See also Henry Jenkins, *Convergence Culture: Where Old and New Media Collide* (New York: New York University Press, 2006).

9 Paolo Bertetti, 'Transmedia Archaeology: Narrative Expansions across Media before the Age of Convergence', in *The Routledge Companion to Transmedia Studies*, ed. Matthew Freeman and Renira Rampazzo Gambarato (London and New York: Routledge, 2019), 263–71 (266). See also Carlos A. Scolari, Paolo Bertetti and Matthew Freeman, 'Introduction: Towards an Archaeology of Transmedia Storytelling', in *Transmedia Archaeology: Storytelling in the Borderlines of Science Fiction, Comics and Pulp Magazines* (Basingstoke and New York: Palgrave Macmillan, 2014), 1–14.

10 For a compelling model of how to examine transmedial fandom and fan studies before the age of media convergence see Erica Haugtvedt, *Transfictional Character and Transmedia Storyworlds in the British Nineteenth Century* (Basingstoke and New York: Palgrave Macmillan, 2022).

11 Matthew Freeman, *Historicising Transmedia Storytelling: Early Twentieth-Century Story Worlds* (London and New York: Routledge, 2017), 9.

12 Freeman, *Historicising Transmedia Storytelling*, 25–6.

13 Pierre Bayle, *A General Dictionary, Historical and Critical*, ed. John Peter Bernard, Thomas Birch and John Lockman, 10 vols (London: G. Strahan, J. Clarke, et al., 1734–41), VI.293.

14 Jonathan Swift, *Gulliver's Travels*, ed. David Womersley (Cambridge: Cambridge University Press, 2012), 437. Hereafter cited in parentheses as *GT*. Most modern editions follow the 1735 text. For the 1726 text see *Gulliver's Travels*, ed. Williams.

15 On ancient and contemporary satiric contexts see Pat Rogers, 'Satire', in *The Cambridge Companion to Gulliver's Travels*, ed. Daniel Cook and Nicholas Seager (Cambridge: Cambridge University Press, 2023), 73–84.

16 Jan-Noël Thon, 'Transmedia Characters: Theory and Analysis', *Frontiers of Narrative Studies* 5, no. 2 (2019): 176–99 (184).

17 Deidre Lynch, 'A Character of Character, in Five Metaphors', in *A Companion to the English Novel*, ed. Stephen Arata, Madigan Haley, J. Paul Hunter and Jennifer Wicke (Oxford: Wiley Blackwell, 2019 [2015]), 209–24 (213).

18 Brian Richardson, 'Transtextual Characters', in *Characters in Fictional Worlds: Understanding Imaginary Beings in Literature, Film, and Other Media*, ed. Jens Eder, Potis Jahnidis and Ralf Schneider (Berlin: De Gruyter, 2010), 527–41.

19 Richardson, 'Transtextual Characters', 534.

20 Marie-Laure Ryan, 'Transmedia Storytelling and Transfictionality', *Poetics Today* 34, no. 3 (2013): 361–88.

21 Paolo Bertetti, 'Toward a Typology of Transmedia Characters', *International Journal of Communication* 8 (2014): 2344–61 (2345).

22 Freeman, *Historicising Transmedia Storytelling*, 23.

23 Tobias Kunz and Lukas R. A. Wilde, *Transmedia Character Studies* (London and New York: Routledge, 2023), 51.

24 Richardson, 'Transtextual Characters', 532.

25 See Stephen Karian, 'The Texts of *Gulliver's Travels*', in *Les Voyages de Gulliver: Mondes Lointains ou Mondes Proches*, ed. Daniel Carey and François Boulaire (Caen: Presses Universitaires de Caen, 2002), 35–50.

26 Frederik N. Smith, 'Vexing Voices: The Telling of Gulliver's Story', *Papers on Language and Literature* 21, no. 4 (1985): 383–98 (394). Robert C. Elliott had earlier proposed that the fictive premise of *Travels* relies on a double point of view, that of the older Gulliver who comments on his past self, and the naïve seaman: 'Gulliver as Literary Artist', *ELH* 19, no. 1 (1952): 49–63 (50).

27 Loyd Douglas, *The Worlds of Lemuel Gulliver* (Stillwater, OK: Oklahoma State University, 1968), 3–19.

28 See W. B. Carnochan, 'Some Roles of Lemuel Gulliver', *Texas Studies in Literature and Language* 5, no. 4 (1964): 520–9, and Raymond J. Smith Jr, 'The "Character" of Lemuel Gulliver', *Tennessee Studies in Literature* 10 (1965): 133–9.

29 For a pertinent discussion of aesthetic considerations in the adaptation of literature to comics and other media see Dirk Vanderbeke, 'It Was the Best of Two Worlds, It Was the Worst of Two Worlds: The Adaptation of Novels in Comics and Graphic Novels', in *The Rise and Reason of Comics and Graphic Literature: Critical Essays on the Form*, ed. Joyce Goggin and Dan Hassler-Forest (Jefferson, NC: McFarland, 2010), 104–18, and Paul Ferstl, 'Novel-based Comics', in *Comics as a Nexus of Cultures: Essays on the Interplay of Media, Disciplines and International Perspectives*, ed. Mark Berninger, Jochen Ecke and Gideon Haberkorn (Jefferson, NC: McFarland, 2010), 60–9.

30 Lionel Basney, 'Gulliver and the Children', in *The Voice of the Narrator in Children's Literature*, ed. Charlotte F. Otten and Gary D. Schmidt (Westport, CT: Greenwood Press, 1989), 148–58 (150).

31 Frederick Bracher suggests Lemuel Gulliver was 'born' late in the creative process as he did not need to be identified until the manuscript went to press: 'The Name "Lemuel Gulliver"', *Huntington Library Quarterly* 12, no. 4 (1949): 409–13 (410).

32 For discussions of Swift's thwarted position in the history of the novel see J. Paul Hunter, '*Gulliver's Travels* and the Novel', in *The Genres of Gulliver's Travels*, ed. Frederik N. Smith (Newark, DE: University of Delaware Press, 1990), 56–74; J. A. Downie, 'Swift and the Making of the English Novel', in *Reading Swift: Papers from The Third Münster Symposium on Jonathan Swift*, ed. Hermann J. Real and Helgard Stöver-Leidig (Munich: Wilhelm Fink, 1998), 179–87; and Clement Hawes, 'Gulliver Effects', in *Reading Swift: Papers from The Sixth Münster Symposium on Jonathan Swift*, ed. Kirsten Juhas, Hermann J. Real and Sandra Simon (Munich: Wilhelm Fink, 2013), 523–41.

33 C. J. Rawson, 'Gulliver and the Gentle Reader', in *Imagined Worlds: Essays on Some English Novels and Novelists in Honor of John Butt*, ed. Maynard Mack and Ian Gregor (London: Methuen, 1968), 51–90 (79–80).

34 Robert C. Elliott, *The Power of Satire: Magic, Ritual, Art* (Princeton, NJ: Princeton University Press, 1972 [1960]), 191.

35 David Fishelov, 'Gulliver as a Novelistic, Quixotic Character? A Response to Aaron R. Hanlon', *Connotations* 23, no. 1 (2013/14): 79–95 (82).

36 Denis Donoghue, 'The Brainwashing of Lemuel Gulliver', *The Southern Review* 32, no. 1 (1996): 128–46.

37 Basney, 'Gulliver and the Children', 152.

38 Rita Felski, 'Identifying with Characters', in Amanda Anderson, Rita Felski and Toril Moi, *Character: Three Inquiries in Literary Studies* (Chicago, IL: The University of Chicago Press, 2019), 77–126 (78).

39 Amie L. Thomasson, *Fiction and Metaphysics* (Cambridge: Cambridge University Press, 1998), 35–42.

40 For a comprehensive cultural history of character see Marjorie Garber, *Character: The History of a Cultural Obsession* (New York: Farrar, Straus and Giroux, 2020).

41 Peter Lamarque, 'How to Create a Fictional Character', in *The Creation of Art: New Essays in Philosophical Aesthetics*, ed. Berys Gaut and Paisley Livingston (Cambridge: Cambridge University Press, 2003), 33–52. For a formalist approach see John Frow, *Character and Person* (Oxford: Oxford University Press, 2016 [2014]).

42 Thomas Docherty, *Reading (Absent) Character: Towards a Theory of Characterization in Fiction* (Oxford: Clarendon Press, 1983), 48.

43 Lynch, 'A Character of Character, in Five Metaphors', 222.

44 Baruch Hochman, *Character in Literature* (Ithaca, NY and London: Cornell University Press, 1985), 105.

45 Shane Denson and Ruth Mayer, 'Border Crossings: Serial Figures and the Evolution of Media', *NECSUS* 7 (2018): 65–84 (67–8).

46 Shane Denson and Ruth Mayer, 'Spectral Seriality: The Sights and Sounds of Count Dracula', in *Media of Serial Narrative*, ed. Frank Kelleter (Columbus, OH: Ohio State University Press, 2017), 108–24 (110).

47 David A. Brewer, *The Afterlife of Character, 1726-1825* (Philadelphia, PA: University of Pennsylvania Press, 2005), 78–120.

48 See Jan-Noël Thon and Roberta Pearson, 'Transmedia Characters', *Narrative* 30, no. 2 (2022): 139–51 (143).

49 See Uri Margolin, 'Characters and Their Versions', in *Fiction Updated: Theories of Fictionality, Narratology, and Poetics*, ed. Calin-Andrei Mihailescu and Walid Hamarneh (Toronto and Buffalo, NY: University of Toronto Press, 1996), 113–32 (117).

50 Freeman, *Historicising Transmedia Storytelling*, 8.

51 Gérard Genette, *Palimpsests: Literature in the Second Degree*, trans. Channa Newman and Claude Doubinsky (Lincoln, NE and London: University of Nebraska Press, 1997 [1982]), 306.

52 Charles Solomon, *The History of Animation: Enchanted Drawings* (Avenel, NJ: Wings Books, 1994), 80.

53 David Cowart, *Literary Symbiosis: The Reconfigured Text in Twentieth-Century Writing* (Athens, GA and London: University of Georgia Press, 1993), 4–5.

54 Christian Moraru, *Rewriting: Postmodern Narrative and Cultural Critique in the Age of Cloning* (Albany, NY: State University of New York Press, 2001), 9.

55 See Abigail Derecho, 'Archontic Literature: A Definition, a History, and Several Theories of Fan Fiction', in *Fan Fiction and Fan Communities in the Age of the Internet*, ed. Karen Hellekson and Kristina Busse (Jefferson, NC: McFarland, 2006), 61–78.

Chapter 1

1 Francisco Solano Constancio, *The Ghost*, no. 35 (27 August 1796), in *The Ghost, by Felix Phantom. Part Second* (Edinburgh: G. Mudie & Son, 1796), 37–40 (37).

2 See Jonathan Swift, *Gulliver's Travels*, ed. David Womersley (Cambridge: Cambridge University Press, 2012), Part 4, Chapter 12. Hereafter cited in parentheses as *GT*.

3 Daniel Defoe refers to an author's published book as the 'Child of his Inventions, the Brat of his Brain' within a complaint that 'these Children of our Heads are seiz'd, captivated, spirited away, and carry'd into Captivity, and there is none to redeem them': see Elizabeth F. Judge, 'Kidnapped and Counterfeit Characters: Eighteenth-Century Fan Fiction, Copyright Law, and the Custody of Fictional Characters', in *Originality and Intellectual Property in the French and English Enlightenment*, ed. Reginald McGinnis (London and New York: Routledge, 2012 [2009]), 22–68 (52–3 and passim).

4 See *Rewriting Crusoe: The Robinsonade across Languages, Cultures, and Media*, ed. Jakub Lipski (Lewisburg, PA: Bucknell University Press, 2020).

5 Constancio, *The Ghost*, 37.

6 Jonathan Swift, *A Tale of a Tub and Other Works*, ed. Marcus Walsh (Cambridge: Cambridge University Press, 2010), 135.

7 Jonathan Smedley, *Gulliveriana: or, a Fourth Volume of Miscellanies* (London: J. Roberts, 1728), 118.

8 Six of the letters are reproduced in *Gulliveriana*, ed. Jeanne K. Welcher and George E. Bush Jr, 8 vols (Gainesville, FL: Scholars' Facsimiles & Reprints, 1970–99), V.219–52.

9 *Blackwood's Edinburgh Magazine* 55 (1844): 98–100.

10 'Appendix to Capt. Lemuel Gulliver's Account of the Famous Empire of Lilliput', in *Samuel Johnson's Parliamentary Reporting: Debates in the Senate of Lilliput*, ed. Benjamin Beard Hoover (Berkeley and Los Angeles, CA: University of California Press, 1953), 172–81 (175, 173).

11 See Daniel Cook, 'Vexed Diversions: *Gulliver's Travels*, the Arts, and Popular Entertainment', in *The Edinburgh Companion to the Eighteenth-Century Novel and the Arts*, ed. Jakub Lipski and M.-C. Newbould (Edinburgh: Edinburgh University Press, 2024), 228–43.

12 For an account of the materials that precede the main narratives of the 1726 and 1735 versions of *Gulliver's Travels*, see Brean Hammond, 'Advertisements and Authorship', in *The Cambridge Companion to Gulliver's Travels*, ed. Daniel Cook and Nicholas Seager (Cambridge: Cambridge University Press, 2023), 111–24.

13 See Michael Treadwell, 'Benjamin Motte, Andrew Tooke and *Gulliver's Travels*', in *Proceedings of The First Münster Symposium on Jonathan Swift*, ed. Hermann J. Real and Heinz J. Vienken (Munich: Wilhelm Fink, 1985), 287–304. See also Treadwell, 'Observations on the Printing of Motte's Octavo Editions of *Gulliver's Travels*', in *Reading Swift: Papers from The Third Münster Symposium on Jonathan Swift*, ed. Hermann J. Real and Helgard Stöver-Leidig (Munich: Wilhelm Fink, 1998), 157–77, and James McLaverty, 'The Revision of the First Edition of *Gulliver's Travels*: Book-Trade Context, Interleaving, Two Cancels, and a Failure to Catch', *The Papers of the Bibliographical Society of America* 106 (2012): 5–35. For a history of bowdlerized versions of *Travels* see Noel Perrin, *Dr Bowdler's Legacy: A History of Expurgated Books in England and America* (New York: Atheneum, 1969), 224–9.

14 See Clauston Jenkins, 'The Ford Changes and the Text of *Gulliver's Travels*', *The Papers of the Bibliographical Society of America* 62 (1968): 1–23.

15 Alan D. Chalmers, *Jonathan Swift and the Burden of the Future* (Newark, DE: University of Delaware Press, 1995), 124–9 (129). See also Antony Easthope, 'The Disappearance of Gulliver: Character and Persona at the End of the "Travels"', *The Southern Review* 2 (1967): 261–6.

16 Stephen Karian, 'Problems and Paratexts in Eighteenth-Century Collections of Swift', *Studies in the Literary Imagination* 32, no. 1 (1999): 59–80 (71).

17 *Gulliveriana*, ed. Welcher and Bush, V.220.

18 *Travels into Several Remote Nations of the World. Faithfully Abridged* (London: J. Stone and R. King, 1727), i. On chapbooks see Michael J. Preston, 'Rethinking Folklore, Rethinking Literature: Looking at *Robinson Crusoe* and *Gulliver's Travels* as Folktales, A Chapbook-Inspired Inquiry', in *The Other Print Tradition: Essays on Chapbooks, Broadsides, and Related Ephemera*, ed. Cathy Lynn Preston and Michael J. Preston (New York: Garland, 1995), 19–73. This includes facsimile images from *The Adventures of Captain Gulliver, in a Voyage to Lilliput* (Glasgow: J. Lumsden & Son, 1815).

19 See Robert Bator, 'Jonathan Swift', in *Writers for Children: Critical Studies of Major Authors Since the Seventeenth Century*, ed. Jane M. Bingham (New York: Scribner's, 1988), 555–9. While dozens of copies of the expanded 1776 version of Newbery's *Adventures* (32mo) have survived, the 1772 edition (12mo) is comparably rarer.

20 Julian Fung, 'Early Condensations of *Gulliver's Travels*: Images of Swift as Satirist in the 1720s', *Studies in Philology* 114, no. 2 (2017): 395–425 (423).

21 See Ulrich Elkmann and Hermann J. Real, 'Gulliver's Travels to Several Remote Nations of the World: A Bibliography of Translations into Remote Languages', *Swift Studies* 32 (2017): 117–32. For a timeline of European translations of *Travels* and related works, among other items, see 'Timeline: European Reception of Jonathan Swift', in *The Reception of Jonathan Swift in Europe*, ed. Hermann J. Real (London and New York: Thoemmes Continuum, 2005), xix–xxxii.

22 M. Sarah Smedman examined fifty-five versions of *Travels* for children published between 1727 and 1985 in the United States and Great Britain: 'Like Me, Like Me Not: *Gulliver's Travels* as Children's Book', in *The Genres of Gulliver's Travels*, ed. Frederik N. Smith (Newark, DE: University of Delaware Press, 1990), 75–100. See also Mary Shine Thompson, '*Gulliver's Travels* in the Lands of Childhood', in *Young Irelands: Studies in Children's Literature*, ed. Mary Shine Thompson (Dublin: Four Courts Press, 2011), 164–86, and Haifeng Hui, 'The Changing Adaptation Strategies of Children's Literature: Two Centuries of Children's Editions of *Gulliver's Travels*', *Hungarian Journal of English and American Studies* 17, no. 2 (2011): 245–62.

23 On such series see Ruth Menzies, 'Children's Versions of *Gulliver's Travels* and the Question of Horizons of Expectation: From Biting Satire to Exciting Adventure Story', in *Horizons*, ed. Catherine Delmas and Isabelle Gadoin, *Représentations: Revue électronique du CEMRA*, 3 (2011): 43–51.

24 Jonathan Coe, *The Story of Gulliver*, illustrated by Sara Oddi (London: Pushkin Press, 2018 [2013]), back cover.

25 *Gulliveriana*, ed. Welcher and Bush, VII.cxvii.

26 *An Account of the State of Learning in the Empire of Lilliput* (1728), in
Gulliveriana, ed. Welcher and Bush, V.183.

27 Jeanne K. Welcher, 'Gulliveriana: Ways of Reading *Gulliver's Travels*', in
Approaches to Teaching Swift's Gulliver's Travels, ed. Edward J. Rielly (New
York: MLA, 1988), 96–101 (97).

28 Brian Richardson, 'Transtextual Characters', in *Characters in Fictional
Worlds: Understanding Imaginary Beings in Literature, Film, and Other
Media*, ed. Jens Eder, Potis Jahnidis and Ralf Schneider (Berlin: De Gruyter,
2010), 527–41 (534).

29 *Gulliveriana*, ed. Welcher and Bush, I.v.

30 Nicholas Seager, '*Gulliver's Travels* Serialized and Continued', in *Reading
Swift: Papers from The Sixth Münster Symposium on Jonathan Swift*, ed.
Kirsten Juhas, Hermann J. Real and Sandra Simon (Munich: Wilhelm Fink,
2013), 543–62 (551).

31 Matthew Freeman, *Historicising Transmedia Storytelling: Early Twentieth-
Century Story Worlds* (London and New York: Routledge, 2017), 9.

32 Marie-Laure Ryan, 'Transmedia Storytelling and Transfictionality', *Poetics
Today* 34, no. 3 (2013): 361–88.

33 David A. Brewer, *The Afterlife of Character, 1726-1825* (Philadelphia, PA:
University of Pennsylvania Press, 2005), 39.

34 See Peter L. Abernathy and Michael C. Stoune, 'Swift, Telemann, and
Gulliver's Travels', *Eighteenth-Century Life* 3 (1977): 71–6, and Jeanne K.
Welcher, *Gulliveriana VIII: An Annotated List of Gulliveriana, 1721-1800*
(New York: Scholars' Facsimiles & Reprints, 1988), 131–2.

35 In a one-page prefatory notice in the collection, Motoyuki Shibati advocates
for 'reading' the illustrations as both translations of and commentaries
on *Travels*: 'I Wish Swift Could See This' (translated by Sam Malissa), in
Asa Hiramatsu, *Travelogue G: Illustrations for Gulliver's Travels* (Tokyo:
Suitchipaburisshingu, 2022).

36 *A Compleat History of the Lives and Robberies of the Most Notorious
Highway-men, Foot-pads, Shop-lifts, and Cheats, of Both Sexes, in and about
London and Westminster* reached a fifth edition as recently as 1719. Captain
Smith had disappeared from the print marketplace by 1726.

37 Quoted in Welcher, *Gulliveriana VIII*, 109.

38 Smedley, *Gulliveriana*, 4–10 (4).

39 Linda Hutcheon, *A Theory of Adaptation*, 2nd edn (London and New York:
Routledge, 2013 [2006]), 84, 88.

40 See Nicholas Seager, 'Samuel Richardson and the Third Volume of *Gulliver's
Travels*', *Swift Studies* 28 (2013): 128–36.

41 Walter Scott, *Sir Walter Scott on Novels and Novelists*, ed. Ioan Williams (London: Routledge and Kegan Paul, 1968), 153.

42 Seager, '*Gulliver's Travels* Serialized and Continued', 557–8.

43 *Gulliveriana*, ed. Welcher and Bush, III.x.

44 Samuel Richardson, *Travels into Several Remote Nations of the World. Vol. III* (London, 1727), 2–3.

45 *Memoirs of the Court of Lilliput* (London: J. Roberts, 1727), viii.

46 On Haywood's authorship see Seager, '*Gulliver's Travels* Serialized and Continued', 552, and *Gulliveriana*, ed. Welcher and Bush, III.ix–x. For de-attribution see Leah Orr, 'The Basis for Attribution in the Canon of Eliza Haywood', *The Library*, 7th series 12 (2011): 335–75 (374).

47 *A Cursory View of the History of Lilliput for these last forty three Years* (1727), in *Gulliveriana*, ed. Welcher and Bush, V.108, 110.

48 *Gulliveriana*, ed. Welcher and Bush, V.xxiv.

49 On authorship see *Gulliveriana*, ed. Welcher and Bush, V.xxviii.

50 Gérard Genette, *Palimpsests: Literature in the Second Degree*, trans. Channa Newman and Claude Doubinsky (Lincoln, NE and London: University of Nebraska Press, 1997 [1982]), 177.

51 *Gulliveriana*, ed. Welcher and Bush, V.194.

52 Seager, '*Gulliver's Travels* Serialized and Continued', 554.

53 *Gulliveriana*, ed. Welcher and Bush, V.201.

54 On Gulliver's language see Paul Odell Clark, 'A Gulliver Dictionary', *Studies in Philology* 50, no. 4 (1953): 592–624.

55 *The Anatomist Dissected: or the Man-Midwife finely brought to Bed* (Westminster: A. Campbell, 1727), 3.

56 *Gulliveriana*, ed. Welcher and Bush, VI(I).lxiii.

57 Henry Fielding, *The Masquerade: A Poem* (London: J. Roberts, 1728), 2–3.

58 J. Roberts had published another verse satire on Heidegger, also called *The Masquerade, A Poem*, two years before the publication of *Travels* and therefore without the timely conflation with Gulliver. Fielding's poem is markedly different, in any case.

59 *The Flying Island, &c. Being a Key to Gulliver's Voyage to Laputa, Balnibarbi, Glubbdubdribb* [sic], *Luggnagg, and Japan* (London, 1726), 20. See also Stephen J. Bernard, 'Jonathan Swift and *A Key, Being Observations and Explanatory Notes, upon the Travels of Lemuel Gulliver*, with a New Edition of the Key', *Swift Studies* 27 (2012): 87–119.

60 See Judge, 'Kidnapped and Counterfeit Characters', 52.

61 *Sequel to Gulliver's Travels. An Eulogy* (London: J. Jaques, 1830), 3–4.

62 Matthew Hodgart, *A New Voyage to the Country of the Houyhnhnms* (New York: G. P. Putnam's Sons, 1969), 7.

63 On Fell and others see Ruth Menzies, 'Re-writing *Gulliver's Travels*: The Demise of a Genre?', *E-Rea* 3, no. 1 (2005): 87–93.

64 Jeremy Rosen discusses the rise of minor-character elaborations from the late 1960s to the 2010s in *Minor Characters Have their Day: Genre and the Contemporary Literary Marketplace* (New York: Columbia University Press, 2016).

65 Modern scholars usually follow Norman Ault's attribution of all five poems to Pope: *New Light on Pope* (Hamden, CT: Archon Books, 1967 [1949]), 231–42. George Sherburn instead suggests Pope may have revised the poems on behalf of the Scriblerian circle, which also included John Arbuthnot and John Gay: 'The "Copies of Verses" about Gulliver', *Texas Studies in Literature and Language* 3, no. 1 (1961): 3–7.

66 Brewer, *The Afterlife of Character, 1726–825*, 36.

67 See Thomas Van der Goten, 'The Lilliputian Ode, 1726-1826', *ANQ* 28, no. 2 (2015): 94–104.

68 Quoted in *Gulliveriana*, ed. Welcher and Bush, VI(I).lxxii.

69 John Gay, *Poetry and Prose*, ed. Vinton A. Dearing with Charles E. Beckwith, 2 vols (Oxford: Clarendon Press, 1974), II.449.

70 Smedley, *Gulliveriana*, 266.

71 For a reading of the poem see Alan T. McKenzie, '"The Lamentation of Glumdalclitch for the Loss of Grildrig. A Pastoral": What We Have Been Missing', *Texas Studies in Literature and Language* 12, no. 4 (1971): 583–94.

72 Sheenagh Pugh, *The Democratic Genre: Fan Fiction in a Literary Context* (Bridgend: Seren, 2015 [2005]), 71.

73 Antony Johae reproduces the poem in full, with contextual analysis, in 'Wole Soyinka's "Gulliver": Swift Transposed', *Comparative Literature* 53, no. 1 (2001): 27–41. See also Peter Sabor, 'Wole Soyinka and the Scriblerians', *Journal of Postcolonial Writing* 29, no. 1 (1989): 43–52.

74 Translation by Michael Düring in 'No Swift beyond Gulliver: Notes on the Polish Reception', in *The Reception of Jonathan Swift in Europe*, ed. Real, 156–69 (156).

75 See Dan Sperrin, 'The Augustan Plath: "Gulliver" and Other Poems', *Journal of Modern Literature* 47, no. 1 (2023): 98–117.

76 Sperrin, 'The Augustan Plath', 110.

77 Michael Düring, 'From Russian "Sviftovedenie" to the Soviet School of Swift Criticism: The Dean's Fate in Russia', in *The Reception of Jonathan Swift in Europe*, ed. Real, 170–213 (211–12).

78 Düring, 'From Russian "Sviftovedenie" to the Soviet School of Swift Criticism', 212.

79 Mortimer Collins, *Squire Silchester's Whim*, 2 vols (London: Henry S. King, 1873), I.48.

80 Lewis Jesse Bridgman, *Gulliver's Bird Book* (Boston, MA: L.C. Page, [*c*.1901]), [i].

81 Louis Hermann, *In the Sealed Cave* (New York: D. Appleton-Century Company, 1935), 28.

82 Thomas Wolfe, 'Gulliver: The Story of a Tall Man', in *The Complete Short Stories of Thomas Wolfe*, ed. Francis E. Skipp (New York: Scribner's, 1989), 241–9 (242).

Chapter 2

1 See Jeanne K. Welcher, 'Horace Walpole and *Gulliver's Travels*', *Studies in Eighteenth-Century Culture* 12 (1983): 45–57, and Peter Sabor, '"St Jonathan" or "wild beast": Horace Walpole's Swift', in *Reading Swift: Papers from The Third Münster Symposium on Jonathan Swift*, ed. Hermann J. Real and Helgard Stöver-Leidig (Munich: Wilhelm Fink, 1998), 321–36.

2 Letter to the editor of *The London Journal* (26 November 1726), in *Gulliveriana*, ed. Jeanne K. Welcher and George E. Bush Jr, 8 vols (Gainesville, FL: Scholars' Facsimiles & Reprints, 1970–99), V.81.

3 *Gulliveriana*, ed. Welcher and Bush, V.xix–xxii, 92–7.

4 On Swift's engagement with the long-established mode of political analogy see David Bywaters, '*Gulliver's Travels* and the Mode of Political Parallel During Walpole's Administration', *ELH* 54, no. 3 (1987): 717–40.

5 *The Flapper* (2 February 1796), in *Gulliveriana*, ed. Welcher and Bush, VI(3).

6 'Gulliver's Last Voyage', *The Monthly Review* (July 1903): 1–17 (11).

7 *Gulliver Joe* (London: Ibister & Company, 1903), 13. The authors have been identified as Cecil Eldred Hughes and E. Harold Begbie in the British Library catalogue.

8 *Gulliver's Last Voyage, describing Ballymugland, or the Floating Island* (London: William Cole, 1825), 10.

9 Matthew Hodgart, *A New Voyage to the Country of the Houyhnhnms* (New York: G. P. Putnam's Sons, 1969), 32.

10 John Paul Brady, *A Voyage to Inishneefa* (Santa Barbara, CA: John Daniel, 1987), 103.

11 Kurt Friedlaender, *A Voyage to Springistan* (Stockholm: AB Seelig & Co, 1972), 11.

12 Jeremy Rosen, *Minor Characters Have their Day: Genre and the Contemporary Literary Marketplace* (New York: Columbia University Press, 2016), 2.

13 Rosen, *Minor Characters Have their Day*, 17. Alternatively, for an historicist reading of Mary Gulliver fictions that charts changing attitudes towards women in literature, see Ruth Menzies, 'Mary Gulliver, an Emblem of Sexual Rebirth?', in *Littérature anglo-saxonne au féminin: (Re)naissance(s) et horizons XVIIIe siècle - XXe siècle*, ed. Claire Bazin and Guyonne Leduc (Paris: L'Harmattan, 2012), 55–68.

14 Rosen, *Minor Characters Have their Day*, 180.

15 Christian Moraru, *Rewriting: Postmodern Narrative and Cultural Critique in the Age of Cloning* (Albany, NY: State University of New York Press, 2001), 9.

16 Rosen, *Minor Characters Have their Day*, 135. See Linda Hutcheon, *A Theory of Adaptation*, 2nd edn (London and New York: Routledge, 2013 [2006]), 4.

17 Jonathan Swift, *Gulliver's Travels*, ed. David Womersley (Cambridge: Cambridge University Press, 2010), 218. Hereafter cited in parentheses as *GT*.

18 Davy King, 'The Woman Gulliver Left Behind' (1978), 1–13 (1), www.davyking.com.

19 John Kessel, 'Gulliver at Home', *The Pure Product* (New York: Tom Doherty, 1997), 329–43 (329).

20 Karen Joy Fowler, 'The Travails', *Black Glass: Short Fictions* (New York: Ballantine Books, 1999), 84–95 (84).

21 See *The Cambridge Companion to Gulliver's Travels*, ed. Daniel Cook and Nicholas Seager (Cambridge: Cambridge University Press, 2023), xvi–xix.

22 For the wider context of minor-character elaborations since the 1960s, along with expanded readings of the Mary Gulliver fictions, see Daniel Cook, 'Mrs Gulliver's Travels: Minor-Character Elaboration in Theory and Practice', *Critical Quarterly* 67 (2024), 1–20 (3).

23 Alison Fell, *The Mistress of Lilliput or The Pursuit* (London: Doubleday, 1999), 43. Monica Germanà examines Fell's feminist engagement with the romantic quest in *Scottish Women's Gothic and Fantastic Writing: Fiction since 1978* (Edinburgh: Edinburgh University Press, 2010), 48–54.

24 For an extended reading of the problematic presentation of the female body in rewritings of canonical texts see Monica Germanà, 'Rewriting Female Monstrosity: (Schizoid) Misogyny in Alison Fell's *The Mistress of Lilliput* and Emma Tennant's *Two Women of London*', in *Women's Writing in Western Europe: Gender, Generation and Legacy*, ed. Adalgisa Giorgio and Julia Waters (Newcastle upon Tyne: Cambridge Scholars Publishing, 2007), 102–17.

25 Lauren Chater, *Gulliver's Wife* (Sydney: Simon & Schuster, 2020), 43.

26 Erga Netz, *Oh, Gulliver! Mrs Gulliver and the Secret of Size* (Arlington, MA: Tough Poets Press, 2023), 11.

27 W. R. Irwin considers T. H. White's *Mistress Masham's Repose* and Walter de la Mare's *Memoirs of a Midget* to be the 'principal exhibits of *Gulliver's Travels* adapted': 'Swift and the Novelists', *Philological Quarterly* 45 (1966): 102–13 (113).

28 Carter Crocker, *Last of the Gullivers* (New York: Philomel Books, 2012), 30.

29 Elbert Perce, *Gulliver Joi: His Three Voyages* (New York: Charles Scribner, 1852), 13.

30 Émile Bouchery, *Les Petits-Neveux de Gulliver* (Paris: Librairie Pittoresque de la Jeunesse, 1845), 9.

31 Algernon Cecil, 'Gulliver Redivivus', *Essays in Imitation* (London: John Murray, 1910), 59–128.

32 Privately printed as *A Fragment of the Voyages of Mr. V. G.* (Middle Hill, 1832) [The British Library, Tab.436.b.1.(10.)].

33 See Paul-Gabriel Boucé, 'Gulliver's Frenchified Travels to Blefescu: The First Two Translations', in *Reading Swift: Papers from The Fourth Münster Symposium on Jonathan Swift*, ed. Hermann J. Real and Helgard Stöver-Leidig (Munich: Wilhelm Fink, 2003), 379–86. See also Mary Helen McMurran, 'Translation as Offence: The Case of Desfontaines', *Translation and Literature* 17 (2008): 150–64.

34 Pierre-François Guyot Desfontaines, *The Travels of Mr. John Gulliver, Son to Capt. Lemuel Gulliver*, trans. John Lockman, 2 vols (London: Sam. Harding, 1731), 'The French Editor's Preface', 1.2–3 (italics reversed).

35 Desfontaines, *The Travels of Mr. John Gulliver*, 'The French Editor's Preface', 1.7.

36 Desfontaines, *The Travels of Mr. John Gulliver*, 'The Travels of John Gulliver, &c', 1.2. The pagination begins again after 'The French Editor's Preface'.

37 Elizabeth Susanna Davenport Graham, *Voyage to Locuta; A Fragment* (London: J. Hatchard, 1818), 9. See Hutcheon, *A Theory of Adaptation*, 4.

38   Colin Milne, *So This Is Glasgow!* (Glasgow: Jackson, Son & Company, 1938), 1.

39   *A Trip to the Moon* (London and Dublin: J. Roberts, 1728), in *Gulliveriana*, ed. Welcher and Bush, I.91.

40   *A Voyage to Cacklogallinia* (London: J. Watson, 1727), 42.

41   See *Gulliveriana*, ed. Welcher and Bush, IV.xxiii–xxvii.

42   Michael Morpurgo, *Boy Giant* (London: HarperCollins, 2019), 57.

43   See Gabriella Hartvig, 'Hungarian Gulliveriads: Gulliver's Travels in Faremidó, Capillária, and Kazohinia', in *Reading Swift: Papers from The Fifth Münster Symposium on Jonathan Swift*, ed. Hermann J. Real (Munich: Wilhelm Fink, 2008), 519–31. An anonymous follow-up to Szathmári's *Voyage* appeared on Amazon's self-publishing platform in 2018: *Gulliver's Return: A Sequel to Voyage to Kazohinia* moves the action forward to 1940, initially, and then a further seventy years.

44   Peter Noçon, 'Rediscovered Gulliveriana from World-War-II Germany', *Swift Studies* 7 (1992): 70–7 (74–7). See also Peter Noçon, 'Versions of the Dean: Swift in Modern German Fiction and Drama', in *The Reception and Reputation of Jonathan Swift in Germany: Essays and Investigations*, ed. Hermann J. Real, with the assistance of Melanie Just, Neil Key and Helga Scholz (Bethesda, MD; Dublin; Oxford and London: Maunsel & Company, 2002), 325–51.

45   Michael Düring, 'From Russian "Sviftovedenie" to the Soviet School of Swift Criticism: The Dean's Fate in Russia', in *The Reception of Jonathan Swift in Europe*, ed. Hermann J. Real (London and New York: Thoemmes Continuum, 2005), 170–213 (210–11).

46   See Astrid Krake, Hermann J. Real and Marie-Luise Spieckermann, 'The Dean's Voyages into Germany', in *The Reception of Jonathan Swift in Europe*, ed. Real, 93–41 (132). For a discussion of twentieth-century German editions of *Travels* for young readers see Heinz Kosok, 'Gulliver's Children: A Classic Transformed for Young Reader', in *Proceedings of The First Münster Symposium on Jonathan Swift*, ed. Hermann J. Real and Heinz J. Vienken (Munich: Wilhelm Fink, 1985), 135–44.

47   Simon Hawke, *The Lilliput Legion* (New York: Ace, 1989), 3.

48   Edward M. Lerner, 'My Fifth and Most Exotic Voyage', *Analog: Science Fiction and Fact* (September/October 2017): 8–27 (12).

49   See Balaka Basu, 'When Worlds Continue: The Doctor's Adventures in Fandom and Metatextuality', in *Ruminations, Peregrinations, and Regenerations: A Critical Approach to Doctor Who*, ed. Christopher J. Hansen (Newcastle upon Tyne: Cambridge Scholars Publishing, 2010), 164–76, and Marcus K. Harmes, *Doctor Who and the Art of Adaptation: Fifty Years of Storytelling* (Lanham, MD: Rowman & Littlefield Publishers, 2014), 24–8.

50 *Doctor Who: The Mind Robber*, dir. by David Maloney (BBC, 1968).

51 Peter Ling, *The Mind Robber* (*Doctor Who Library*: 115) (London: W. H. Allen & Co, 1986), 47.

52 Marc Platt, 'Future Imperfect', in *Doctor Who Year Book* (London: Marvel Comics, 1991), 18.

53 *Gulliver's Fugitives* was reissued in 1991 and 1993. An audiobook version was released in 1994, 1996 and 1999, and an e-book in 2000. On authorship in the *Star Trek* franchise novels see Sean Guynes and Gerry Canavan, 'Novels', in *The Routledge Handbook of Star Trek*, ed. Leimar Garcia-Siino, Sabrina Mittermeier and Stefan Rabitsch (London and New York: Routledge, 2022), 176–84.

54 Keith Sharee, *Gulliver's Fugitives* (*Star Trek: The Next Generation*: 11) (London: Titan Books, 1990), 5.

Chapter 3

1 See Ruth Menzies, 'Visual Culture', in *The Cambridge Companion to Gulliver's Travels*, ed. Daniel Cook and Nicholas Seager (Cambridge: Cambridge University Press, 2023), 206–23, and Nathalie Collé, '"[T] o Mix Colours for Painters" and Illustrate and Adapt *Gulliver's Travels* Worldwide: Street Murals, Adaptability and Transmediality', in *Adaptation and Illustration: New Cartographies*, ed. Shannon Wells-Lassange and Sophie Aymes (Basingstoke and New York: Palgrave Macmillan, 2024), 47–68.

2 Isaac Asimov's *The Annotated Gulliver's Travels* (New York: Clarkson N. Potter, 1980) includes more than two hundred illustrations from Gulliverian artists. See also David S. Lenfest, 'A Checklist of Illustrated Editions of *Gulliver's Travels*, 1727–1914', *The Papers of the Bibliographical Society of America* 62 (1968): 85–123, and 'Lefebvre's Illustrations of *Gulliver's Travels*', *New York Public Library Bulletin* 76 (1972): 199–213; Jeanne K. Welcher, 'Eighteenth-Century Views of Gulliver: Illustrations and Prints', in *Imagination on a Long Rein: English Literature Illustrated*, ed. Joachim Moller (Marburg: Jonas Verlag, 1988), 82–93; John F. Sena, '*Gulliver's Travels* and the Genre of the Illustrated Book', in *The Genres of Gulliver's Travels*, ed. Frederik N. Smith (Newark, DE: University of Delaware Press, 1990), 101–38; and Russell Palmer, 'Illustrating Gulliver and the Lilliputians in 1727 and 1728', *ANQ* 34, no. 3 (2021): 311–18.

3 See David S. Lenfest, 'Grandville's Gulliver', *Satire Newsletter* 10 (1973): 12–24, and Alice Colombo, 'Rewriting *Gulliver's Travels* under the Influence of J. J. Grandville's Illustrations', *Word & Image* 30, no. 4 (2014): 401–15.

4   On the contrasting styles of J. J. Grandville, Thomas Morten, Edward Bawden and other Gulliverian illustrators see Simon Cooke, 'Illustrating *Gulliver's Travels*: Fantasy and Satire', *The Book Collector* 70, no. 3 (2021): 437–48.

5   See Robert Halsband, 'Eighteenth-Century Illustrations of *Gulliver's Travels*', in *Proceedings of The First Münster Symposium on Jonathan Swift*, ed. Hermann J. Real and Heinz J. Vienken (Munich: Wilhelm Fink, 1985), 83–112 (88–9).

6   For a contrastive juxtaposition of illustrations by Morten and Whistler, albeit in black and white, see *The Annotated Gulliver's Travels*, 44.

7   Quoted in Richard D. Altick, *Paintings from Books: Art and Literature in Britain, 1760-1900* (Columbus, OH: Ohio State University Press, 1985), 382.

8   See Thierry Groensteen, *The System of Comics* (Jackson, MS: University Press of Mississippi, 2007 [1999]) and Scott McCloud, *Understanding Comics: The Invisible Art* (New York: HarperCollins, 1994).

9   John Traugott, 'The Yahoo in the Doll's House: *Gulliver's Travels* the Children's Classic', in *English Satire and the Satiric Tradition*, ed. Claude Rawson (Oxford: Basil Blackwell, 1984), 127–50.

10 For Arthur Rackham's image see *The Annotated Gulliver's Travels*, 99.

11 On collecting as a fundamental trope in *Travels* see Barbara M. Benedict, 'Material Ideas: Things and Collections in *Gulliver's Travels*', in *Reading Swift: Papers from The Sixth Münster Symposium on Jonathan Swift*, ed. Kirsten Juhas, Hermann J. Real and Sandra Simon (Munich: Wilhelm Fink, 2013), 461–81.

12 *Gulliveriana*, ed. Jeanne K. Welcher and George E. Bush Jr, 8 vols (Gainesville, FL: Scholars' Facsimiles & Reprints, 1970–99), VII.303.

13 See *Gulliveriana*, ed. Welcher and Bush, VII.42–53.

14 See Xiao Yang, 'On the History of the Chinese Translations of *Gulliver's Travels*', *ANQ* 34, no. 1 (2021): 36–61, and Te-hsing Shan, 'Gulliver's Travels to the Centre of the Earth: Three Early Translations of *Gulliver's Travels*', *Swift Studies* 17 (2022): 109–24.

15 See Sandro Jung, '*Gulliver's Travels* in China: The Illustrations for *Han Man You*', *The Book Collector* 70, no. 4 (2021): 665–79.

16 On Chris Riddell and other recent Gulliverian illustrators and adapters see Remi Majersdorf, 'Adapting Swift for an Imagined Audience: A Comparative Study of the Adaptational Strategies and Implied Child Readers of Four Twenty-First-Century Children's Versions of *Gulliver's Travels*', *Swift Studies* 35 (2020): 83–105.

17 *Les Voyages de Gulliver: De Laputa au Japon*, adapted by Bertrand Galic and illustrated by Paul Echegoyen (Paris: Soleil, 2020), 9.

18 For William Hogarth's graphic satire see *The Annotated Gulliver's Travels*, 288. See also Jeanne K. Welcher, 'Hogarth's Reading of *Gulliver's Travels*', in *Hogarth in Context: Ten Essays and a Bibliography*, ed. Joachim Möller (Marburg: Jonag Verlag, 1996), 106–16. On Hogarth's imaginative expansion of Swift's materials see Leigh G. Dillard, 'Drawing Outside the Book: Parallel Illustration and the Creation of a Visual Culture', in *Book Illustration in the Long Eighteenth Century: Reconfiguring the Visual Periphery of the Text*, ed. Christina Ionescu and Renata Schellenberg (Newcastle upon Tyne: Cambridge Scholars Publishing, 2011), 195–241 (232–5).

19 See Ads of the World, www.adsoftheworld.com/campaigns/gulliver -edf5944b-3278-4e7b-9939-c884d0fe7784.

20 For a discussion of Gulliverian political caricatures see David Francis Taylor, 'Gillray's Gulliver and the 1803 Invasion Scare', in *The Afterlives of Eighteenth-Century Fiction*, ed. Daniel Cook and Nicholas Seager (Cambridge: Cambridge University Press, 2015), 212–32, and Kirsten Juhas, 'Gulliver as a Vehicle of Satire in Twenty-First-Century Political Cartoons', *Swift Studies* 38 (2023): 105–25.

21 Thomas Kingsley Troupe and Xavier Bonet, *Midnight Library: The Gulliver Giant* (Oxford: Raintree, 2020), 37.

22 See AdForum, www.adforum.com/creative-work/ad/player/37166/talisman /breil.

23 For bibliographical accounts of the portraits see Jonathan Swift, *Gulliver's Travels*, ed. David Womersley (Cambridge: Cambridge University Press, 2012), 567–72, hereafter cited in parentheses as *GT*; H. Teerink, *A Bibliography of the Writings of Jonathan Swift*, ed. Arthur H. Scouten, 2nd edn (Philadelphia, PA: University of Pennsylvania Press, 1963), 193–4; and *Gulliveriana*, ed. Welcher and Bush, VII.xxvi–xxxiii, 1–11 and 143–7. For commentary see Peter Wagner, *Reading Iconotexts: From Swift to the French Revolution* (London: Reaktion Books, 1995), 37–74 (44–62), and Janine Barchas, *Graphic Design, Print Culture, and the Eighteenth-Century Novel* (Cambridge: Cambridge University Press, 2003), 19–59 (28–34).

24 Richard H. Rodino, '"Splendide Mendax": Authors, Characters, and Readers in *Gulliver's Travels*', *PMLA* 106, no. 5 (1991): 1054–70 (1058).

25 Jenny Mezciems, 'Utopia and "the Thing which Is Not": More, Swift, and Other Lying Idealists', *University of Toronto Quarterly* 52, no. 1 (1982): 40–62 (46), and A. W. F. Edwards, 'Is the Frontispiece of *Gulliver's Travels* a Likeness of Newton?', *Notes and Records of the Royal Society of London* 50, no. 2 (1996): 191–4. For Philippus Baldaeus see *Gulliveriana*, ed. Welcher and Bush, VII.xxix.

26 Swift, *Gulliver's Travels*, ed. Womersley, 572.

27 Wagner, *Reading Iconotexts*, 57.

28 Grant Holly, 'Travel and Translation: Textuality in *Gulliver's Travels*', *Criticism* 21, no. 2 (1979): 134–52 (149).

29 See *Gulliveriana*, ed. Welcher and Bush, VII.236–9.

30 For a book-historical approach to illustration studies focused on the early images of Robinson Crusoe see Sandro Jung, *Transnational Crusoe, Illustration and Reading History, 1719–1722* (Cambridge: Cambridge University Press, 2025). Like Gulliver, Crusoe has also been endlessly updated by artists. See David Blewett, *The Illustration of Robinson Crusoe, 1719–1920* (Gerrards Cross: Colin Smythe, 1995) and 'The Iconic Crusoe: Illustrations and Images of Robinson Crusoe', in *The Cambridge Companion to Robinson Crusoe*, ed. John Richetti (Cambridge: Cambridge University Press, 2018), 159–90; Simon Cooke, 'Illustrating *Robinson Crusoe* over Three Centuries', *The Book Collector* 73, no. 3 (2024): 267–80; and Nathalie Collé, 'From Visual to Material Culture: The Afterlives of Frontispieces to *Robinson Crusoe*', in *The Edinburgh Companion to the Eighteenth-Century Novel and the Arts*, ed. Jakub Lipski and M.-C. Newbould (Edinburgh: Edinburgh University Press, 2024), 397–413.

31 See William B. Jones Jr, *Classics Illustrated: A Cultural History*, 2nd edn (Jefferson, NC: McFarland, 2017), 37–9.

32 Jones, *Classics Illustrated*, 39. On the series' target readership see Kristin L. Matthews, 'Making Reading Popular: Cold War Literacy and *Classics Illustrated*', *Book History* 22 (2019): 320–41.

33 *Gulliver's Travels: Classics Illustrated*, adapted by Daniel Kushner and illustrated by Lillian Chestney Zuckerberg (New York: Gilberton Company, 1965 [1943]). The tagline, 'Featuring Stories by the World's Greatest Authors', appears in a black box directly beneath the series title, *Classics Illustrated*. On the 1943 version the tagline appears to the right and in a sky-blue box that matches the background.

34 Delmore Schwartz, 'Masterpieces as Cartoons', in *Arguing Comics: Literary Masters on a Popular Medium*, ed. Jeet Heer (Jackson, MS: University Press of Mississippi, 2004), 52–62 (58). This article first appeared in *Partisan Review* in 1952.

35 *Gulliver's Travels: Classics Illustrated*, adapted by Daniel Kushner and illustrated by Lillian Chestney [Zuckerberg] (New York: Gilberton Company, 1943), inside back cover. Unless stated otherwise, I will be referring to the 1965 version from now on.

36 I am indebted to Professor Chris Murray at the University of Dundee for his technical insights into the comic's form.

37 On the fraught commercial and technological history of colour in comics see McCloud, *Understanding Comics*, 185–92.

38 Jones, *Classics Illustrated*, 39.

39 *Gulliver's Travels: Dell Junior Treasury*, illustrated by Alberto Giolitti (New York: Dell Publishing Company, 1956), untitled foreword.

40 *Gulliver's Travels: Thriller Comics*, adapted by Peter O'Donnell and illustrated by Selby Donnison (London: Fleetway, 1952), 62 (bottom panel).

41 *Treasure Chest of Fun & Facts*, vol. 3, no. 12 (Dayton, OH: George A. Pflaum, 1948), 27–31.

42 *Gulliver's Travels: 3-D Color Classics*, adapted by Peter Stone and illustrated by Neal Adams, Rodolfo Damaggio, Andres Klasic and John Nyberg (Racine, WI: WPC, 1995), 5 (bottom panel).

43 *Gulliver's Travels: Marvel Classics Comics*, adapted by John Norwood Fago and illustrated by E. R. Cruz (New York: Marvel Comics, 1976), 48.

44 *Gulliver's Travels: Classics Illustrated*, 46 (bottom frame).

45 *Gulliver's Travels: King Classics*, adapted by Anne Mueser, scripted by Antonio Vidal Sales and drawn by Alfonso Cerón Núñez (Barcelona: Editorial Bruguera; New York: King Features Syndicate, 1978), 1 (top left).

46 *Gulliver in the Country of Dwarfs (Gulliver Bono ke Desh me)* (HardPress, 2019), 4 (bottom panels).

47 'Editor's Introduction to Volume 1', in *The Graphic Canon: The World's Great Literature as Comics and Visuals*, ed. Russ Kick, 3 vols (New York: Seven Stories Press, 2012–13), 1.1.

48 Gareth Hinds, 'Gulliver's Travels; Part II: A Voyage to Brobdingnag' (2003), in *The Graphic Canon*, ed. Kick, 1.448–59.

49 *Jonathan Swift's Gulliver's Travels*, retold by Donald Lemke and illustrated by Cynthia Martin (North Mankato, MN: Stone Arch Books, 2014 [2008]), back cover.

50 Salariya reissued this iteration in 2022 under the branding of the *Classic Comix* series, where Gulliver appears more prominently on the cover art and in the illustrated list of characters. The reissued version has coloured gutters and enlarged images, but the educational apparatus at the back has been removed.

51 Shane Denson and Ruth Mayer, 'Spectral Seriality: The Sights and Sounds of Count Dracula', in *Media of Serial Narrative*, ed. Frank Kelleter (Columbus, OH: Ohio State University Press, 2017), 108–24 (110).

52 *Jonathan Swift's Gulliver's Travels*, adapted by Lewis Helfand and illustrated by Vinod Kumar (New Delhi: Campfire, 2010), 68. Swift's Gulliver writes: 'Thus, gentle Reader, I have given thee a faithful History of my Travels for Sixteen Years, and above Seven Months', *Gulliver's Travels*, ed. Womersley, 436.

53 *Gulliver's Travels*, adapted by John Malam and illustrated by Penko Gelev (Brighton: Salariya, 2022), 63.

54 Martin Rowson, *Gulliver's Travels: Adapted & Updated* (London: Atlantic Books, 2012), I.9. The book is not paginated. My numbering refers to the four separate voyages and begins again on the title page of each.

55 Jonathan Swift, *The Correspondence of Jonathan Swift*, ed. Harold Williams, 5 vols (Oxford: Clarendon Press, 1963–5), III.257–8.

56 See Gary Spencer Millidge, *Alan Moore: Storyteller* (Lewes: Ilex, 2011), 212–19.

57 Alan Moore and Kevin O'Neill, *The League of Extraordinary Gentlemen: Black Dossier* (Burbank, CA: DC Comics, 2007), 16. My numbering here refers to the internal comic (i.e. *The Trump*).

58 Elizabeth Susanna Davenport Graham, *Voyage to Locuta; A Fragment* (London: J. Hatchard, 1818), vi.

59 Alan Moore and Kevin O'Neill, *The League of Extraordinary Gentlemen*, 4 vols (Burbank, CA: America's Best Comics; DC Comics, 1999–2021), 2.14. The numbering refers to *The New Traveller's Almanac*, located towards the end of the volume, and begins on its title page.

Chapter 4

1 Quoted in Dan Torre, *Animation: Process, Cognition and Actuality* (London and New York: Bloomsbury Academic, 2017), 148.

2 See Richard D. Altick, *The Shows of London: A Panoramic History of Exhibitions, 1600–1862* (Cambridge, MA and London: The Belknap Press, 1978), 43, and Dennis Todd, *Imagining Monsters: Miscreations of the Self in Eighteenth-Century England* (Chicago, IL and London: The University of Chicago Press, 1995), 140–8.

3 Jonathan Swift, *Gulliver's Travels*, ed. David Womersley (Cambridge: Cambridge University Press, 2012), 36. Hereafter cited parenthetically as *GT*.

4 See Daniel Cook, 'Vexed Diversions: *Gulliver's Travels*, the Arts, and Popular Entertainment', in *The Edinburgh Companion to the Eighteenth-Century Novel and the Arts*, ed. Jakub Lipski and M.-C. Newbould (Edinburgh: Edinburgh University Press, 2024), 228–43.

5 Paul Goring, '*Gulliver's Travels* on the Mid-Eighteenth-Century Stage; or, What is an Adaptation?', *Forum for Modern Language Studies* 51, no. 2 (2015): 100–15 (104–8).

6 David Garrick, *Lilliput. A Dramatic Entertainment* (1757), in *Gulliveriana*, ed. Jeanne K. Welcher and George E. Bush Jr, 8 vols (Gainesville, FL: Scholars' Facsimiles & Reprints, 1970–99), V.307. On the problem caused by

the novelistic demands of the Lady Flimnap episode in *Travels* see Robert
M. Ryley, 'Gulliver, Flimnap's Wife, and the Critics', *Studies in the Literary
Imagination* 5, no. 2 (1972): 53–63.

7 See *The London Magazine, Or, Gentleman's Monthly Intelligencer* 52 (1783):
556–7 (557).

8 See Heinz Kosok, 'Stage Versions of *Gulliver's Travels*', *Swift Studies* 7 (2002):
88–99.

9 Richard Findlater, *Joe Grimaldi: His Life and Theatre*, 2nd edn (Cambridge:
Cambridge University Press, 1978), 191.

10 Mary Barnard Horne, *Gulliver and the Lilliputians Up to Date* (Boston, MA:
Walter H. Baker, 1903), 5.

11 Heinz Kosok, *Explorations in Irish Literature* (Trier: Wissenschaftlicher
Verlag Trier, 2008), 9–25 (11–12).

12 William A. Eddy, '*Gulliver's Travels* and *Le Théâtre Italien*', *Modern Language
Notes* 44, no. 6 (1929): 356–61 (361n11). A 1734 version of *L'Isle de la Folie*
is reproduced in *Gulliveriana*, ed. Welcher and Bush, V.129-80. A total of
eighty performances, including revivals, followed the premiere, according
to Mary Cyr, 'Gulliver in France: Voyage to the Island of Folly', *The Musical
Times* 163 (2022): 65–84 (67).

13 See Allardyce Nicoll, *A History of English Drama 1660–1900*, 6 vols
(Cambridge: Cambridge University Press, 1965–70), passim.

14 *Gulliver's Travels! Or, Harlequin Prince Rover and the Princess Tricksy
Wicksy!* (Birmingham: James Upton, 1875), 19.

15 H. J. Byron, *The Gaiety Gulliver*, in *Plays by H. J. Byron*, ed. Jim Davis
(Cambridge: Cambridge University Press, 2008 [1984]), 163.

16 Kosok, *Explorations in Irish Literature*, 16–24 (16).

17 See Michael Düring, 'No Swift beyond Gulliver: Notes on the Polish
Reception', in *The Reception of Jonathan Swift in Europe*, ed. Hermann J.
Real (London and New York: Thoemmes Continuum, 2005), 156–69 (166).

18 Farhana Sheikh, *Gulliver's Travels: A Play* (Bath: Brown Dog Books, 2020),
21 (pagination refers to the e-book numbering on Kindle).

19 See Sergei Obraztsov Puppet Theatre's website, https://puppet.ru/en/
performances/gullivers-travels.

20 In her annotated bibliography of Spanish adaptations, Ana Maria Hornero
Corisco notes that Brobdingnag features more often in Spanish-language
productions: '*Gulliver's Travels* on the Screen: Spanish Film Versions', *Swift
Studies* 20 (2005): 111–23. On book adaptations in Spanish see María Pilar
González Vera, '*Gulliver's Travels*: The World of Adaptations', in *Crossing*

Textual Boundaries in International Children's Literature, ed. Lance Weldy (Newcastle upon Tyne: Cambridge Scholars Publishing, 2011), 25–43.

21 Bruno Edera, *Full Length Animated Feature Films*, ed. John Halas (New York: Hastings House Publishers, 1977), 88.

22 Gregory M. Colón Semenza and Robert J. Hasenfratz, *The History of British Literature on Film, 1895–2015* (London and New York: Bloomsbury Academic, 2015), 175.

23 See Ana Hornero, '*Gulliver's Travels*, or All's Well: Film Versions for a Young Audience', in *Crossing Textual Boundaries in International Children's Literature*, ed. Lance Weldy (Newcastle upon Tyne: Cambridge Scholars Publishing, 2011), 123–34.

24 Katie Lanning, 'Spectacle and Satire: American Film Adaptations of Gulliver's Travels', *BSECS Criticks* (17 January 2012), www.bsecs.org.uk /criticks-reviews/spectacle-and-satire-american-film-adaptations-of -gullivers-travels. See also Emrys Jones, 'Screen Media', in *The Cambridge Companion to Gulliver's Travels*, ed. Daniel Cook and Nicholas Seager (Cambridge: Cambridge University Press, 2023), 224–36.

25 On the immediate cultural impact of Walt Disney's *Snow White and the Seven Dwarfs* see James Clarke, *Animated Films* (London: Virgin Books, 2004), 29–42.

26 Vito Adriaensens, 'Ovidian Violence: Georges Méliès's Explosive Screen Bodies', in *Corporeality in Early Cinema: Viscera, Skin, and Physical Form*, ed. Marina Dahlquist, Doron Galili, Jan Olsson and Valentine Robert (Bloomington, IN: Indiana University Press, 2018), 25–34. See also Semenza and Hasenfratz, *The History of British Literature on Film*, 61–5.

27 Semenza and Hasenfratz, *The History of British Literature on Film*, 61–2.

28 William Davenport Adams has identified seven plays and pantomimes that were performed before 1901 and therefore may have been on Méliès's watchlist, including Albert Monnier's *Les Voyages de Gulliver, Piece Fantastique en 4 Actes et 30 Tableaux* (1867). See *A Dictionary of the Drama: A Guide to the Plays, Play-wrights, Players, and Playhouses of the United Kingdom and America* (London: Chatto and Windus, 1904), 385–6.n85.

29 *Gulliver's Travels* broke the attendance record of the Paramount Theatre in New York City. By the second week of its screening in 1939, a reported 264,798 people had come to see it (including 72,927 children). See Leslie Cabarga, *The Fleischer Story* (New York: DaCapo Press, 1988), 163. Forest Light Productions produced a comic book version of the 1939 animation to mark the 60th anniversary: *Max Fleischer's Gulliver's Travels*, adapted by Mitchell Perkins and illustrated by George Broderick Jr (Plymouth, MI: Forest Light Productions, 2000). Perkins and Broderick broadly adhere to

the narrative structure of the film, but their Gulliver has become noticeably more chiselled in his looks.

30 *Motion Picture Herald* (25 November 1939): 18.

31 For details and images see BoardGameGeek, https://boardgamegeek.com/ boardgame/96399/gullivers-travels. In Milton Bradley's tie-in board game, which was also produced in 1939, Gulliver is a tad more tangential: see https://boardgamegeek.com/boardgame/43051/gullivers-travels.

32 See Michael Barrier, *Hollywood Cartoons: American Animation in its Golden Age* (Oxford: Oxford University Press, 2003 [1999]), 292–6 (296).

33 The profits have been estimated at $3.2 million (based on US and Canada rentals only). See '1959: Probable Domestic Take', *Variety* (6 January 1960): 34.

34 Steve Swires, 'Maestro of the Magicks Part Two', *Starlog* (February 1990): 66.

35 *Gulliver in Lilliput*, dir. by Barry Letts (BBC, 1982).

36 For a discussion of the film's satiric strategies see John Price, 'Modernizing Augustan Satire on Screen: *Gulliver's Travels* (1996)', in *Jonathan Swift and Philosophy*, ed. Janelle Pötzsch (Lanham, MD: Lexington Books, 2016), 237–49.

37 Alan D. Chalmers, 'Film, Censorship, and the "Corrupt Original" of *Gulliver's Travels*', in *Eighteenth-Century Fiction on Screen*, ed. Robert Mayer (Cambridge: Cambridge University Press, 2002), 70–87 (72).

38 See Michael DePorte, 'Novelizing the *Travels*: Simon Moore's Gulliver', *Swift Studies* 12 (1997): 99–102.

39 DePorte, 'Novelizing the *Travels*', 102.

40 *Gulliver's Travels*, dir. by Charles Sturridge (Hallmark Entertainment, 1996).

41 *Gulliver's Travels*, dir. by Rob Letterman (20th Century Fox, 2010).

42 See also Karen Bloom Gevirtz, *Representing the Eighteenth Century in Film and Television, 2000–2015* (Basingstoke: Palgrave Macmillan, 2017), 17–38.

43 See William Lewin, 'A Guide to the Discussion of the Technicolor Animated Screen Version of Gulliver's Travels', *Photoplay Studies* 6, no. 2 (1940): 1–16.

44 Aleksandr Ptushko received a special prize at the International Cinema Festival in Milan.

45 For a discussion of the importance of *The New Gulliver* for Soviet cinema, particularly its presentation of *kinotriuki* (film tricks) see Anne Eakin Moss, 'Cinema's "Miracles": Film Tricks and the Production of Soviet Wonder', *Film History* 32, no. 4 (2020): 33–59.

46 See *Monthly Film Bulletin* 37, no. 432 (1970): 128.

47 *Gulliver's Travels Beyond the Moon* [*Garibā no Uchū Ryokō*], dir. by Masao Kuroda and Sanae Yamamoto (Toei & Continental Distributing, 1965).

48 IMDB, www.imdb.com/title/tt1473040.

49 Jan-Noël Thon, 'Transmedia Characters: Theory and Analysis', *Frontiers of Narrative Studies* 5, no. 2 (2019): 176–99 (184).

50 'Return of Gulliver', *Journey to the Center of the Earth*, dir. by Hal Sutherland, Norm McCabe and Lou Zukor (ABC, 1967). See IMDB, www .imdb.com/title/tt5894320.

51 *Gulliver Returns*, dir. by Ilya Maksimov (All Rights Entertainment, 2021).

52 See Nicole Sheriko, 'Patchwork Play: Nineteenth-Century Toy Theater and Participatory Media Culture', *Nineteenth-Century Studies* 30 (2019): 25–44. Toy theatre sheets and accoutrement can be found in the Arthur Weyhe Toy Theatre Collection (New York Public Library), the Juvenile Drama Collection (University of Toronto), and the theatre history holdings at Harvard.

53 The British Museum holds 1815 and 1818 copies of Jameson's 'Theatrical Characters' sheets [nos 1886,0513.1743-1744 and 1886,0513.1735], which feature Gulliver and related characters, as well as West's 1825 version [no. 1886,0513.991-994]. These were acquired from the Victorian collector Ralph Thomas Jr in 1886.

54 Ads of the World, www.adsoftheworld.com/campaigns/metamorphosis.

Conclusion

1 Jonathan Swift, *Gulliver's Travels*, ed. David Womersley (Cambridge: Cambridge University Press, 2012), 437.

2 Swift, *Gulliver's Travels*, ed. Womersley, 452.

3 Thomas Docherty, *Reading (Absent) Character: Towards a Theory of Characterization in Fiction* (Oxford: Clarendon Press, 1983), 48. See also Deidre Lynch, 'A Character of Character, in Five Metaphors', in *A Companion to the English Novel*, ed. Stephen Arata, Madigan Haley, J. Paul Hunter and Jennifer Wicke (Oxford: Wiley Blackwell, 2019 [2015]), 209–24 (222).

4 See Henry Jenkins, 'Transmedia Storytelling 101', *Pop Junctions* (21 March 2007), http://henryjenkins.org/blog/2007/03/transmedia_storytelling_101 .html.

5 CherryFlavoredSpades, 'Gulliver in Attenation' (2021), *Archive of Our Own*, https://archiveofourown.org/works/30331272.

6 Alex Ritman, '*Gulliver's Travels* Getting Contemporary TV Remake From Moonriver, Federation Studios', *Variety* (22 January 2025), https://variety.com/2025/tv/global/gullivers-travels-tv-remake-moonriver-federation-1236281797.

7 Nick Vivarelli, '*Gulliver's Travels* Set for "Fun" TV Series Adaptation With *Full Monty* Producer Uberto Pasolini as Showrunner', *Variety* (24 March 2025), https://variety.com/2025/tv/global/gullivers-travels-tv-series-adaptation-uberto-pasolini-1236344645.

BIBLIOGRAPHY

Primary Resources

Archives and Databases

AdForum <www.adforum.com>
Ads of the World <www.adsoftheworld.com>
Archive of Herbert Davis, Bodleian Library
Archive of Our Own <archiveofourown.org>
Arthur Weyhe Toy Theatre Collection, New York Public Library
ARTstor <www.artstor.org>
Australian Performing Arts Collection, Arts Centre Melbourne
BBC Archive <www.bbc.co.uk/archive>
BD Gest: Le portail BD de reference <www.bedetheque.com>
Beinecke Library, Yale University
BFI National Archive
The Billy Ireland Cartoon Library and Museum, Ohio State University
BoardGameGeek [BGG] <boardgamegeek.com>
Bodleian Library, University of Oxford
The British Library, London
The British Library Images Online <imagesonline.bl.uk>
The British Museum Collection Online <www.britishmuseum.org/collection>
Children's Literature and Culture (Adam Matthew Digital)
Comicbook+ <comicbookplus.com>
Comics Collection, University of Pennsylvania
Cudequest Family Collection, Academy Film Archive
Digital Bodleian <digital.bodleian.ox.ac.uk>
The Digital Comic Museum <digitalcomicmuseum.com>
Doollee: The Playwrights Database <www.doollee.com>
eBay <www.ebay.co.uk>
Ehrenpreis Centre for Swift Studies, University of Münster
Eighteenth-Century Collections Online (Gale)
Eighteenth-Century Drama (Adam Matthew Digital)
European Film Gateway [EFG] <www.europeanfilmgateway.eu>
FanFiction <www.fanfiction.net>
Geoffrey Denison Gulliver's Travels Collection, University of Pennsylvania
The Grand Comics Database <www.comics.org>

Harvard Theater Collection, Houghton Library (Harvard University)
Internet Archive <archive.org>
Internet Game Database [IGDB] <www.igdb.com>
Internet Movie Database [IMDB] <www.imdb.com>
Jisc Library Hub Discover <discover.libraryhub.jisc.ac.uk>
The John Johnson Collection, Bodleian Library
Juvenile Drama Collection, University of Toronto
Laing Comics Collection, University of Dundee
The Lewis Walpole Library, Yale University
The Library of Congress, Washington DC
London Stage Database <londonstagedatabase.uoregon.edu>
Marsh's Library, Dublin
Media History Digital Library <mediahistoryproject.org>
The Morgan Library & Museum, New York
The National Library of Ireland, Dublin
The National Library of Scotland, Edinburgh
National Trust Collections <www.nationaltrustcollections.org.uk>
Nineteenth-Century Collections Online (Gale)
Oxford Dictionary of National Biography [ODNB]
Sterling Memorial Library, Yale University
Trinity College Dublin
Victoria and Albert Museum [V&A], London
Victorian Popular Culture (Adam Matthew Digital)
William Andrews Clark Memorial Library, UCLA
Williams Collection, University of Cambridge
Wisconsin Center for Film & Theater Research
Worldcat <www.worldcat.org>
Yale Film Archive, Sterling Memorial Library
Yale University Digital Collections <collections.library.yale.edu>
YouTube <www.youtube.com>

Bibliographies and Gulliveriana

Eddy, William A., 'Gulliveriana: The Minor Works of Lemuel Gulliver', in
    Gulliver's Travels: A Critical Study, 193–200, Gloucester, MA: Peter Smith,
    1963.
Elkmann, Ulrich and Hermann J. Real, 'Gulliver's Travels to Several Remote
    Nations of the World: A Bibliography of Translations into Remote
    Languages', *Swift Studies* 32 (2017): 117–32.
Lenfest, David S., 'A Checklist of Illustrated Editions of *Gulliver's Travels*, 1727-
    1914', *The Papers of the Bibliographical Society of America* 62 (1968): 85–123.
Teerink, H., *A Bibliography of the Writings of Jonathan Swift*, edited by Arthur H.
    Scouten, 2nd edn, Philadelphia, PA: University of Pennsylvania Press, 1963.
Welcher, Jeanne K., *Gulliveriana VIII: An Annotated List of Gulliveriana,
    1721–1800*, New York: Scholars' Facsimiles & Reprints, 1988.

Welcher, Jeanne K. and George E. Bush Jr (ed.), *Gulliveriana*, 8 vols, Gainesville, FL: Scholars' Facsimiles & Reprints, 1970–99.

Comics and Graphic Novels

Anon., *Treasure Chest of Fun & Facts*, vol. 3, nos 12 and 13, Dayton, OH: George A. Pflaum, 1948.

Kick, Russ (ed.), *The Graphic Canon: The World's Great Literature as Comics and Visuals*, 3 vols, New York: Seven Stories Press, 2012–13.

Manara, Milo, *Gullivera*, translated by Jacinthe Leclerc, New York: Nantier-Beall-Minoustchine Publishing, 1996.

Moore, Alan and Kevin O'Neill, *The League of Extraordinary Gentlemen*, 4 vols, Burbank, CA: America's Best Comics; DC Comics, 1999–2021.

Moore, Alan and Kevin O'Neill, *The League of Extraordinary Gentlemen: Black Dossier*, Burbank, CA: DC Comics, 2007.

Rowson, Martin, *Gulliver's Travels: Adapted & Updated*, London: Atlantic Books, 2012.

Swift, Jonathan, *The 3 Worlds of Gulliver*, adapted by Paul S. Newman and illustrated by Mike Sekowsky, New York: Dell Publishing Company, 1960.

Swift, Jonathan, *Gulliver in the Country of Dwarfs (Gulliver Bono ke Desh me)*, HardPress, 2019.

Swift, Jonathan, *Gulliver chez les Géants*, illustrated by Gaston Niezab, Les Merveilleuses Histoires, *c.*1935.

Swift, Jonathan, *Gulliver à Lilliput*, illustrated by Gaston Niezab, Les Merveilleuses Histoires, *c.*1934.

Swift, Jonathan, *Gulliver's Travels*, adapted by John Malam and illustrated by Penko Gelev, Brighton: Salariya, 2022.

Swift, Jonathan, *Gulliver's Travels: 3-D Color Classics*, adapted by Peter Stone and illustrated by Neal Adams, Rodolfo Damaggio, Andres Klasic and John Nyberg, Racine, WI: WPC, 1995.

Swift, Jonathan, *Gulliver's Travels: Classics Illustrated*, adapted by Daniel Kushner and illustrated by Lillian Chestney Zuckerberg, New York: Gilberton Company, 1965 [1943].

Swift, Jonathan, *Gulliver's Travels: Dell Junior Treasury*, illustrated by Alberto Giolitti, New York: Dell Publishing Company, 1956.

Swift, Jonathan, *Gulliver's Travels: Great Illustrated Classics*, adapted by Malvina G. Vogel and illustrated by Pablo Marcos, New York: Baronet Books, 1995.

Swift, Jonathan, *Gulliver's Travels: King Classics*, adapted by Anne Mueser, scripted by Antonio Vidal Sales and drawn by Alfonso Cerón Núñez, Barcelona: Editorial Bruguera; New York: King Features Syndicate, 1978.

Swift, Jonathan, *Gulliver's Travels: Manga Literary Classics*, adapted by Jun Wang and illustrated by Ben Wong and Art Lim, Republic of Korea: Y.kids, 2007.

Swift, Jonathan, *Gulliver's Travels: Marvel Classics Comics*, adapted by John Norwood Fago and illustrated by E. R. Cruz, New York: Marvel Comics, 1976.

Swift, Jonathan, *Gulliver's Travels: Thriller Comics*, adapted by Peter O'Donnell
and illustrated by Selby Donnison, London: Fleetway, 1952.
Swift, Jonathan, *Jonathan Swift's Gulliver*, adapted by Martin Jenkins and
illustrated by Chris Riddell, London: Walker Books, 2004.
Swift, Jonathan, *Jonathan Swift's Gulliver's Travels*, adapted by Lewis Helfand and
illustrated by Vinod Kumar, New Delhi: Campfire, 2010.
Swift, Jonathan, *Jonathan Swift's Gulliver's Travels*, adapted by Donald Lemke
and illustrated by Cynthia Martin, North Mankato, MN: Stone Arch Books,
2014 [2008].
Swift, Jonathan, *Max Fleischer's Gulliver's Travels*, adapted by Mitchell Perkins
and illustrated by George Broderick Jr, Plymouth, MI: Forest Light
Productions, 2000.
Swift, Jonathan, *Les Voyages du Docteur Gulliver*, adapted by Kokor [Alain
Koch], 3 vols, Paris: Vents D'Ouest, 2006–2009.
Swift, Jonathan, *Les Voyages de Gulliver*, adapted by Kiyokazu Chiba, translated by
Fabien Dautriche and illustrated by Catherine Bouvier, Paris: nobi nobi!, 2017.
Swift, Jonathan, *Les Voyages de Gulliver: De Laputa au Japon*, adapted by
Bertrand Galic and illustrated by Paul Echegoyen, Paris: Soleil, 2020.

Fiction

Anon., *A Cursory View of the History of Lilliput For these last forty three Years*,
London: A. Moore, 1727 [*Gulliveriana*, V.105–28].
Anon., 'Gulliver's Last Voyage', *The Monthly Review* (July 1903): 1–17.
Anon., *Gulliver's Last Voyage, describing Ballymugland, or the Floating Island*,
London: William Cole, 1825.
Ariazad [Varoujan Kazanjian], *Gulliver in Cloneland: The Fifth Travel of Gulliver*,
Sussex: The Book Guild, 2000.
Bouchery, Émile, *Les Petits-Neveux de Gulliver*, Paris: Librairie Pittoresque de la
Jeunesse, 1845.
'Brunt, Samuel', *A Voyage to Cacklogallinia*, London: J. Watson, 1727
[*Gulliveriana*, IV. 1–43].
Cecil, Algernon, 'Gulliver Redivivus', *Essays in Imitation*, 59–128, London: John
Murray, 1910.
Chater, Lauren, *Gulliver's Wife*, Sydney: Simon & Schuster, 2020.
Coe, Jonathan, *The Story of Gulliver*, illustrated by Sara Oddi, London: Pushkin
Press, 2018 [2013].
Collins, Mortimer, *Squire Silchester's Whim*, 2 vols, London: Henry S. King, 1873.
Constancio, Francisco Solano, *The Ghost, by Felix Phantom. Part Second*,
Edinburgh: G. Mudie & Son, 1796.
Crocker, Carter, *Last of the Gullivers*, New York: Philomel Books, 2012.
Dare, Bill, *Brian Gulliver's Travels*, Edinburgh: Pilrig Press, 2013.
Desfontaines, Pierre-François Guyot, *The Travels of Mr. John Gulliver, Son to
Capt. Lemuel Gulliver*, translated by John Lockman, 2 vols, London: Sam.
Harding, 1731 [*Gulliveriana*, II].

Desfontaines, Pierre-François Guyot, *Les Voyages de Gulliver*, Paris: J. Guérin, 1727.

Dodderidge, Esmé, *The New Gulliver; or, The Adventures of Lemuel Gulliver Jr in Capovolta*, London: The Women's Press, 1988 [1979].

Druery, Charles Thomas, *The New Gulliver: Or Travels in Athomia*, Westminster: The Roxburghe Press, 1897.

Édouard-Bauer, Edmond, 'Le neveu de Gulliver', *Je sais tout* 187 (15 July 1921): 849–92.

Fell, Alison, *The Mistress of Lilliput or The Pursuit*, London: Doubleday, 1999.

Fowler, Karen Joy, 'The Travails', *Black Glass: Short Fictions*, 84–95, New York: Ballantine Books, 1999.

Gasbarra, Felix, *Schule der Planeten*, München: Heyne, 1968.

Gayton, Sam, *Lilliput*, London: Andersen Press, 2013.

'Gulliver, Lemuel' [John Arbuthnot?], *An Account of the State of Learning in the Empire of Lilliput*, London: J. Roberts, 1728 [*Gulliveriana*, V.181–217].

'Gulliver, Lemuel', *The Anatomist Dissected: or the Man-Midwife finely brought to Bed*, Westminster: A. Campbell, 1727 [*Gulliveriana*, VI(I)].

'Gulliver, Lemuel', *Applebee's Original Weekly Journal* (13 April–5 October 1728) [letters to the editor] [*Gulliveriana*, V.219–52].

'Gulliver, Lemuel' [Lewis Jesse Bridgman], *Gulliver's Bird Book*, Boston, MA: L.C. Page, [*c*.1901].

'Gulliver, Lemuel' [Volter Kilpi], *Gulliver's Voyage to Phantomimia*, translated by Douglas Robinson, Bucharest: Zeta Books, 2020.

'Gulliver, Lemuel' [Eliza Haywood?], *Memoirs of the Court of Lilliput*, London: J. Roberts, 1727 [*Gulliveriana*, III.297–463].

'Gulliver, Lemuel' [Matthew Hodgart], *A New Voyage to the Country of the Houyhnhnms*, New York: G. P. Putnam's Sons, 1969.

'Gulliver, Lemuel', *Sequel to Gulliver's Travels. An Eulogy*, London: J. Jaques, 1830.

'Gulliver, Lemuel' [Samuel Richardson], *Travels into Several Remote Nations of the World. Vol. III*, London, 1727 [*Gulliveriana*, III.1–295].

'Gulliver, Lemuel' [John Paul Brady], *A Voyage to Inishneefa*, Santa Barbara, CA: John Daniel, 1987.

'Gulliver, Lemuel' ['Conrad Peregrinus', i.e. Kurt Friedlaender], *A Voyage to Springistan*, Stockholm: AB Seelig & Co, 1972.

'Gulliver Jr, Lemuel' [H. Whitmore], *Modern Gulliver's Travels*, London: T. Chapman, 1796 [*Gulliveriana*, II].

'Gulliver Jr, Lemuel' [Elizabeth Susanna Davenport Graham], *Voyage to Locuta; A Fragment*, London: J. Hatchard, 1818.

'Gulliver, Lemuel Swift' [Colin Milne], *So This Is Glasgow!*, Glasgow: Jackson, Son & Company, 1938.

'Gulliver, Verigull', *A Fragment of the Voyages of Mr. V. G.*, Middle Hill, 1832.

Hawke, Simon, *The Lilliput Legion*, New York: Ace, 1989.

Hermann, Louis, *In the Sealed Cave*, New York: D. Appleton-Century Company, 1935.

Karinthy, Frigyes, *Voyage to Faremido & Capillaria*, translated by Paul Tabori, London: New English Library/Times Mirror, 1978.

Kessel, John, 'Gulliver at Home', *The Pure Product*, 329–43, New York: Tom Doherty, 1997.

King, Davy, 'The Woman Gulliver Left Behind', 1978, 1–13, www.davyking.com.

Lerner, Edward M., 'My Fifth and Most Exotic Voyage', *Analog: Science Fiction and Fact* (September/October 2017): 8–27.

Ling, Peter, *The Mind Robber* (*Doctor Who Library*: 115), London: W. H. Allen & Co, 1986.

'McDermot, Murtagh', *A Trip to the Moon*, London and Dublin: J. Roberts, 1728 [*Gulliveriana*, I.1–96].

Morpurgo, Michael, *Boy Giant*, London: HarperCollins, 2019.

Munro, William, *Daniel Thomson: The Scottish Gulliver: A Stirring Tale of His Travels and Adventures in a' Airts an' Pairts*, Kilmarnock: D. Brown; Glasgow: John Menzies, *c*.1905 [1892].

Netz, Erga, *Oh, Gulliver! Mrs Gulliver and the Secret of Size*, Arlington, MA: Tough Poets Press, 2023.

Orme, Joseph, *The Adventures of Gulliver Redivivus*, London: J. Blackwood, 1881.

Pain, Barry, *The New Gulliver and Other Stories*, London: T. Werner Laurie, 1913.

Perce, Elbert, *Gulliver Joi: His Three Voyages*, New York: Charles Scribner, 1852.

Perry, Walter Copland, *The Revolt of the Horses*, London: Grant Richards, 1898.

Platt, Marc, 'Future Imperfect', in *Doctor Who Year Book*, 18, London: Marvel Comics, 1991.

'Quick, Jonathan' [Cecil Eldred Hughes and Harold Begbie], *Gulliver Joe*, London: Ibister & Company, 1903.

[Raspe, Rudolf Erich], *The Travels of Baron Münchausen: Gulliver Revived, or, the Vice of Lying Properly Exposed; Together with the Sequel Containing the Adventures of Baron Münchausen in Russia*, edited by William Rose, London: George Routledge and Sons; New York: E. P. Dutton, 1930 [1923].

Roberts, Adam, *Swiftly: A Novel*, London: Gollancz, 2008.

Ryan, Michael, *Gulliver*, New York: Autonomedia, 1993.

Sharee, Keith, *Gulliver's Fugitives* (*Star Trek: The Next Generation*: 11), London: Titan Books, 1990.

Sonderegger, Leo, *Glumdalclitch*, Lincoln, NE: Writer's Showcase, 2000.

Swift, Jonathan, *The Adventures of Captain Gulliver, in a Voyage to the Islands of Lilliput and Brobdignag* [*sic*], adapted by Francis Newbery, London: F. Newbery, 1776 [1772].

Swift, Jonathan, *The Adventures of Captain Gulliver, in a Voyage to Lilliput*, Glasgow: J. Lumsden & Son, 1815.

Swift, Jonathan, *The Annotated Gulliver's Travels*, edited by Isaac Asimov, New York: Clarkson N. Potter, 1980.

Swift, Jonathan, *Gulliver's Travels*, edited by Harold Williams, London: First Edition Club, 1926.

Swift, Jonathan, *Gulliver's Travels*, edited by David Womersley, Cambridge: Cambridge University Press, 2012.

Swift, Jonathan, *Travels into Several Remote Nations of the World. Faithfully Abridged*, London: J. Stone and R. King, 1727.

Szathmári, Sándor, *Voyage to Kazohinia*, translated by Inez Kemenes, North Adams, MA: New Europe Books, 2012.

Troupe, Thomas Kingsley, and Xavier Bonet, *Midnight Library: The Gulliver Giant*, Oxford: Raintree, 2020.

Wittkop, Justus Franz, *Gullivers letzte Reise: die Insel der Vergänglichen*, Nürnberg: Schrag-Verlag Nürnberg, 1941.

Wolfe, Thomas, *The Complete Short Stories of Thomas Wolfe*, edited by Francis E. Skipp, New York: Scribner's, 1989.

Film and Television

The 3 Worlds of Gulliver, dir. by Jack Sher (Columbia Pictures, 1960).

The Adventures of Gulliver, dir. by Joseph Barbera and William Hanna (Hanna-Barbera Productions, 1968).

Doctor Who: The Mind Robber, dir. by David Maloney (BBC, 1968).

Enchanted Tales: Gulliver's Travels, dir. by Diane Eskenazi (Golden Films, 1996).

Guliver, dir. by Zdenko Basic (In Fine, 2009).

Gulliver, dir. by María Alché (FiGa Films, 2015).

Gulliver in Lilliput, dir. by Barry Letts (BBC, 1982).

Gulliver Mickey, dir. by Burt Gillett (United Artists, 1934).

Gulliver Returns, dir. by Ilya Maksimov (All Rights Entertainment, 2021).

Gulliver's Travels, dir. by Dave Fleischer (Paramount Pictures, 1939).

Gulliver's Travels, dir. by Peter R. Hunt (Paramount Pictures, 1977).

Gulliver's Travels, dir. by Art Scott (Hanna-Barbera Productions, 1979).

Gulliver's Travels, dir. by Charles Sturridge (Hallmark Entertainment, 1996).

Gulliver's Travels, dir. by Anita Udeep (Mayajaal, 2005).

Gulliver's Travels, dir. by Rob Letterman (20th Century Fox, 2010).

Gulliver's Travels Beyond the Moon [*Garibā no Uchū Ryokō*], dir. by Masao Kuroda and Sanae Yamamoto (Toei & Continental Distributing, 1965).

Jajantaram Mamantaram, dir. by Soumitra Ranade (SPE Films India, 2003).

Manga Sekai Mukashi Banashi: Gulliver's Travels (TBS, 1977).

Novyy Gulliver [*The New Gulliver*], dir. by Aleksandr Ptushko (Serlin-Burstyn, 1935).

Rani aur Lalpari, dir. by Ravikant Nagaich (Guru Enterprising Movies, 1975).

'Return of Gulliver', *Journey to the Center of the Earth*, dir. by Hal Sutherland, Norm McCabe and Lou Zukor (ABC, 1967).

Saban's Gulliver's Travels, dir. by Bruno Bianchi (Saban International Paris, 1992–3).

Tales of Gulliver's Travels, dir. by Michael Kruzan (SFK Media Corp., 2004 [1997]).

Le Voyage de Gulliver à Lilliput et chez les Géants, dir. by Georges Méliès (Star-Film, 1902).

Playtexts and Poems

Anon., *A Fable Founded upon Fact, Translated from a Manuscript, Found in an Old Castle, May 10th, 1784*, London, 1784.

Anon., *Gulliver's Travels! Or, Harlequin Prince Rover and the Princess Tricksy Wicksy!*, Birmingham: James Upton, 1875.

Bovell, Andrew, *Gulliver's Travels*, Melbourne: Melbourne Theatre Company, 1992.

Byron, H. J., *The Gaiety Gulliver*, in *Plays by H. J. Byron*, edited by Jim Davis, Cambridge: Cambridge University Press, 2008 [1984].

Carter, Lonnie, *Plays by Lonnie Carter: The Gulliver Trilogy*, New York: Broadway Play Publishing, 1997.

Coralli, Jean, *Gulliver, ballet-pantomime en deux tableaux*, Paris, 1826.

Garrick, David, *Lilliput. A Dramatic Entertainment*, London: Paul Vaillant, 1757 [*Gulliveriana*, V.303–50].

Gay, John, *Poetry and Prose*, edited by Vinton A. Dearing with Charles E. Beckwith, 2 vols, Oxford: Clarendon Press, 1974.

'Gulliver, Captain' [Joseph Mitchell], *The Totness Address Transversed*, London, 1727.

'Gulliver, Lemuel' [Elizabeth Susanna Davenport Graham], *The Eo-nauts, or The Spirit of Delusion*, London: Chapple, 1813.

'Gulliver, Lemuel' [Henry Fielding], *The Masquerade, A Poem*, London: J. Roberts, 1728.

Horne, Mary Barnard, *Gulliver and the Lilliputians Up to Date*, Boston, MA: Walter H. Baker, 1903.

Marivaux, Pierre Carlet de Chamblain de, *L'Ile de la Raison ou Les Petits Hommes: Comédie en trois actes, en prose*, Paris: La Comédie française, 1975.

Sheikh, Farhana, *Gulliver's Travels: A Play*, Bath: Brown Dog Books, 2020.

Woolland, Brian, *Gulliver*, Surrey: Nelson, 1993.

Other

Bayle, Pierre, *A General Dictionary, Historical and Critical*, edited by John Peter Bernard, Thomas Birch and John Lockman, 10 vols, London: G. Strahan, J. Clarke, et al., 1734–41.

'Corolini, Signor' [Edmund Curll?], *The Flying Island, &c. Being a Key to Gulliver's Voyage to Laputa, Balnibarbi, Glubbdubdribb* [sic]*, Luggnagg, and Japan*, London, 1726.

Hiramatsu, Asa, *Travelogue G: Illustrations for Gulliver's Travels*, Tokyo: Suitchipaburisshingu, 2022.

Johnson, Samuel, *Samuel Johnson's Parliamentary Reporting: Debates in the Senate of Lilliput*, edited by Benjamin Beard Hoover, Berkeley and Los Angeles, CA: University of California Press, 1953.

Smedley, Jonathan, *Gulliveriana: or, a Fourth Volume of Miscellanies*, London: J. Roberts, 1728.

Swift, Jonathan, *The Correspondence of Jonathan Swift*, edited by Harold
    Williams, 5 vols, Oxford: Clarendon Press, 1963–5.
Swift, Jonathan, *A Tale of a Tub and Other Works*, edited by Marcus Walsh,
    Cambridge: Cambridge University Press, 2010.
Telemann, Georg Philipp, *XII Fantasias: Gulliver Suite*, Los Angeles, CA:
    Harmonia Mundi, 1995.

Secondary Resources

Abernathy, Peter L. and Michael C. Stoune, 'Swift, Telemann, and *Gulliver's
    Travels*', *Eighteenth-Century Life* 3 (1977): 71–6.
Adriaensens, Vito, 'Ovidian Violence: Georges Méliès's Explosive Screen Bodies',
    in *Corporeality in Early Cinema: Viscera, Skin, and Physical Form*, 25–34,
    edited by Marina Dahlquist, Doron Galili, Jan Olsson and Valentine Robert,
    Bloomington, IN: Indiana University Press, 2018.
Altick, Richard D., *Paintings from Books: Art and Literature in Britain,
    1760–1900*, Columbus, OH: Ohio State University Press, 1985.
Altick, Richard D., *The Shows of London: A Panoramic History of Exhibitions,
    1600–1862*, Cambridge, MA and London: The Belknap Press, 1978.
Anderson, Amanda, Rita Felski and Toril Moi, *Character: Three Inquiries in
    Literary Studies*, Chicago, IL: The University of Chicago Press, 2019.
Apke, Bernd, 'When Nature Took Sides: Richard Janthur's Expressionist
    Illustrations of Gulliver's Voyage to the Country of the Houyhnhnms', *Swift
    Studies* 28 (2013): 115–27.
Ault, Norman, *New Light on Pope*, Hamden, CT: Archon Books, 1967 [1949].
Baltes, Sabine, 'Swiftian Material Culture', in *The Reception of Jonathan Swift
    in Europe*, edited by Hermann J. Real, 273–83, London and New York:
    Thoemmes Continuum, 2005.
Barchas, Janine, *Graphic Design, Print Culture, and the Eighteenth-Century
    Novel*, Cambridge: Cambridge University Press, 2003.
Barrier, Michael, *Hollywood Cartoons: American Animation in its Golden Age*,
    Oxford: Oxford University Press, 2003 [1999].
Basney, Lionel, 'Gulliver and the Children', in *The Voice of the Narrator in
    Children's Literature*, edited by Charlotte F. Otten and Gary D. Schmidt,
    148–58, Westport, CT: Greenwood Press, 1989.
Basu, Balaka, 'When Worlds Continue: The Doctor's Adventures in
    Fandom and Metatextuality', in *Ruminations, Peregrinations, and
    Regenerations: A Critical Approach to Doctor Who*, edited by Christopher
    J. Hansen, 164–76, Newcastle upon Tyne: Cambridge Scholars
    Publishing, 2010.
Bator, Robert, 'Jonathan Swift', in *Writers for Children: Critical Studies of Major
    Authors Since the Seventeenth Century*, edited by Jane M. Bingham, 555–9,
    New York: Scribner's, 1988.
Benedict, Barbara M., 'Material Ideas: Things and Collections in *Gulliver's
    Travels*', in *Reading Swift: Papers from The Sixth Münster Symposium on*

Jonathan Swift, edited by Kirsten Juhas, Hermann J. Real and Sandra Simon, 461–81, Munich: Wilhelm Fink, 2013.

Bernard, Stephen J., 'Jonathan Swift and *A Key, Being Observations and Explanatory Notes, upon the Travels of Lemuel Gulliver*, with a New Edition of the Key', *Swift Studies* 27 (2012): 87–119.

Bertetti, Paolo, 'Toward a Typology of Transmedia Characters', *International Journal of Communication* 8 (2014): 2344–61.

Bertetti, Paolo, 'Transmedia Archaeology: Narrative Expansions across Media before the Age of Convergence', in *The Routledge Companion to Transmedia Studies*, edited by Matthew Freeman and Renira Rampazzo Gambarato, 263–71, London and New York: Routledge, 2019.

Blewett, David, 'The Iconic Crusoe: Illustrations and Images of *Robinson Crusoe*', in *The Cambridge Companion to Robinson Crusoe*, edited by John Richetti, 159–90, Cambridge: Cambridge University Press, 2018.

Blewett, David, *The Illustration of Robinson Crusoe, 1719–1920*, Gerrards Cross: Colin Smythe, 1995.

Block, Edward A., 'Lemuel Gulliver: Middle-Class Englishman', *Modern Language Notes* 68, no. 7 (1953): 474–7.

Boucé, Paul-Gabriel, 'Gulliver's Frenchified Travels to Blefescu: The First Two Translations', in *Reading Swift: Papers from The Fourth Münster Symposium on Jonathan Swift*, edited by Hermann J. Real and Helgard Stöver-Leidig, 379–86, Munich: Wilhelm Fink, 2003.

Bracher, Frederick, 'The Name "Lemuel Gulliver"', *Huntington Library Quarterly* 12, no. 4 (1949): 409–13.

Brewer, David A., *The Afterlife of Character, 1726–1825*, Philadelphia, PA: University of Pennsylvania Press, 2005.

Bywaters, David, '*Gulliver's Travels* and the Mode of Political Parallel During Walpole's Administration', *ELH* 54, no. 3 (1987): 717–40.

Cabarga, Leslie, *The Fleischer Story*, New York: DaCapo Press, 1988.

Carnochan, W. B., 'Some Roles of Lemuel Gulliver', *Texas Studies in Literature and Language* 5, no. 4 (1964): 520–9.

Chalmers, Alan D., 'Film, Censorship, and the "Corrupt Original" of *Gulliver's Travels*', in *Eighteenth-Century Fiction on Screen*, edited by Robert Mayer, 70–87, Cambridge: Cambridge University Press, 2002.

Chalmers, Alan D., *Jonathan Swift and the Burden of the Future*, Newark, DE: University of Delaware Press, 1995.

Clark, Paul Odell, 'A Gulliver Dictionary', *Studies in Philology* 50, no. 4 (1953): 592–624.

Clarke, James, *Animated Films*, London: Virgin Books, 2004.

Collé, Nathalie, 'From Visual to Material Culture: The Afterlives of Frontispieces to *Robinson Crusoe*', in *The Edinburgh Companion to the Eighteenth-Century Novel and the Arts*, edited by Jakub Lipski and M.-C. Newbould, 397–413, Edinburgh: Edinburgh University Press, 2024.

Collé, Nathalie, '"[T]o Mix Colours for Painters" and Illustrate and Adapt Gulliver's Travels Worldwide: Street Murals, Adaptability and Transmediality', in *Adaptation and Illustration: New Cartographies*, edited by

Shannon Wells-Lassange and Sophie Aymes, 47–68, Basingstoke and New York: Palgrave Macmillan, 2024.

Colombo, Alice, 'Rewriting *Gulliver's Travels* under the Influence of J. J. Grandville's Illustrations', *Word & Image* 30, no. 4 (2014): 401–15.

Cook, Daniel, 'Mrs Gulliver's Travels: Minor-Character Elaboration in Theory and Practice', *Critical Quarterly* 67 (2024): 1–20.

Cook, Daniel, 'Vexed Diversions: *Gulliver's Travels*, the Arts, and Popular Entertainment', in *The Edinburgh Companion to the Eighteenth-Century Novel and the Arts*, edited by Jakub Lipski and M.-C. Newbould, 228–43, Edinburgh: Edinburgh University Press, 2024.

Cook, Daniel and Nicholas Seager (ed.), *The Cambridge Companion to Gulliver's Travels*, Cambridge: Cambridge University Press, 2023.

Cooke, Simon, 'Illustrating *Gulliver's Travels*: Fantasy and Satire', *The Book Collector* 70, no. 3 (2021): 437–48.

Cooke, Simon, 'Illustrating *Robinson Crusoe* over Three Centuries', *The Book Collector* 73, no. 3 (2024): 267–80.

Corisco, Ana Maria Hornero, '*Gulliver's Travels* on the Screen: Spanish Film Versions', *Swift Studies* 20 (2005): 111–23.

Cowart, David, *Literary Symbiosis: The Reconfigured Text in Twentieth-Century Writing*, Athens, GA and London: University of Georgia Press, 1993.

Cyr, Mary, 'Gulliver in France: Voyage to the Island of Folly', *The Musical Times* 163 (2022): 65–84.

Denson, Shane and Ruth Mayer, 'Border Crossings: Serial Figures and the Evolution of Media', *NECSUS* 7 (2018): 65–84.

Denson, Shane and Ruth Mayer, 'Spectral Seriality: The Sights and Sounds of Count Dracula', in *Media of Serial Narrative*, edited by Frank Kelleter, 108–24, Columbus, OH: Ohio State University Press, 2017.

DePorte, Michael, 'Novelizing the *Travels*: Simon Moore's Gulliver', *Swift Studies* 12 (1997): 99–102.

Derecho, Abigail, 'Archontic Literature: A Definition, a History, and Several Theories of Fan Fiction', in *Fan Fiction and Fan Communities in the Age of the Internet*, edited by Karen Hellekson and Kristina Busse, 61–78, Jefferson, NC: McFarland, 2006.

Dillard, Leigh G., 'Drawing Outside the Book: Parallel Illustration and the Creation of a Visual Culture', in *Book Illustration in the Long Eighteenth Century: Reconfiguring the Visual Periphery of the Text*, edited by Christina Ionescu and Renata Schellenberg, 195–241, Newcastle upon Tyne: Cambridge Scholars Publishing, 2011.

Docherty, Thomas, *Reading (Absent) Character: Towards a Theory of Characterization in Fiction*, Oxford: Clarendon Press, 1983.

Donoghue, Denis, 'The Brainwashing of Lemuel Gulliver', *The Southern Review* 32, no. 1 (1996): 128–46.

Douglas, Aileen, 'Borders: Reading *Gulliver's Travels* in 2020', *Journal of Irish Studies* 35 (2021): 3–14.

Douglas, Loyd, *The Worlds of Lemuel Gulliver*, Stillwater, OK: Oklahoma State University, 1968.

Downie, J. A., 'Swift and the Making of the English Novel', in *Reading Swift: Papers from The Third Münster Symposium on Jonathan Swift*, edited by Hermann J. Real and Helgard Stöver-Leidig, 179–87, Munich: Wilhelm Fink, 1998.

Düring, Michael, 'From Russian "Sviftovedenie" to the Soviet School of Swift Criticism: The Dean's Fate in Russia', in *The Reception of Jonathan Swift in Europe*, edited by Hermann J. Real, 170–213, London and New York: Thoemmes Continuum, 2005.

Düring, Michael, 'No Swift beyond Gulliver: Notes on the Polish Reception', in *The Reception of Jonathan Swift in Europe*, edited by Hermann J. Real, 156–69, London and New York: Thoemmes Continuum, 2005.

Easthope, Antony, 'The Disappearance of Gulliver: Character and Persona at the End of the "Travels"', *The Southern Review* 2 (1967): 261–6.

Eddy, William A., 'The Anatomist Dissected—by Lemuel Gulliver', *Modern Language Notes* 41, no. 5 (1926): 330–1.

Eddy, William A., '*Gulliver's Travels* and *Le Théâtre Italien*', *Modern Language Notes* 44, no. 6 (1929): 356–61.

Edera, Bruno, *Full Length Animated Feature Films*, edited by John Halas, New York: Hastings House Publishers, 1977.

Edwards, A. W. F., 'Is the Frontispiece of *Gulliver's Travels* a Likeness of Newton?', *Notes and Records of the Royal Society of London* 50, no. 2 (1996): 191–4.

Elleström, Lars, *Transmedial Narration: Narratives and Stories in Different Media*, Basingstoke and New York: Palgrave Macmillan, 2019.

Elliott, Robert C., 'Gulliver as Literary Artist', *ELH* 19, no. 1 (1952): 49–63.

Elliott, Robert C., *The Power of Satire: Magic, Ritual, Art*, Princeton, NJ: Princeton University Press, 1972 [1960].

Ferstl, Paul, 'Novel-based Comics', in *Comics as a Nexus of Cultures: Essays on the Interplay of Media, Disciplines and International Perspectives*, edited by Mark Berninger, Jochen Ecke and Gideon Haberkorn, 60–9, Jefferson, NC: McFarland, 2010.

Findlater, Richard, *Joe Grimaldi: His Life and Theatre*, 2nd edn, Cambridge: Cambridge University Press, 1978.

Fishelov, David, 'Gulliver as a Novelistic, Quixotic Character? A Response to Aaron R. Hanlon', *Connotations* 23, no. 1 (2013/14): 79–95.

Freeman, Matthew, *Historicising Transmedia Storytelling: Early Twentieth-Century Story Worlds*, London and New York: Routledge, 2017.

Frow, John, *Character and Person*, Oxford: Oxford University Press, 2016 [2014].

Fung, Julian, 'Early Condensations of *Gulliver's Travels*: Images of Swift as Satirist in the 1720s', *Studies in Philology* 114, no. 2 (2017): 395–425.

Garber, Marjorie, *Character: The History of a Cultural Obsession*, New York: Farrar, Straus and Giroux, 2020.

Genette, Gérard, *Palimpsests: Literature in the Second Degree*, translated by Channa Newman and Claude Doubinsky, Lincoln, NE and London: University of Nebraska Press, 1997 [1982].

Germanà, Monica, 'Rewriting Female Monstrosity: (Schizoid) Misogyny in Alison Fell's *The Mistress of Lilliput* and Emma Tennant's *Two Women of London*', in *Women's Writing in Western Europe: Gender, Generation and Legacy*, edited by Adalgisa Giorgio and Julia Waters, 102–17, Newcastle upon Tyne: Cambridge Scholars Publishing, 2007.

Germanà, Monica, *Scottish Women's Gothic and Fantastic Writing: Fiction since 1978*, Edinburgh: Edinburgh University Press, 2010.

Gevirtz, Karen Bloom, *Representing the Eighteenth Century in Film and Television, 2000–2015*, Basingstoke: Palgrave Macmillan, 2017.

Goring, Paul, '*Gulliver's Travels* on the Mid-Eighteenth-Century Stage; or, What is an Adaptation?', *Forum for Modern Language Studies* 51, no. 2 (2015): 100–15.

Gottlieb, Gerald, *Early Children's Books and Their Illustration*, New York: Pierpont Morgan Library, 1975.

Gove, Philip Babcock, *The Imaginary Voyage in Prose Fiction*, London: The Holland Press, 1961 [1941].

Groensteen, Thierry, *The System of Comics*, Jackson, MS: University Press of Mississippi, 2007 [1999].

Guynes, Sean and Gerry Canavan, 'Novels', in *The Routledge Handbook of Star Trek*, edited by Leimar Garcia-Siino, Sabrina Mittermeier and Stefan Rabitsch, 176–84, London and New York: Routledge, 2022.

Halsband, Robert, 'Eighteenth-Century Illustrations of *Gulliver's Travels*', in *Proceedings of The First Münster Symposium on Jonathan Swift*, edited by Hermann J. Real and Heinz J. Vienken, 83–112, Munich: Wilhelm Fink, 1985.

Hammond, Brean, 'Advertisements and Authorship', in *The Cambridge Companion to Gulliver's Travels*, edited by Daniel Cook and Nicholas Seager, 111–24, Cambridge: Cambridge University Press, 2023.

Hanlon, Aaron R., 'Re-reading Gulliver as Quixote: Toward a Theory of Quixotic Exceptionalism', *Connotations* 21, no. 2–3 (2011/12): 278–303.

Harmes, Marcus K., *Doctor Who and the Art of Adaptation: Fifty Years of Storytelling*, Lanham, MD: Rowman & Littlefield Publishers, 2014.

Hartvig, Gabriella, 'Hungarian Gulliveriads: Gulliver's Travels in Faremidó, Capillária, and Kazohinia', in *Reading Swift: Papers from The Fifth Münster Symposium on Jonathan Swift*, edited by Hermann J. Real, 519–31, Munich: Wilhelm Fink, 2008.

Haugtvedt, Erica, *Transfictional Character and Transmedia Storyworlds in the British Nineteenth Century*, Basingstoke and New York: Palgrave Macmillan, 2022.

Hawes, Clement, 'Gulliver Effects', in *Reading Swift: Papers from The Sixth Münster Symposium on Jonathan Swift*, edited by Kirsten Juhas, Hermann J. Real and Sandra Simon, 523–41, Munich: Wilhelm Fink, 2013.

Hochman, Baruch, *Character in Literature*, Ithaca, NY and London: Cornell University Press, 1985.

Holly, Grant, 'Travel and Translation: Textuality in *Gulliver's Travels*', *Criticism* 21, no. 2 (1979): 134–52.

Hornero, Ana, '*Gulliver's Travels*, or All's Well: Film Versions for a Young Audience', in *Crossing Textual Boundaries in International Children's Literature*, edited by Lance Weldy, 123–34, Newcastle upon Tyne: Cambridge Scholars Publishing, 2011.

Horrell, Joe, 'What Gulliver Knew', *The Sewanee Review* 51, no. 4 (1943): 476–504.

Hui, Haifeng, 'The Changing Adaptation Strategies of Children's Literature: Two Centuries of Children's Editions of *Gulliver's Travels*', *Hungarian Journal of English and American Studies* 17, no. 2 (2011): 245–62.

Hui, Haifeng and Lei Fan, 'Words Not in the Story: Paratextual Analysis of Moral Education in a School Edition of *Gulliver's Travels* in China', *International Research in Children's Literature* 8, no. 1 (2015): 31–44.

Hunter, J. Paul, '*Gulliver's Travels* and the Novel', in *The Genres of Gulliver's Travels*, edited by Frederik N. Smith, 56–74, Newark, DE: University of Delaware Press, 1990.

Hutcheon, Linda, *A Theory of Adaptation*, 2nd edn, London and New York: Routledge, 2013 [2006].

Irwin, W. R., 'Swift and the Novelists', *Philological Quarterly* 45 (1966): 102–13.

Jenkins, Clauston, 'The Ford Changes and the Text of *Gulliver's Travels*', *The Papers of the Bibliographical Society of America* 62 (1968): 1–23.

Jenkins, Henry, *Convergence Culture: Where Old and New Media Collide*, New York: New York University Press, 2006.

Johae, Antony, 'Wole Soyinka's "Gulliver": Swift Transposed', *Comparative Literature* 53, no. 1 (2001): 27–41.

Jones, Emrys, 'Screen Media', in *The Cambridge Companion to Gulliver's Travels*, edited by Daniel Cook and Nicholas Seager, 224–36, Cambridge: Cambridge University Press, 2023.

Jones Jr, William B., *Classics Illustrated: A Cultural History*, 2nd edn, Jefferson, NC: McFarland, 2017.

Judge, Elizabeth F., 'Kidnapped and Counterfeit Characters: Eighteenth-Century Fan Fiction, Copyright Law, and the Custody of Fictional Characters', in *Originality and Intellectual Property in the French and English Enlightenment*, edited by Reginald McGinnis, 22–68, London and New York: Routledge, 2012 [2009].

Juhas, Kirsten, 'Gulliver as a Vehicle of Satire in Twenty-First-Century Political Cartoons', *Swift Studies* 38 (2023): 105–25.

Jung, Sandro, '*Gulliver's Travels* in China: The Illustrations for *Han Man You*', *The Book Collector* 70, no. 4 (2021): 665–79.

Jung, Sandro, *Transnational Crusoe, Illustration and Reading History, 1719–1722*, Cambridge: Cambridge University Press, 2025.

Karian, Stephen, 'Problems and Paratexts in Eighteenth-Century Collections of Swift', *Studies in the Literary Imagination* 32, no. 1 (1999): 59–80.

Karian, Stephen, 'The Texts of *Gulliver's Travels*', in *Les Voyages de Gulliver: Mondes Lointains ou Mondes Proches*, edited by Daniel Carey and François Boulaire, 35–50, Caen: Presses Universitaires de Caen, 2002.

Kelly, Ann Cline, *Jonathan Swift and Popular Culture: Myth, Media, and the Man*, Basingstoke: Palgrave Macmillan, 2002.

Kosok, Heinz, *Explorations in Irish Literature*, Trier: Wissenschaftlicher Verlag Trier, 2008.

Kosok, Heinz, 'Gulliver's Children: A Classic Transformed for Young Reader', in *Proceedings of The First Münster Symposium on Jonathan Swift*, edited by Hermann J. Real and Heinz J. Vienken, 135–44, Munich: Wilhelm Fink, 1985.

Kosok, Heinz, 'Stage Versions of *Gulliver's Travels*', *Swift Studies* 7 (2002): 88–99.

Krake, Astrid, Hermann J. Real and Marie-Luise Spieckermann, 'The Dean's Voyages into Germany', in *The Reception of Jonathan Swift in Europe*, edited by Hermann J. Real, 93–41, London and New York: Thoemmes Continuum, 2005.

Kunz, Tobias and Lukas R. A. Wilde, *Transmedia Character Studies*, London and New York: Routledge, 2023.

Lamarque, Peter, 'How to Create a Fictional Character', in *The Creation of Art: New Essays in Philosophical Aesthetics*, edited by Berys Gaut and Paisley Livingston, 33–52, Cambridge: Cambridge University Press, 2003.

Lanning, Katie, 'Spectacle and Satire: American Film Adaptations of Gulliver's Travels', *BSECS Criticks* (17 January 2012), www.bsecs.org.uk/criticks -reviews/spectacle-and-satire-american-film-adaptations-of-gullivers -travels.

Lenfest, David S., 'Grandville's Gulliver', *Satire Newsletter* 10 (1973): 12–24.

Lenfest, David S., 'Lefebvre's Illustrations of *Gulliver's Travels*', *New York Public Library Bulletin* 76 (1972): 199–213.

Lewin, William, 'A Guide to the Discussion of the Technicolor Animated Screen Version of Gulliver's Travels', *Photoplay Studies* 6, no. 2 (1940): 1–16.

Lipski, Jakub (ed.), *Rewriting Crusoe: The Robinsonade across Languages, Cultures, and Media*, Lewisburg, PA: Bucknell University Press, 2020.

Lynch, Deidre, 'A Character of Character, in Five Metaphors', in *A Companion to the English Novel*, edited by Stephen Arata, Madigan Haley, J. Paul Hunter and Jennifer Wicke, 209–24, Oxford: Wiley Blackwell, 2019 [2015].

McCloud, Scott, *Understanding Comics: The Invisible Art*, New York: HarperCollins, 1994.

McCormack, W. J., 'On *Gulliver's Travels*', in *Narrative: From Malory to Motion Pictures*, edited by Jeremy Hawthorn, 70–84, London: Edward Arnold, 1985.

McKenzie, Alan T., '"The Lamentation of Glumdalclitch for the Loss of Grildrig. A Pastoral": What We Have Been Missing', *Texas Studies in Literature and Language* 12, no. 4 (1971): 583–94.

McLaverty, James, 'The Revision of the First Edition of *Gulliver's Travels*: Book-Trade Context, Interleaving, Two Cancels, and a Failure to Catch', *The Papers of the Bibliographical Society of America* 106 (2012): 5–35.

McMurran, Mary Helen, 'Translation as Offence: The Case of Desfontaines', *Translation and Literature* 17 (2008): 150–64.

Majersdorf, Remi, 'Adapting Swift for an Imagined Audience: A Comparative Study of the Adaptational Strategies and Implied Child Readers of Four

Twenty-First-Century Children's Versions of *Gulliver's Travels*', *Swift Studies* 35 (2020): 83–105.

Margolin, Uri, 'Characters and Their Versions', in *Fiction Updated: Theories of Fictionality, Narratology, and Poetics*, edited by Calin-Andrei Mihailescu and Walid Hamarneh, 113–32, Toronto and Buffalo, NY: University of Toronto Press, 1996.

Marshall, Ashley, 'Gulliver, Gulliveriana, and the Problem of Swiftian Satire', *Philological Quarterly* 84, no. 2 (2005): 211–39.

Matthews, Kristin L., 'Making Reading Popular: Cold War Literacy and *Classics Illustrated*', *Book History* 22 (2019): 320–41.

Menzies, Ruth, 'Children's Versions of *Gulliver's Travels* and the Question of Horizons of Expectation: From Biting Satire to Exciting Adventure Story', in *Horizons*, edited by Catherine Delmas and Isabelle Gadoin, *Représentations: Revue électronique du CEMRA* 3 (2011): 43–51.

Menzies, Ruth, 'Mary Gulliver, an Emblem of Sexual Rebirth?', in *Littérature anglo-saxonne au féminin: (Re)naissance(s) et horizons XVIIIe siècle - XXe siècle*, edited by Claire Bazin and Guyonne Leduc, 55–68, Paris: L'Harmattan, 2012.

Menzies, Ruth, 'Re-writing *Gulliver's Travels*: The Demise of a Genre?', *E-Rea* 3, no. 1 (2005): 87–93.

Menzies, Ruth, 'Visual Culture', in *The Cambridge Companion to Gulliver's Travels*, edited by Daniel Cook and Nicholas Seager, 206–23, Cambridge: Cambridge University Press, 2023.

Meyer, Christina and Monika Pietrzak-Franger (ed.), *Transmedia Practices in the Long Nineteenth Century*, London and New York: Routledge, 2022.

Mezciems, Jenny, 'Utopia and "the Thing which is not": More, Swift, and Other Lying Idealists', *University of Toronto Quarterly* 52, no. 1 (1982): 40–62.

Millidge, Gary Spencer, *Alan Moore: Storyteller*, Lewes: Ilex, 2011.

Moore, John Brooks, 'The Rôle of Gulliver', *Modern Philology* 25, no. 4 (1928): 469–80.

Moraru, Christian, *Rewriting: Postmodern Narrative and Cultural Critique in the Age of Cloning*, Albany, NY: State University of New York Press, 2001.

Moss, Anne Eakin, 'Cinema's "Miracles": Film Tricks and the Production of Soviet Wonder', *Film History* 32, no. 4 (2020): 33–59.

Nicoll, Allardyce, *A History of English Drama 1660–1900*, 6 vols, Cambridge: Cambridge University Press, 1965–70.

Noçon, Peter, 'Rediscovered Gulliveriana from World-War-II Germany', *Swift Studies* 7 (1992): 70–7.

Noçon, Peter, 'Versions of the Dean: Swift in Modern German Fiction and Drama', in *The Reception and Reputation of Jonathan Swift in Germany: Essays and Investigations*, edited by Hermann J. Real, with the assistance of Melanie Just, Neil Key and Helga Scholz, 325–51. Bethesda, MD; Dublin; Oxford and London: Maunsel & Company, 2002.

Orr, Leah, 'The Basis for Attribution in the Canon of Eliza Haywood', *The Library*, 7th Series 12 (2011): 335–75.

Palmer, Russell, 'Illustrating Gulliver and the Lilliputians in 1727 and 1728', *ANQ* 34, no. 3 (2021): 311–18.

Parey, Armelle (ed.), *Prequels, Coquels and Sequels in Contemporary Anglophone Fiction*, London and New York: Routledge, 2019.

Perrin, Noel, *Dr Bowdler's Legacy: A History of Expurgated Books in England and America*, New York: Atheneum, 1969.

Preston, Michael J., 'Rethinking Folklore, Rethinking Literature: Looking at *Robinson Crusoe* and *Gulliver's Travels* as Folktales, A Chapbook-Inspired Inquiry', in *The Other Print Tradition: Essays on Chapbooks, Broadsides, and Related Ephemera*, edited by Cathy Lynn Preston and Michael J. Preston, 19–73, New York: Garland, 1995.

Price, John, 'Modernizing Augustan Satire on Screen: *Gulliver's Travels* (1996)', in *Jonathan Swift and Philosophy*, edited by Janelle Pötzsch, 237–49, Lanham, MD: Lexington Books, 2016.

Pugh, Sheenagh, *The Democratic Genre: Fan Fiction in a Literary Context*, Bridgend: Seren, 2015 [2005].

Rawson, C. J., 'Gulliver and the Gentle Reader', in *Imagined Worlds: Essays on Some English Novels and Novelists in Honor of John Butt*, edited by Maynard Mack and Ian Gregor, 51–90, London: Methuen, 1968.

Real, Hermann J. (ed.), *The Reception of Jonathan Swift in Europe*, London and New York: Thoemmes Continuum, 2005.

Richardson, Brian, 'Transtextual Characters', in *Characters in Fictional Worlds: Understanding Imaginary Beings in Literature, Film, and Other Media*, edited by Jens Eder, Potis Jahnidis and Ralf Schneider, 527–41, Berlin: De Gruyter, 2010.

Rodino, Richard H., '"Splendide Mendax": Authors, Characters, and Readers in *Gulliver's Travels*', *PMLA* 106, no. 5 (1991): 1054–70.

Rogers, Pat, 'Satire', in *The Cambridge Companion to Gulliver's Travels*, edited by Daniel Cook and Nicholas Seager, 73–84, Cambridge: Cambridge University Press, 2023.

Rosen, Jeremy, *Minor Characters Have their Day: Genre and the Contemporary Literary Marketplace*, New York: Columbia University Press, 2016.

Ryan, Marie-Laure, 'Transmedia Storytelling and Transfictionality', *Poetics Today* 34, no. 3 (2013): 361–88.

Ryley, Robert M., 'Gulliver, Flimnap's Wife, and the Critics', *Studies in the Literary Imagination* 5, no. 2 (1972): 53–63.

Sabor, Peter, '"St Jonathan" or "wild beast": Horace Walpole's Swift', in *Reading Swift: Papers from The Third Münster Symposium on Jonathan Swift*, edited by Hermann J. Real and Helgard Stöver-Leidig, 321–36, Munich: Wilhelm Fink, 1998.

Sabor, Peter, 'Wole Soyinka and the Scriblerians', *Journal of Postcolonial Writing* 29, no. 1 (1989): 43–52.

Saint-Gelais, Richard, 'Transfictionality', in *Routledge Encyclopedia of Narrative Theory*, edited by David Herman, Manfred Jahn and Marie-Laure Ryan, 612–3, New York: Routledge, 2005.

Sanders, Julie, *Adaptation and Appropriation (The New Critical Idiom)*, London and New York: Routledge, 2005.

Schwartz, Delmore, 'Masterpieces as Cartoons', in *Arguing Comics: Literary Masters on a Popular Medium*, edited by Jeet Heer, 52–62, Jackson, MS: University Press of Mississippi, 2004.

Scolari, Carlos A., Paolo Bertetti and Matthew Freeman, *Transmedia Archaeology: Storytelling in the Borderlines of Science Fiction, Comics and Pulp Magazines*, Basingstoke and New York: Palgrave Macmillan, 2014.

Scott, Walter, *Sir Walter Scott on Novels and Novelists*, edited by Ioan Williams, London: Routledge and Kegan Paul, 1968.

Seager, Nicholas, '*Gulliver's Travels* Serialized and Continued', in *Reading Swift: Papers from The Sixth Münster Symposium on Jonathan Swift*, edited by Kirsten Juhas, Hermann J. Real and Sandra Simon, 543–62, Munich: Wilhelm Fink, 2013.

Seager, Nicholas, 'Samuel Richardson and the Third Volume of *Gulliver's Travels*', *Swift Studies* 28 (2013): 128–36.

Seidel, Michael, '*Gulliver's Travels* and the Contracts of Fiction', in *The Cambridge Companion to the Eighteenth Century Novel*, edited by John Richetti, 72–89, Cambridge: Cambridge University Press, 1996.

Semenza, Gregory M. Colón and Robert J. Hasenfratz, *The History of British Literature on Film, 1895–2015*, London and New York: Bloomsbury Academic, 2015.

Sena, John F., '*Gulliver's Travels* and the Genre of the Illustrated Book', in *The Genres of Gulliver's Travels*, edited by Frederik N. Smith, 101–38, Newark, DE: University of Delaware Press, 1990.

Shan, Te-hsing, 'Gulliver's Travels to the Centre of the Earth: Three Early Translations of *Gulliver's Travels*', *Swift Studies* 17 (2022): 109–24.

Sherburn, George, 'The "Copies of Verses" about Gulliver', *Texas Studies in Literature and Language* 3, no. 1 (1961): 3–7.

Sheriko, Nicole, 'Patchwork Play: Nineteenth-Century Toy Theater and Participatory Media Culture', *Nineteenth-Century Studies* 30 (2019): 25–44.

Smedman, M. Sarah, 'Like Me, Like Me Not: *Gulliver's Travels* as Children's Book', in *The Genres of Gulliver's Travels*, edited by Frederik N. Smith, 75–100, Newark, DE: University of Delaware Press, 1990.

Smith, Frederik N., 'Vexing Voices: The Telling of Gulliver's Story', *Papers on Language and Literature* 21, no. 4 (1985): 383–98.

Smith Jr, Raymond J., 'The "Character" of Lemuel Gulliver', *Tennessee Studies in Literature* 10 (1965): 133–9.

Solomon, Charles, *The History of Animation: Enchanted Drawings*, Avenel, NJ: Wings Books, 1994.

Sperrin, Dan, 'The Augustan Plath: "Gulliver" and Other Poems', *Journal of Modern Literature* 47, no. 1 (2023): 98–117.

Stallcup, Jackie E., 'Inescapable Bodies, Disquieting Perception: Why Adults Seek to Tame and Harness Swift's Excremental Satire in *Gulliver's Travels*', *Children's Literature in Education* 35, no. 2 (2004): 87–111.

Swires, Steve, 'Maestro of the Magicks Part Two', *Starlog* (February 1990): 66.

Tabachnick, Stephen E. and Esther Bendit Saltzman (ed.), *Drawn from the Classics: Essays on Graphic Adaptations of Literary Works*, Jefferson, NC: McFarland, 2015.

Taylor, David Francis, 'Gillray's Gulliver and the 1803 Invasion Scare', in *The Afterlives of Eighteenth-Century Fiction*, edited by Daniel Cook and Nicholas Seager, 212–32, Cambridge: Cambridge University Press, 2015.

Thomasson, Amie L., *Fiction and Metaphysics*, Cambridge: Cambridge University Press, 1998.

Thompson, Mary Shine, '*Gulliver's Travels* in the Lands of Childhood', in *Young Irelands: Studies in Children's Literature*, edited by Mary Shine Thompson, 164–86, Dublin: Four Courts Press, 2011.

Thon, Jan-Noël, 'Transmedia Characters: Theory and Analysis', *Frontiers of Narrative Studies* 5, no. 2 (2019): 176–99.

Thon, Jan-Noël and Roberta Pearson, 'Transmedia Characters', *Narrative* 30, no. 2 (2022): 139–51.

Tilton, John W., '*Gulliver's Travels* as a Work of Art', *The Bucknell Review* 8, no. 4 (1959): 246–59.

Todd, Dennis, *Imagining Monsters: Miscreations of the Self in Eighteenth-Century England*, Chicago, IL and London: The University of Chicago Press, 1995.

Torre, Dan, *Animation: Process, Cognition and Actuality*, London and New York: Bloomsbury Academic, 2017.

Traugott, John, 'The Yahoo in the Doll's House: *Gulliver's Travels* the Children's Classic', in *English Satire and the Satiric Tradition*, edited by Claude Rawson, 127–50, Oxford: Basil Blackwell, 1984.

Treadwell, Michael, 'Benjamin Motte, Andrew Tooke and *Gulliver's Travels*', in *Proceedings of The First Münster Symposium on Jonathan Swift*, edited by Hermann J. Real and Heinz J. Vienken, 287–304, Munich: Wilhelm Fink, 1985.

Treadwell, Michael, 'Observations on the Printing of Motte's Octavo Editions of *Gulliver's Travels*', in *Reading Swift: Papers from The Third Münster Symposium on Jonathan Swift*, edited by Hermann J. Real and Helgard Stöver-Leidig, 157–77, Munich: Wilhelm Fink, 1998.

Treadwell, Michael, 'Swift, Richard Coleire, and the Origins of *Gulliver's Travels*', *The Review of English Studies* 34, no. 135 (1983): 304–11.

Van der Goten, Thomas, 'The Lilliputian Ode, 1726-1826', *ANQ* 28, no. 2 (2015): 94–104.

Vanderbeke, Dirk, 'It Was the Best of Two Worlds, It Was the Worst of Two Worlds: The Adaptation of Novels in Comics and Graphic Novels', in *The Rise and Reason of Comics and Graphic Literature: Critical Essays on the Form*, edited by Joyce Goggin and Dan Hassler-Forest, 104–18, Jefferson, NC: McFarland, 2010.

Vera, María Pilar González, '*Gulliver's Travels*: The World of Adaptations', in *Crossing Textual Boundaries in International Children's Literature*, edited by Lance Weldy, 25–43, Newcastle upon Tyne: Cambridge Scholars Publishing, 2011.

Vermeule, Blakey, *Why Do We Care about Literary Characters?*, Baltimore, MD: Johns Hopkins University Press, 2011 [2010].

Wagner, Peter, *Reading Iconotexts: From Swift to the French Revolution*, London: Reaktion Books, 1995, 37–74.

Welcher, Jeanne K., 'Eighteenth-Century Views of Gulliver: Illustrations and Prints', in *Imagination on a Long Rein: English Literature Illustrated*, edited by Joachim Moller, 82–93, Marburg: Jonas Verlag, 1988.

Welcher, Jeanne K., 'Gulliver in the Marketplace', *Studies on Voltaire and the Eighteenth Century* 217 (1983): 125–39.

Welcher, Jeanne K., 'Gulliveriana: Ways of Reading *Gulliver's Travels*', in *Approaches to Teaching Swift's Gulliver's Travels*, edited by Edward J. Rielly, 96–101, New York: MLA, 1988.

Welcher, Jeanne K., 'Hogarth's Reading of *Gulliver's Travels*', in *Hogarth in Context: Ten Essays and a Bibliography*, edited by Joachim Möller, 106–16, Marburg: Jonag Verlag, 1996.

Welcher, Jeanne K., 'Horace Walpole and *Gulliver's Travels*', *Studies in Eighteenth-Century Culture* 12 (1983): 45–57.

Williams, Kathleen, *Jonathan Swift: The Critical Heritage*, London and New York: Routledge, 2009 [1970].

Yang, Xiao, 'On the History of the Chinese Translations of *Gulliver's Travels*', *ANQ* 34, no. 1 (2021): 36–61.

Zimmerman, Everett, 'Gulliver the Preacher', *PMLA* 89, no. 5 (1974): 1024–32.

Zimmerman, Lester F., 'Lemuel Gulliver', in *Jonathan Swift: Tercentenary Essays*, 61–73, edited by David P. French et al., Tulsa, OK: University of Tulsa, 1967.

INDEX